CAMBRIDGE SENIOR HISTORY

# CONFLICT in Indochina

## 1954–1979

**Sean Brawley, Chris Dixon and Jeffrey Green**

CAMBRIDGE
UNIVERSITY PRESS

# CAMBRIDGE
## UNIVERSITY PRESS

Shaftesbury Road, Cambridge CB2 8EA, United Kingdom

One Liberty Plaza, 20th Floor, New York, NY 10006, USA

477 Williamstown Road, Port Melbourne, VIC 3207, Australia

314–321, 3rd Floor, Plot 3, Splendor Forum, Jasola District Centre, New Delhi – 110025, India

103 Penang Road, #05–06/07, Visioncrest Commercial, Singapore 238467

Cambridge University Press is part of the University of Cambridge.

It furthers the University's mission by disseminating knowledge in the pursuit of
education, learning and research at the highest international levels of excellence.

www.cambridge.org
Information on this title: www.cambridge.org/9780521618625

First published 2005

20  19  18  17  16  15  14  13  12  11  10  9  8  7  6

Cover designed by Sylvia Witte

*A Cataloguing-in-Publication entry is available from the catalogue
of the National Library of Australia at* www.nla.gov.au

ISBN  978-0-521-61862-5  Paperback

# Contents

For
Caitlin Brawley,
Sam Dixon and Michael Remilton
and
Nicholas, Emily, Caleb and Jacob Green

# Acknowledgments

The authors would like to acknowledge a number of people who helped in the process of writing and producing this book. At Cambridge University Press, Martin Ford, and then Allison Scott, have been enthusiastic and energetic editors. Bree DeRoche has been a sympathetic and careful copyeditor. Closer to home, we would like to thank Susan Shaw, Lorna Davin and Renee Green. Although we were not excused from our domestic obligations, writing was made much easier by the support and encouragement they provided. Finally, we would like to dedicate this book to Nat and Caitlin Brawley, Sam Dixon, Michael Remilton, and Nicholas, Emily, Caleb and Jacob Green. May the closest they come to war be through the pages of a book.

**Cover Image:** Australian War Memorial Negative Number EKT/67/0036/VN.

**Page 16:** Library of Congress [LC-USZ62-62808]; **18**, **23**: © AFP/Viet Nam News Agency; **33**: Courtesy Ngo Vinh Long Collection; **38**, **53**, **57**, **66**, **73**, **103**, **109**, **145**, **153**, **154** both, **156**, **162**, **163**, **166**, **170**, **175**, **182**, **185**, **194** top, **210**: © CORBIS/Australian Picture Library; **39**: Imperial War Museum Neg. HU 30992/Vietnam Department of Culture & Information; **42**: National Park Service, Dwight D. Eisenhower Library; **49**, **97**: Courtesy US National Archives & Records Administration; **51**: Imperial War Museum Neg. HU 73010; **60**: Courtesy US Navy; **61**: Courtesy of art-hanoi.com/collection; **75**, **111**, **126**, **131**, **132**, **139**, **150**: LBJ Library photo by Yoichi R. Okamoto; **80**: LBJ Library photo by Cecil Stoughton; **81**: Courtesy US Naval Historical Centre; **86**, **141**: LBJ Library photo by Frank Wolfe; **99**: © AP Photo; **114**: © AP Photo/Peter Arnett; **127**: © AP Photo/Hong Seong-Chan; **129**: © AP Photo/Eddie Adams; **133**: LBJ Library photo by Jack Kightlinger; **151** bottom: By permission of the National Library of Australia; **165**: Courtesy Gerald R. Ford Library; **168**: © AP Photo/File/Nick Ut; **187**: Courtesy Richard Nixon Library; **194** bottom: © AFP/Pressens Bild; **195**, **199**: Photograph by Ben Kiernan, 1980; **202**: Photograph of Phnom Penh in 1979 is by Marcus Thompson and is reproduced with the permission of Oxfam GB, 274 Banbury Road, Oxford, OX2 7DZ; **211**: © Brendan Read/Fairfaxphotos;

**Australian War Memorial**
**Page 117:** Neg. P00508.008; **120**: Neg. FOR/66/0661/VN; **151** top: Neg. 044368; **157**: Neg. PJE/71/0398/VN; **203**: Neg. P02570.008.

# Introduction: Themes, Issues and Approaches

## The Significance of the Conflict in Indochina

Between 1945 and 1979 Indochina (the former French colonial region comprising the present-day nations of Vietnam, Cambodia and Laos) was racked by warfare. This book traces the origins, nature and legacies of those conflicts, which were wars of independence, as well as civil wars. While there are no absolutely reliable casualty figures for these conflicts, an estimated four million people were killed in Indochina between 1945 and 1979, with a much larger number physically or psychologically wounded. The vast majority of those casualties were Vietnamese, Cambodian or Lao. The conflict also led to the deaths of nearly 60,000 Americans, and thousands of troops from America's allies (principally South Korea, Australia and New Zealand) became casualties.

Why did the United States sacrifice so much in its failed attempt to thwart Vietnamese nationalism? American historians have written hundreds of books analysing the reasons behind their nation's involvement in Indochina. On one point, however, there is no argument: the overriding factor behind US intervention was the Cold War. The 30-year conflict in Vietnam, which began as a struggle for independence from French colonial authority, became entangled in the post-World War II contest between 'the West', led by the United States, and the 'communist world', dominated by the Soviet Union (USSR) and (after 1949) by 'Red' China.

From the late 1940s, successive American presidents, initially with widespread public support, were convinced the Vietnamese (and, by extension, the Cambodian and Lao) struggle for independence was one component of a worldwide quest for communist domination. US policymakers, driven by their unshakeable fears of communism, were unwilling to accept the nationalist aspirations of the Indochinese people. This confusion between 'nationalism' (an aspiration Americans understood) and 'communism' (an ideology they despised) clouded the judgements of American policymakers and led them into a conflict from which there was no easy exit. Once committed to the struggle, the United States could not withdraw without losing face. In the end, however, the world's

1

major superpower was defeated, and for the last three decades has grappled with the legacies of that humiliating defeat.

## Ho Chi Minh and Vietnamese Nationalism

Paradoxically, the United States had initially expressed sympathy for the nationalist aspirations of the Vietnamese people and collaborated with the leaders of the Vietnamese independence movement. During World War II, when Vietnam was occupied by Japan, US forces had worked alongside Ho Chi Minh (the leader of the 'Viet Minh') who was resisting the Japanese occupation – and who was equally determined to prevent a return of French power. A long-time opponent of French colonialism, Ho was the undisputed leader of the Vietnamese struggle for independence. Ho himself shunned adulation, and it would be going too far to suggest Vietnam's struggle for independence would not have occurred without him. Nevertheless, Ho was a figure of enormous significance – a hero to his people, but the nemesis of American policymakers and strategists. Accordingly, this book will pay specific attention to Ho's role in the long struggle for Vietnamese independence.

*Vietnam*

A frequently asked question concerns Ho's motivations: was he first and foremost a communist or was he a nationalist? There is no straightforward answer to this question, but as you learn about the conflict in Indochina, you will reach a clearer understanding of the nature and role of both 'communism' and 'nationalism'.

The Indochinese conflict was shaped by competing versions of Vietnamese nationalism. Americans convinced themselves that Ho and Vietnamese communism were controlled by Moscow and China. That analysis, however, reflected Americans' deep misunderstanding of Vietnamese history: China has exercised a significant impact on Vietnam, but Vietnam's history was long dominated by a determination to establish and maintain its independence from China. For their part, Ho and his supporters – including millions of Vietnamese civilians, in southern as well as northern Vietnam – were convinced they were fighting for Vietnamese nationalism, by fighting to eject the French colonisers and then the Americans who followed, and by striving to unite the 'two' Vietnams that nominally existed from the mid-1950s until 1975.

American policymakers were equally insistent that they were fighting for Vietnamese nationalism. But the form of Vietnamese nationalism for which they were fighting existed in only the southern part of the country. During the 1960s, the United States engaged in 'nation building' in South Vietnam (the Republic of Vietnam): a major theme of this book is the contest between these competing forms of Vietnamese nationalism: one led by Ho and based on the assumption that a genuine form of Vietnamese nationalism required the reunification of the two 'Vietnams'; the other based in Saigon, and extending only so far as the 17th parallel dividing 'North Vietnam' from 'South Vietnam'. One of the issues confronting American policymakers (and American soldiers who complained frequently that their South Vietnamese allies were uninterested in taking the fight up to their adversaries) was how to build support for the South Vietnamese nation amongst a population that was, at best, indifferent about the conflict – and often sympathetic to the enemy's goals, if not their methods.

## Waging War: A Military and Civil Conflict

As well as exploring the path to war, this book will examine the nature of the Indochinese conflict: how was the war fought and what impact did it have on civilians, as well as soldiers? When the United States launched its large-scale intervention in Vietnam during the mid-1960s, few Americans assumed they would be defeated by an enemy President Lyndon Johnson derided as a 'third-rate pissant little country'. Yet that is precisely what happened. Despite a massive intervention of American firepower and forces – which by early 1969 numbered nearly 543,000 men – the USA did not prevail. It is important to understand, therefore, how the war in Vietnam, and by extension in Laos and Cambodia, was waged. What tactics and strategies did the various combatants use? What was it like to be a part of this unconventional and messy war, where every part of Vietnam could become the front line?

## How Not to Lose a War: The United States Confronts its Defeat in Vietnam

Americans have spent a long time analysing 'what went wrong' in Vietnam. Historians have addressed this question at length, and it has also been a theme in American political and cultural life. American movies about the Indochinese conflict often represent the war as a 'dreadful mistake' – or a 'quagmire' – from which innocent Americans could not extricate themselves. And Americans have often asked: 'how could we have done things differently'? As some of those films imply, many Americans refuse to concede they were defeated in Vietnam. If they do accept they were defeated, they attribute that defeat to various factors:

• weak-willed politicians in Washington, who allegedly did not allow American forces to fight in ways that would have guaranteed victory

- the antiwar movement in the United States, which turned American public opinion against the war and gave heart to the enemy forces
- the American media, which is blamed for presenting the war in a 'negative' way
- the inability, or unwillingness, of the South Vietnamese to fight effectively against a ruthless and highly motivated foe.

This book explores the reasons behind America's defeat in Indochina, and traces the long and frustrating efforts to secure a peaceful solution to the war.

It is also important to analyse the war from another perspective: how did the Vietnamese win the war? At the outset, it is important to appreciate that 'Vietnam' refers to a country, as well as a war. It is important, too, to understand that Vietnamese have a different name for what Americans and Australians call 'the Vietnam War'. To the Vietnamese, the conflict was fought in two parts, the 'French War' and then the 'American War'. Consequently, this book pays due attention to Vietnamese perspectives, including the Vietnamese way of war, which frustrated and infuriated many Americans, who not only misunderstood the long history of Vietnamese nationalism, but who also failed to comprehend the connections Vietnamese drew between their political and military struggles for independence and reunification. Confronting a society and a culture they neither valued nor understood, most Americans assumed Ho Chi Minh and the Vietnamese would have a 'breaking point': When that point was reached, the Vietnamese would yield to American demands and accept the permanent partition of Vietnam into two separate nations. But Ho was serious when he declared his willingness to fight on, regardless of the cost.

## HISTORICAL DOCUMENT

### Ho Chi Minh, 1966

The Americans ... can wipe out all the principal towns in Tonkin [the northern part of Vietnam] ... We expect it, and besides, we are prepared for it. But that does not weaken our determination to fight to the very end. You know, we've already had that experience, and you have seen how that conflict ended.

In trying to reconcile themselves to their defeat in Vietnam, Americans have focussed on the divisions the war inflicted on the United States. By the late 1960s, the USA was a deeply divided society:

- proponents of the war clashed with those who believed the United States should withdraw from an immoral and futile conflict
- politicians blamed each other for leading the nation into the war and debated the best means of extricating the USA from the conflict
- veterans of the war debated whether the war was necessary and were widely blamed for atrocities against the Vietnamese
- there was a generation gap, with some younger Americans increasingly persuaded that their nation's social and cultural systems were as flawed as the politicians who had led the United States into the war
- there were increasingly visible, and sometimes violent, differences between

African–Americans (who believed they were doing a disproportionate amount of the fighting – and dying – in Vietnam) and white Americans, over civil rights and 'Black Power'.

The conflict in Indochina, therefore, had a dramatic impact on American society and politics during the 1960s and 1970s. But those divisions, and American casualties, must be viewed alongside the massive destruction inflicted upon Vietnam, Cambodia and Laos. In addition to the massive loss of life, Indochina was economically and physically devastated during the 1960s and 1970s, when the United States dropped millions of tonnes of bombs, as well as vast quantities of Agent Orange, on Indochina. Three decades after the United States was defeated in Indochina, unexploded bombs and the long-term effects of herbicides continue to take their toll.

# The Wider War: Conflict in Cambodia and Laos

When Americans (and Australians) refer to the 'Indochinese Conflict', they usually mean the war in Vietnam. Vietnam is the largest of the three Indochinese nations and it was where the United States suffered most of its casualties. But the conflict in Indochina also encompassed Laos and Cambodia. Laos was significant partly because it served as a conduit through which North Vietnam channelled troops and supplies to the conflict in southern Vietnam. But Laos also endured a long, three-way conflict between the 'Pathet Lao' communist forces and anti-communist and neutralist factions.

For most of the 1950s and 1960s, the third Indochinese nation, Cambodia, was able to avoid the worst excesses of the conflicts raging in Vietnam and Laos.

*Laos*

Americans regarded Cambodia as a 'sideshow' to the conflict in Vietnam. The Cambodian leader, Norodom Sihanouk, pursued a policy of neutrality, playing a careful balancing act between the United States, North Vietnam and South Vietnam, with which it shared a border. By the late 1960s, however, Cambodia was increasingly entangled in the Vietnamese conflict: this not only fuelled the communist rebellion in Cambodia, led by Pol Pot and the Khmer Rouge (KR), but also precipitated the overthrow in 1970 of Sihanouk by Lon Nol. Determined to subdue the KR rebellion, Lon Nol forged a closer relationship with the United States, which had already commenced bombing eastern Cambodia and, in 1970, launched an 'incursion' into Cambodia in an effort to ensure Vietnamese communist forces could no longer seek sanctuary in the region.

From 1970 to 1975 Cambodia was subjected to a brutal civil war between Lon Nol's forces (backed by the United States) and the Khmer Rouge. The brutality of that civil war was just a foretaste of the horror that

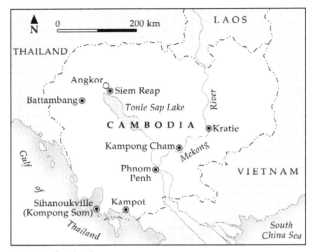

Cambodia

followed after the KR gained control in April 1975. Obsessed with building a 'model' society, based around a peculiar interpretation of Maoist theory, the KR were determined to purge Cambodia ('Democratic Kampuchea') of any Western influence. In practice, this led to the murder of at least a million Cambodians and the deaths of hundreds of thousands of others through starvation and maltreatment. The latter chapters of this text trace the rise and fall of the Khmer Rouge, whose brutal amalgam of nationalism and communism left a terrible scar on Cambodia.

# Thinking as Historians: Interpreting Sources

In learning about the issues raised throughout the various chapters, we will be encouraging you to *think* and *act* as historians. This applies to secondary sources – the work of historians and others writing *after* the events being described – as well as the primary sources that were produced *during* the conflict in Indochina. On some issues, you will be introduced to differing interpretations by historians: any historical subject – but particularly one as contentious as the Indochinese conflict – inevitably prompts a range of interpretations and arguments amongst historians.

Sometimes, these different views reflect the different sources to which historians have access. The declassification of 'official' government sources, can sometimes lead to fresh interpretations. In other instances, historians' views reflect their fundamentally different perspectives. We would anticipate, for example, that Vietnamese and American historians would approach the same topic from different points of view. But we should not assume that Americans will agree amongst themselves. Just as the war was divisive during the 1960s and 1970s, so too historians – some of whom opposed the war and some of whom fought in the conflict – will reflect those divisions. And, of course, people's views often change over time.

It is important, therefore, to *think critically* about the sources you consult. This is particularly the case when you examine the documentary sources included throughout the book. When you *interrogate* the primary sources, it is always helpful to begin with several questions:

• Who was writing the document?
• Why – and when – was the document written?
• Was it a 'public' document or was it intended for a more restricted audience?

Before we turn to the conflict that raged across Indochina during the post–World War II period, it is necessary to trace the origins of Vietnamese nationalism and France's impact upon the region from the mid-19th century.

# Timeline

## 1959

**Apr. 4**    Eisenhower connects America's vital national interests to the survival of the non-communist state in South Vietnam
760 American military personnel in Vietnam

## 1960

**Dec. 20**    NLF formed in South Vietnam

## 1961

**Jan. 21**    John F. Kennedy inaugurated President of USA
Kennedy approves Vietnam counter-insurgency plan

**May 9–15**    Vice President Johnson visits South Vietnam

**Nov. 3**    General Maxwell Taylor believes US aid will bring victory without it taking over the war
3,205 US military personnel in Vietnam

## 1962

**Feb. 6**    MACV (US Military Assistance Command Vietnam) established in Saigon; major US build-up begins

**Feb. 14**    Kennedy authorises US forces to return fire if fired on

**Mar. 22**    Strategic Hamlet program begins

**July 23**    Geneva Accords on Laos signed
11,300 US military personnel in Vietnam

## 1963

**Aug. 21**    South Vietnamese troops attack Buddhist pagodas

**Nov. 1**    Military coup removes Ngo Dinh Diem from government

**Nov. 2**    Diem and his brother assassinated

**Nov. 22**    President Kennedy assassinated
16,300 US military personnel in Vietnam

## 1964

**June 20**    General William Westmoreland becomes head of MACV

**Aug. 2**    US destroyer *Maddox* attacked by North Vietnamese patrol boats

**Aug. 4**    US destroyer *Turner Joy* reports attack from North Vietnamese patrol boats

**Aug. 7**    US Congress passes Gulf of Tonkin Resolution

**Oct. 1**    US Army Fifth Special Forces Group arrives in Vietnam

**Nov. 1**    Viet Cong attack Bien Hoa Air Base destroying six US bombers and killing five American personnel
23,300 US military personnel in Vietnam

## 1965

**Feb. 7**    Viet Cong launch attacks on US military installations

**Mar. 2**    Operation Rolling Thunder starts

**Mar. 8**    First US combat troops arrive in Danang

**Mar. 15**    National teach-in

**Mar. 24**    First teach-in at University of Michigan

**Apr. 6**    Johnson permits US troops to conduct offensive operations in South Vietnam

**Oct. 15–16**    Antiwar protests in 40 American cities

**Dec. 25**    Bombing of North Vietnam halts; Johnson invites North Vietnam to negotiate
184,300 US military personnel in Vietnam
636 US military personnel killed
22,420 Allied troops in Vietnam

## 1966

**Jan. 31**    Rolling Thunder resumes

**Feb. 4**    Senate Foreign Relations Committee holds televised hearings on the war

**Mar. 20**    Johnson convenes Guam Conference

**May 1**    USA bombs Viet Cong in Cambodia

**June 29**    USA bombs oil installations in Haiphong and Hanoi

**Oct. 26**    Johnson visits American troops in Vietnam
385,300 US military personnel in Vietnam
6,644 US military personnel killed
52,500 Allied Troops in Vietnam

## 1967

**Jan. 8–26**    Operation Cedar Falls

**Feb. 22**    Operation Junction City starts

**Apr. 15**    100,000 antiwar protesters in New York

| May 19 | USA bombs power plant in Hanoi |
| Sept. 3 | Nguyen Van Thieu elected President of South Vietnam |
| Oct. 21 | 50,000 protest outside the Pentagon |
| | 485,600 military personnel in Vietnam |
| | 16,021 US military personnel killed |

# 1968

| Jan. 3 | Senator Eugene McCarthy announces he is running for Democratic Party presidential nomination |
| Jan. 30 | Tet Offensive |
| Feb. 1 | Nixon to run for President |
| Feb. 25 | ARVN and US troops recapture Hue |
| Feb. 27 | Westmoreland requests an extra 206,000 troops; Walter Cronkite concludes on national television that the war cannot be won |
| Mar. 16 | Senator Robert Kennedy to run for Democratic presidential nomination |
| Mar. 31 | Johnson decides not to seek re-election |
| May 12 | Peace talks begin in Paris |
| June 6 | Robert Kennedy assassinated |
| July 1 | General Abrams replaces Westmoreland |
| Oct. 31 | Operation Rolling Thunder ends |
| Nov. 5 | Nixon wins presidential election |
| | 536,000 military personnel in Vietnam |
| | 30,610 US military personnel killed |
| | 65,600 Allied troops in Vietnam |

# 1969

| Jan. 22 | Nixon inaugurated as President |
| May 10 | Operation Apache Snow begins – ends June 7 |
| June 8 | Nixon announces withdrawal of 25,000 troops from Vietnam |
| July 25 | The Nixon Doctrine |
| Sept. 3 | Ho Chi Minh dies |
| Oct. 15 | National Moratorium |
| Nov. 16 | My Lai massacre reported in US press |
| | 475,200 military personnel in Vietnam |
| | 40,024 US military personnel killed |
| | 70,000 Allied troops in Vietnam |

# 1970

| Feb. 20 | Kissinger begins secret peace talks in Paris |
| Mar. 18 | Lon Nol stages coup in Cambodia |
| Apr. 30 | USA invades Cambodia |

| May 4 | Kent State University demonstration – four killed |
| June 30 | Operations in Cambodia end |
| Dec. 22 | US Congress prohibits US forces in Cambodia or Laos |
| | 334,600 military personnel in Vietnam |
| | 44,245 US military personnel killed |
| | 67,700 Allied troops in Vietnam |

# 1971

| Jan. 30 | Operation Lam Son 719 begins |
| Jan. 31 | Winter Soldier Investigation starts in Detroit |
| Mar. 29 | Lieutenant William L. Calley, Jr. found guilty of murder |
| June 13 | *New York Times* publishes the Pentagon Papers |
| Nov. 12 | US forces take a defensive role |
| Dec. 26 | Nixon orders the resumption of bombing of North Vietnam |
| | 156,800 military personnel in Vietnam |
| | 45,626 US military personnel killed |
| | 53,900 Allied troops in Vietnam |

# 1972

| Feb. 21 | Nixon seeks détente with China |
| Mar. 23 | Peace talks suspended by USA |
| Mar. 30 | Easter Offensive begins |
| Apr. 15 | USA bombs Hanoi |
| Apr. 27 | Paris peace talks resume |
| May 4 | Peace talks suspended |
| May 8 | USA mines North Vietnamese ports |
| June 22 | Watergate break-in and arrests |
| July 13 | Paris peace talks resume |
| Sept. 26–27 | Kissinger holds secret talks with North Vietnamese in Paris |
| Nov. 7 | Nixon is re-elected in a landslide |
| Dec. 13 | Peace talks stop |
| Dec. 18-29 | Operation Linebacker II conducted |
| | 24,000 US military personnel in Vietnam |
| | 45,926 US military personnel killed |
| | 35,500 Allied troops in Vietnam |
| | SVNAF 195,847 military personnel killed in action |

# 1973

| Jan. 8-12 | Kissinger and Le Duc Tho hold private meetings |
| Jan. 15 | Nixon halts offensive actions against North Vietnam |

Jan. 27   Peace treaty signed in Paris
Feb. 12   First US POWs released
Mar. 29   MACV headquarters removed
June 24   Congress prohibits all US bombing in Cambodia after August
Aug. 14   All US military operations end in Indochina
Nov. 7   War Powers Resolution becomes law
Only 50 US military personnel in Vietnam; no Allied Military personnel in Vietnam

# 1974

Aug. 9   Nixon resigns as President
Aug. 20   Congress reduces aid to South Vietnam from $1 billion to $700 million
Sept. 16   President Ford offers clemency to draft evaders and deserters
Dec. 13   Major fighting begins between PAVN and ARVN

# 1975

Jan. 6   NVA captures Phuoc Long Province
Jan. 8   North Vietnam decides to invade South Vietnam
Mar. 14   ARVN forces withdraw from Central Highlands
Apr. 1   Khmer Rouge makes military advances in Cambodia
Apr. 11–3   Operation Eagle removes US embassy personnel from Phnom Penh
Apr. 12   President Nguyen Van Thieu reigns
Apr. 17   Cambodia falls to Khmer Rouge
Apr. 29–30   Operation Frequent Wind evacuates all

American personnel and some South Vietnamese from Vietnam; NVA captures Saigon
May 7   President Ford formally declares an end to the 'Vietnam era'
Aug. 11   USA vetoed the proposed admission of North and South Vietnam to the United Nations, following the Security Council's refusal to consider South Korea's application.

# 1976

July 2   North and South Vietnam officially reunified
Sept. 13   USA reaffirms it will veto Vietnam's UN bid

# 1977

July 18   Vietnam became a member of UN

# 1978

Dec. 25   Vietnam invades Cambodia

# 1979

Jan. 5   Vietnamese troops occupy Phnom Penh and Pol Pot is ousted
Jan. 15   USSR calls for withdrawal of Vietnamese troops from Cambodia
Feb. 17   China begins a 'pedagogical' war against Vietnam
Mar. 8   China withdraws troops from Vietnam

# PART 1

## INDOCHINA AND FRANCE

# Ho Chi Minh and the Development of Vietnamese Nationalism

**IN THIS CHAPTER YOU WILL:**

- be introduced to the long history of Vietnamese resistance to foreign rule
- gain an understanding of French colonialism in Indochina
- follow the major trends in the development of Vietnamese nationalism
- be introduced to Ho Chi Minh
- explore the consequences of World War II for Vietnamese independence
- learn about the 'August Revolution'.

## Background

Vietnamese history dates to at least 500 BCE. Around this time the Nam people, a sub-group of a broader group known as the Viet, moved south from the Yangste Basin in present-day China to escape the influence of the dominant ethnic group, the Han.

The refugees from Han China settled on the fringes of Chinese civilisation in the Red River Delta in present-day North Vietnam. These early settlers, however, could not long avoid Chinese influence. By 258 BCE they had been brought back into the Chinese sphere of influence as a 'vassal state', which paid 'tribute' to the Chinese emperor, thereby securing his protection.

For the next 1,000 years the Vietnamese resisted periodic attempts by the Chinese to re-incorporate them. They were relatively successful in maintaining their own cultural identity because of three factors:

1 The Vietnamese were very far from the centre of Chinese power.
2 Vietnamese trade with other communities meant a number of diverse cultural influences competed with the Chinese influence.
3 In Vietnamese tradition, the people themselves wished to maintain their identity. They embraced the spirit of independence (*Doc Lap/Zoc Lap*).

Following the 10th-century Mongol invasion of China, Chinese influence in Vietnam declined. Following a period of instability, the Li (Ly) Dynasty was established in 1010 CE, with its base in Hanoi. This represented Vietnam's first central government and imperial family.

The Li Dynasty followed the Chinese model of government. Day-to-day affairs of state were conducted by a strong civil service chosen from a Scholar Gentry class. Unlike the Chinese system, however, the bureaucrats often displayed little loyalty to the dynasty.

Armed clashes between 'warlords' were frequent. Many warlords who were defeated in such clashes, or who rejected the authority of the Imperial court, headed south down the coast, trying to escape Hanoi's influence.

# Civil War

By the 17th century Hanoi's influence over central and southern Vietnam had waned. In the north, the Trinh family ruled. In central Vietnam the Nguyen family asserted control. The claims of these two families eventually led to civil war. After 50 years of struggle, however, neither side achieved the ascendancy, and Vietnam was roughly divided at the 17th parallel.

The civil war took place at a time when Europe was becoming increasingly interested in Asia as a new centre for trade. The Dutch and the Portuguese took sides in the Vietnamese conflict in the hope of securing some economic benefit.

Vietnam remained partitioned into the 18th century. But a third centre of power emerged, around the trading city of Saigon, where the Tay-son family dominated. In 1776 tensions between these competing families again erupted into civil war. With significant assistance from France, which was taking a newfound interest in Asian affairs, the Tay-sons won the 10-year civil war. By 1786 they had reunited Vietnam under the new Dynasty Nguyen-Anh.

# French Colonialism

The French remained interested in Vietnam. This attention was welcomed by the Nguyen Court: with French support, it was hoped that any Chinese plans for Vietnam would be thwarted. French interest was based on three factors:
1   The race to build colonial empires that delivered power and prestige to European nations.
2   The belief that colonial empires delivered economic advantages, by providing raw materials for industrial economies and closed markets for manufacturers.
3   Advocates of colonialism insisted it was part of Europe's obligation to the world to help develop poorer, less 'civilised' nations.

In 1847 France used the excuse of protecting Vietnamese converts to Catholicism to begin exerting influence and control. By 1859 the French had captured Saigon, and by 1862 the Vietnamese had been forced to cede large sections of south-eastern Vietnam to France. By 1867 the entire southern region of Vietnam ('Cochin-china') had been annexed by France. The French next looked north. In 1883 they attacked the Imperial Court in Hue, forcing the Emperor to sign a 'Treaty of Protectorate'. By 1887 the independent state of

*French administrative regions of Vietnam: Tonkin, Annam, Cochin China*

Vietnam ceased to exist: along with Cambodia and Laos, Vietnam was folded into a new colonial enterprise – the Union of French Indochina.

# Vietnamese Nationalism

The Vietnamese resisted French control. Resistance was led by the Scholar Gentry, who equated colonialism with 'national extinction'. Opposition ranged from refusal to serve the new colonial bureaucracy to open rebellion. The most famous of these rebellions was the 'Scholars' Revolt' of 1885–1888. By 1897, however, France had quelled all armed resistance.

The next generation of scholars (born at the time of French usurpation) accepted the limitations of their fathers' training and, influenced by developments in China and Japan, sought new methods of resistance, by exploring European and American historical experiences. By understanding the nature and power of the Western world they hoped to find ways of circumventing it. This 'Reform Movement' dominated Vietnamese nationalism during the early 20th century.

The most important of these Reform Movement scholars were Phan Boi Chau and Phan Chu Trinh. Phan Boi Chau, who formed the Reformation Society in 1904, regarded the lack of unity as the major impediment facing Vietnamese nationalists: if nationalists were united, and supported by the imperial family, a rebellion would succeed. Phan Chu Trinh disagreed, seeing armed insurrection as futile: peaceful and gradual national reform, with French assistance, would enable Vietnam to evolve into a modern democracy in the European mould.

In 1908, another uprising was thwarted. The rebellion's leaders fled. Some went to France, Hong Kong or Thailand, but a larger group found refuge in the southern Chinese city of Guangshou (Canton). There, in 1912, Phan Boi Chau formed the Vietnam Restoration Society. Under pressure from France, the Chinese imprisoned Phan Boi Chau.

## World War I

World War I had a major impact on Vietnamese nationalism. The French sought the support of their empire to fight and fund the war. France barely acknowledged Vietnam's sacrifices.

Disenchanted with their colonial masters, some Vietnamese soldiers in the colonial army planned a revolt, with the support of the 16-year-old emperor Duy Tan. But the French foiled the May 1916 insurrection. The ringleaders were executed and the young emperor was removed from the throne and charged with committing treason – against himself.

Following World War I, as opportunities arose for the development of indigenous industry, and as additional lands in the Mekong Delta were opened for private ownership, a French-educated Vietnamese elite emerged in Vietnam. This elite sought political power, while maintaining their economic advantages resulting from French rule. This group became a new force in Vietnamese nationalism.

In 1917, Bui Quang Chieu, a French-trained agricultural engineer, formed the Constitutionalist Party, Vietnam's first legal political party. With members including wealthy landowners, merchants, industrialists and senior civil servants, the Party's aims were modest and reflected the stake this elite held within the colonial system. It sought greater political representation within the colonial system and the same legal rights enjoyed by all French citizens.

In France, exiled Vietnamese nationalists, soldiers, workers and students were also agitating for change in their homeland. They saw the French Republic in action and sought to extend French democratic principles to their own lives. Towards the end of the war a group of Vietnamese living in France formed the 'Groupe Des Patriotes Annamités' ('Annamités' was the term used by the French to describe Vietnamese). Among their members was Phan Chu Trinh.

The group aimed to present their case at the Paris Peace Conference of 1919, which ended World War I. Reflecting the philosophy of Phan Chu Trinh and the new economic elite, its demands were very modest. They urged France to allow the formation of political parties in Vietnam and permanent representation in the French parliament. Although Vietnamese nationalists sought accommodation with France, neither the French, nor the rest of the world, listened.

By the end of World War I there was little cause for optimism among Vietnamese nationalists. Armed struggle had failed again. But so too had the efforts of moderate nationalists. Some moderates turned their attention to extending their economic privileges. Others, however, were increasingly radicalised by their inability to effect change. If the French would not grant even the most modest of changes, then their overthrow remained the only alternative. Many nationalists concluded that revolution was the only path forward. But how could the mistakes of the past be avoided?

# Ho Chi Minh

One young nationalist radicalised by the frustrations of World War I was Nguyen Tat Thanh. Born on 19 May 1890 in Kimlien, Annam, Nguyen Tat Thanh was familiar with the Vietnamese nationalist struggle. His scholar-father was a friend of Phan Boi Chau. Yet the young Nguyen Tat Thanh was not a radical nationalist. Indeed, at one time he applied for training with the French Colonial School, which prepared Vietnamese to work in colonial administration.

**Diary of Nguyen Tat Thanh, 12 February 1918 (Paris, France)**

The so-called 'recruitment' of our people out of Vietnam to fight alongside the French in the trenches is really a forced roundup, but yesterday Nguyen Chanh, who lost his leg fighting, told us that on the 'front line' there was never any difference between the French and Vietnamese. They got the same pay, same food, same treatment. Perhaps, I said, but we are still being used as cannon fodder here by a country that is still treating us like dirt back home. But I'm beginning to see France in a new light. There is much to admire about the country, and I have made many French friends here. In Vietnam forming such friendships was nearly impossible.

(The authenticity of this diary has long been debated. Many assume it was written long after the events described therein.)

In 1911 he left Vietnam, employed as a cook/steward on a French steamship. He sailed the world for six years, before settling in wartime France. During this period in France Nguyen Tat Thanh become a revolutionary. He realised Vietnamese sacrifices for France's war effort were not being rewarded.

Nguyen Tat Thanh joined the Groupe Des Patriotes and changed his name to Nguyen Ai Quoc (Nguyen the Patriot). It was a pen name once used by Phan Chu Trinh.

While the failure to bring change at the peace conference was a factor in Nguyen Tat Thanh's radicalisation, perhaps more important for his conversion was the rise of communism in wartime Europe, culminating in the Russian Revolution. While many Vietnamese had used French revolutionary history and rhetoric to champion their cause, communism spoke to many nationalists because it suggested European colonialism was driven by capitalism. A challenge to capitalism, therefore, was also a challenge to colonialism. Nguyen Ai Quoc accepted these ideas. Already a member of the Socialist Party, in 1920 he became a founding member of the French Communist Party.

The French Communist Party, however, was more interested in domestic affairs than in challenging colonialism. Unable to persuade French communists to champion his cause in practical ways, Nguyen Ai Quoc headed to Moscow, the 'birthplace of the revolution'. As part of its desire to encourage the overthrow of capitalism, the Soviet Union assisted Asian nationalists.

After spending several years in Moscow, Nguyen Ai Quoc was sent to Guangshou in late 1924. In Guangshou, Nguyen Ai Quoc's first task was to build a cadre amongst

*Nguyen the Patriot (Ho Chi Minh), as a member of the French Socialist Party, speaks at the Versailles Peace Conference, 1919*

Vietnamese sympathetic to 'revolution'. This required enticing potential supporters away from non-communist groups and leaders, the most important of whom was Phan Boi Chau who, after being freed, had stayed in Guangshou.

To remove a rival and provide a rallying point for Vietnamese nationalists Nguyen Ai Quoc betrayed Phan Boi Chau to the French authorities for 10,000 Hong Kong dollars. The French kidnapped the nationalist leader from Shanghai and returned him to Hanoi for trial and life imprisonment. The sentence was later amended to house arrest until Phan Boi Chau's death in 1940.

Following his role as a French collaborator in the downfall of Phan Boi Chau, Nguyen Ai Quoc was forced to again change his name to protect himself from vengeful opponents. This time, however, there was little choice with regard to a name. Adopting the identity papers of an old Chinese man who had died without family, he used the name 'Ho Chi Minh'.

# Assessing Phan Boi Chau

While Vietnamese historians value Phan Boi Chau's contribution to their country's independence, they identified two flaws in his nationalist campaign:
1   Although he dedicated his life to the nationalist cause, he had no concrete plan to evict the French.
2   Believing the peasantry was insignificant to the nationalist struggle and would follow the Vietnamese elite, he confined his efforts to the Vietnamese elite.

Perhaps because of his long exile, Phan Boi Chau was unaware of several developments transforming his homeland. First, while French rule initially had little impact on the Vietnamese peasantry and their traditional lifestyle, this changed during the early 20th century. Large tracts of land were confiscated and allocated to French investors to build large plantations, and taxes on the peasantry were increased dramatically. In addition, French land reforms gave more power to local landowners, and fuelled corruption. The peasantry became increasingly alienated from French rule. This groundswell of dissatisfaction, however, was not marshalled by the scholar-gentry nationalists, nor by the early French-educated nationalists.

Second, Phan Boi Chau appeared unaware of how World War I had helped transform the economy and produce a new social and economic class. The development of indigenous industry helped create a working class in Vietnam. This class was mostly confined to cities and regional centres, and differed from the traditional rural peasantry. During the 1920s these workers began to organise themselves to protect their economic interests. Primarily using strikes to protect their interests, by the mid-1920s these workers were also engaging in industrial action for political reasons.

Others learned from Phan Boi Chau's mistakes. It was among the peasantry and the new working class that Ho Chi Minh saw the best chance of ending French colonialism in Vietnam.

# The Road to Revolution

Ho Chi Minh's political beliefs and motivations continue to fascinate historians. For decades their analyses were influenced by the Cold War. Superpower rivalries that helped start the Vietnam War saw an earlier generation of historians debate Ho's motivations: was he driven primarily by a commitment to communism or to nationalism? Sympathetic historians portrayed him primarily as a nationalist, who regarded communism as the means to securing his nation's independence. They pointed to the absence of communist rhetoric in his editorship of the journal *Thanh-Nien* during the mid-1920s. Unsympathetic historians portrayed him as a ruthless communist, dedicated to the overthrow of not only the French in Vietnam, but the whole 'free world'. They cited his 1926 book *The Road to Revolution*. After the end of the Cold War in the early 1990s this labelling of Ho became less important. Most historians now accept that Ho was both a communist and a nationalist, and do not see the two goals as mutually exclusive.

---

**HISTORICAL DOCUMENT**

### Ho Chi Minh Discusses Workers' and Peasants' Commitment to Revolution, 1926

One becomes a revolutionary because one is oppressed ... The workers and peasants constitute the most considerable revolutionary force in society because they are the most oppressed and the most numerous. Being without property, they have nothing to lose but their chains – but they have a world to gain. So they constitute the most resolute forces, the basic constituents of revolution.

From *Road to Revolution*, reprinted in *Ho Chi Minh*, Hanoi, 1961.

---

Ho believed revolution in Vietnam would take place in two stages:

- in the first stage, nationalists from all social classes (but most importantly the 'masses') would unite to produce a bourgeois–democratic regime that might exist for decades

*Ho Chi Minh, 1924*

- only in the second stage would a socialist revolution take place, led by a communist party that deftly positioned itself at the vanguard of the nationalist struggle.

In Guangshou in the 1920s Ho's main aim was to secure the first stage of Vietnamese revolution, and establish the political apparatus to secure the second. He collaborated with the next generation of Vietnamese nationalists. During the mid-1920s students were the new vanguard of the nationalist movement. Their participation in the 'quit school movement' led to many of them being expelled from school; their radical agenda led to many being exiled outside Vietnam. Many of these young men sought refuge in Guangshou. Appealing to this group, Ho helped establish the 'Association of Vietnamese Revolutionary Youth'.

Ho's work in southern China, however, lasted only a few

years. The governing Chinese Nationalist Party (the Guomindang) was increasingly in conflict with the Chinese Communist Party; the Vietnamese nationalist leader's socialist credentials left him *persona non grata*. Ho returned to Moscow in late 1927, before embarking on an extended study tour of Europe.

# The Indochinese Communist Party (ICP)

Industrial unrest amongst the Vietnamese working classes was growing. Strikes were taking place across Vietnam. Some communist–nationalists were convinced Ho's first stage could be effectively leap-frogged: the time had come to move to the second stage, beginning with the formation of a Vietnamese communist party. Others argued the formation of such a party was premature and would alienate non-communist nationalists who were still crucial to the cause. Differences over the issue destroyed unity and led in 1929 to the establishment of three disparate Vietnamese communist parties.

Ho Chi Minh was not party to these debates as he had been sent by Moscow to work in Siam (Thailand). Unhappy with the situation in Vietnam, the Communist International (Comintern), which oversaw Moscow's desire for worldwide revolution, then sent Ho to Hong Kong to unite the various Vietnamese communist parties.

It was agreed that a new and united communist party must be formed. The new party was called the 'Vietnamese Communist Party', although in October 1930 Ho decided the name should be changed to the 'Indochinese Communist Party'.

## HISTORICAL DOCUMENT

### *Manifesto of the Indochinese Communist Party*

1  To overthrow imperialism, the feudal system and the reactionary bourgeoisie in Vietnam.

2  To win complete independence for Indochina.

3  To form a government made up of workers, peasants and soldiers.

4  To nationalise the banks and other imperialist concerns and place them under the control of the proletarian government.

5  To confiscate the agricultural concessions and other estates owned by the imperialists and bourgeois reactionaries, in order to share them out among the poor peasants.

6  To introduce an eight-hour working day.

7  To abolish compulsory loans, the poll tax and all the iniquitous taxes afflicting the poor.

8  To accord the people democratic liberties.

9  To provide education for all.

10  To achieve sexual equality.

While communists were united, their new party was only one of a number of nationalist groups in Vietnam. The most important group of the late 1920s was the Vietnam Nationalist Party (VNQDD). The new party set out to force change through direct action.

The Nationalist Party commenced a program of political assassination in 1929, and in 1930 planned a general revolt of Vietnamese soldiers in the colonial army. The rebellion, however, was a disaster. Poor communications, and hesitation on the part of some participants, meant only one section of the colonial army mutinied. The brutal and bloody manner with which France ended the mutiny, however, gained international attention. For many people in France the mutiny marked their first awareness of the anti-colonial struggle in Vietnam.

With the suppression of the rebellion, the Nationalist Party's importance waned, leaving the communists well placed to become the leading political party of national revolution. Ho regarded the failed 1930 revolt as clear evidence that the time for full-scale armed revolution remained far distant.

There were, however, more encouraging signs for Ho. In mid-1930 the first mass protests staged by peasants took place in Central Vietnam. Angered at the widespread poverty, the 'Nghe Tinh Soviets' – as they became known – were well organised. In September 1930, 6,000 peasants protested, demanding that the large landholdings be broken up and that people's councils be established. Vietnamese communists hoped to energise and radicalise the peasantry. But French rule was already achieving that goal.

## The Popular Front

Living in Hong Kong under the name Tong Van So, Ho Chi Minh's prominence in Asian communist circles made him a danger to all European interests in Asia. In June 1931 he was arrested by the British. Leading communists in Europe and Asia, fearing Ho would be turned over to the colonial French secret police (the *Sureté*), urged the left-wing British Government to prevent this happening. For the French, Ho was a major prize. Almost since its inception, and in the wake of the Nationalist Party's decline, the *Sureté* identified the Communist Party as the greatest danger to French rule in Vietnam.

Suffering a recurrence of the tuberculosis that had dogged him since the 1920s, Ho was admitted to a British prison hospital. In 1933 French authorities were told he had succumbed to his illness and died. In France and the USSR the death was reported in the press. The *Sureté* file on Nguyen Ai Quoc was closed.

Reports of Ho Chi Minh's death, however, were premature – as they would be on other occasions. The British released Ho in July 1932, for reasons that remain unclear. It has been suggested his release was due primarily to the actions of a prominent British anti-colonial lawyer, who lobbied the British authorities. Other, less plausible, arguments suggest Ho was released on condition he would work for British intelligence.

After his release Ho returned to the USSR. Still ill, he did not reappear in public until 1935, when he attended the Seventh Congress of the

Communist International. He studied and taught in Moscow, before replacing his friend Le Hong Phong on the Central Committee of the Communist International.

Ho did not return to Asia until 1938. By then, north-east Asia had been transformed by the continuing civil war in China and Japanese expansionism. Seeing Chinese instability as both a problem and an opportunity, Japan sought to exert its influence, first in 1931, by annexing Manchuria, and then, in 1937, by commencing an undeclared war on China.

The situation in north-east Asia encouraged a shift already underway in Europe. To counter the rise of German Nazism and Italian Fascism the USSR sought to cooperate with the liberal democracies such as Britain and France. Moscow instructed European communists to establish 'Popular Fronts' with non-communist political parties and groups opposing fascism.

After Japan signed the Anti-Comintern Pact (1936–1937) with Germany and Italy, it was clear that Japanese expansion threatened both the USSR and communist groups in Asia. Moscow instructed Asian communists to unite with non-communist forces who were resisting Japanese expansion. Asian communists would have to defer their plans for revolution. Moscow did not want its emerging relationship with the Western democracies harmed by Asian communists' anti-colonial rebellions.

These instructions outraged many Asian communists, especially members of the Indochinese Communist Party (ICP), who had become increasingly militant. One of the reasons Ho returned to China was to explain the importance of the Popular Front approach to his Asian colleagues. In 1939 Ho told the ICP that its plans for revolution must be deferred: 'The Party cannot at present put forward excessive demands (national independence, parliament) without risk of falling into the Japanese trap.'

In Hanoi, the French moderated their persecution of the ICP. This was possible because nationalist movements had not gained widespread popular support during the 1930s. On the eve of World War II the Vietnamese appeared docile subject peoples: French interests were protected by a colonial army of just 27,000 men, most of whom were Vietnamese.

# World War II

In 1939 France declared war on Nazi Germany. The Vietnamese were again expected to support France. By mid-1940, however, France was beaten. With a pro-Nazi French government established in southern France, colonial administrators in Indochina had to decide whether they would support the exiled 'Free French', led by Charles de Gaulle, or the new 'Vichy' Government. In Indochina colonial authorities aligned themselves with Vichy: Vietnam became an ally of Japan.

By 1940 Vietnam was of great strategic importance to Japan as a conflict with the United States and Britain looked increasingly inevitable. Vietnam provided the perfect location from which Japan could project its power into South-East Asia. Japan's decision to place troops in southern Vietnam in early 1941 set off a chain of events that culminated with the attack on Pearl Harbour and the outbreak of the Pacific War.

# The Viet Minh

In 1941 Ho returned to Vietnam for the first time in 30 years. The Eighth Plenum of the ICP was held in caves in the far north of the country. Still committed to securing the first stage of revolution through the formation of a broad-based nationalist movement, Ho formed a new organisation – the 'Revolutionary League for the Independence of Vietnam'. The group would become enshrined in history as the 'Viet Minh'.

---

**HISTORICAL DOCUMENT**

### Ho Chi Minh Announces the Formation of the Viet Minh, June 1941

Elders! Prominent personalities! Intellectuals, peasants, workers, traders and soldiers! Dear compatriots!

Since the French were defeated by the Germans, their forces have been completely disintegrated. However, with regard to our people, they continue to plunder us pitifully … they heartlessly offer our interests to Japan. As a result our people suffer under a double yoke; they serve not only as buffaloes and horses to the French invaders but also as slaves to the Japanese plunderers …

Now, the opportunity has come for our liberation. France itself is unable to dominate our country. As to the Japanese, on the one hand they are bogged in China, on the other, they are hamstrung by the British and American forces …

Some hundreds of years ago, when our country was endangered by the Mongolian invasion, our elders under the Tran dynasty rose up indignantly and called on their sons and daughters throughout the country to rise as one in order to kill the enemy. Finally they saved their people from danger, and their good name will be carried into posterity for all time …

Rich people, soldiers, workers, peasants, intellectuals, employees, traders, youth, and women who warmly love your country! At present time national liberation is the most important problem. Let us unite together! As one mind and strength we shall overthrow the Japanese and French and their jackals in order to save people from the situation between boiling water and boiling heat.

---

Now seeing the Vichy French and the Japanese as their enemy, the Viet Minh set about building an army. This task was placed in the hands of a former history teacher, Vo Nguyen Giap. These soldiers were trained with two missions in mind: To close with the enemy when the opportunity arose, but, in the meantime, to move through the countryside gathering intelligence and converting the people of Vietnam to the nationalist cause. Their function, therefore, was *political* as well as *military*.

In July 1942 Ho travelled to China to make contact with Jiang Jieshi and unite the Viet Minh with the Chinese in their struggle against Japan. He hoped also to re-open channels of communication with the Chinese Communist Party and Moscow.

Ho's mission was a total failure. Soon after entering southern China he was arrested and imprisoned by the local Guomindang warlord Marshal Chang Fa-kwei. Wishing to spread his influence into northern Vietnam, Chang had been developing his own Vietnamese nationalist organisation –

## PERSONALITY

## Vo Nguyen Giap

Vo Nguyen Giap was born in Quang Binh Province, in central Vietnam, in 1912. Like Ho Chi Minh, the young Giap was educated at the Lycée National, in Hue.

Giap played a role in the establishment of the Viet Minh and became the pre-eminent Viet Minh military leader during the First Indochina War. Ho decided Giap was the best-placed of the Vietnamese communists to assume military command.

Giap's qualifications for such an office were few, although he was an admirer of Napoleon Bonaparte. With a group of 40 men, Giap began his military career, training others in the tactics of guerrilla war. He was helped not only by Ho, who had received some military training in Moscow, but also by the Chinese communists, who were well versed in the ways of war.

Nicknamed *Nui Lua* ('Volcano under Snow'), Giap's cold exterior gave nothing away and concealed a fiery passion. Cautious and calculating, but with explosive and untiring energy, he was described as forceful, arrogant and dogmatic. Giap's military leadership was a crucial ingredient in the success of the Vietnamese communists.

the Revolutionary League of Vietnam. Ho's Viet Minh were perceived as a threat to this group.

Following Ho's arrest, reports reached Vietnam that he had died in a Chinese prison. Ho was saved from such a fate, however, because the Revolutionary League failed to live up to Chang's expectations and because the Vietnamese leader convinced the Chinese warlord that he was best placed to lead the organisation that was supposed to supplant the Viet Minh.

# The United States and Indochina

*Ho Chi Minh (second right) with General Vo Nguyen Giap (back left) during a military campaign in Vietnam, 1950*

Although the United States was an Asian colonial power (controlling the Philippines), many Americans had been critical of French exploitation in Indochina and of the colonial government's cooperation with Japan. Amongst these critics was President Franklin Delano Roosevelt.

From as early as 1943 Roosevelt was suggesting to British, Chinese and Russian leaders that France should not be allowed to return to Indochina. While some American intelligence reports suggested the Vietnamese were ready for self-government, Roosevelt believed that a period of 'trusteeship' was required. China and the United States would provide leadership and guidance to Vietnam until it was ready to manage its own affairs.

While Ho was in China he realised that many Americans were sympathetic to Vietnamese nationalism. Before Chang granted him freedom of movement, Ho was a regular visitor at the local branch of the US Office of War Information in the Chinese city of Kunming. Having lived in New York City for six months during his sea-going days, Ho had a grasp of English and was an avid reader of the publications in the OWI Library.

So impressed were local American authorities with Ho that they hoped to send him to San Francisco, from where he could broadcast in Vietnamese to his countrymen and women. Fearful of offending France, however, the State Department refused to grant a visa to Ho.

### HISTORICAL ISSUE

#### The United States in the Vietnamese Mind

The United States had always figured prominently in the thoughts of Vietnamese nationalists. The Reform Movement scholars were interested in the United States as the first modern republic. Men such as George Washington had successfully resisted colonial rule.

Having lived in New York City, Ho Chi Minh was fascinated by American history. He wrote about the lessons of the American experience in *Road to Revolution* (1926). Influenced, perhaps, by the disappointment of the Groupe de Patriotes, who were inspired by US President Woodrow Wilson's notion of self-determination, Ho believed the United States was betraying its revolutionary past. The Russian Revolution, he argued, was now closer to the Vietnamese experience.

During World War II, however, American rhetoric again spoke of freedom. The Atlantic Charter, signed between Britain and the United States in 1941, offered hope that Wilsonian self-determination would this time be delivered to colonial peoples.

# The Japanese Coup

In 1944 Allied forces liberated France from Nazi rule. This placed pressure on Japan's relationship with the Vichy French colonials in Indochina. Was the new government of Charles de Gaulle legitimate in the eyes of the French colonials? While the French sent mixed messages on this issue, the repeated use of the word 'liberated' to describe the situation in France was considered by Japan as clear proof of where Vichy allegiances now lay. With American forces having returned to the Philippines, Japan feared that France's colonial army might turn against them.

Claiming that the French use of the word 'liberated' was tantamount to a declaration of war, the Japanese staged a coup d'etat against the French on 9 March 1945. French colonial forces were expelled quickly from the major urban centres.

Even before the coup, Japan had been in discussion with leading non-communist nationalists and had supported a number of organisations. Seeking support from the Vietnamese population, Japan quickly announced that Vietnam had now been freed.

Japan maintained the French imperial system. The emperor was Bao Dai. Assuming the position in 1925 (when he was just 13) Bao Dai had been educated in France, before returning to Hue, where he found his position an irrelevance within the French colonial system. He spent most of his time hunting, gambling and womanising. The Japanese allowed Bai Dai to declare his nation's independence. But his rights and responsibilities remained unclear. For the position of Prime Minister, the Japanese overlooked the prominent non-communist Catholic nationalist Ngo Dinh Diem. Instead, they appointed the conservative Tran Trong Kim. The new Cabinet's powers, however, were greatly limited. The Japanese remained very much in control.

# Uncle Ho and Uncle Sam

The Japanese coup smashed the Free French and Allied intelligence networks that had provided information during the war. Fearing that Japanese troops in Indochina might now join the campaign against American air bases in southern China, it was crucial for the Allies to re-establish reliable intelligence networks.

Before returning to Vietnam in 1944, Ho Chi Minh met with officials of the American intelligence agency, the Office of Strategic Services (OSS), and began providing information regarding Viet Minh forces in northern Vietnam. Could these forces provide military intelligence to the United States?

Prior to the Japanese coup, Allied intelligence operatives believed these Vietnamese nationalist groups could not be trusted. Repeated requests from these groups to be armed by the Allies to fight the Japanese had also been ignored. But the escalation of Allied bombing campaigns in Vietnam, and the intelligence blackout, compelled a change of heart.

Fortuitously for the Viet Minh, Ho Chi Minh had returned to Kunming in February 1945. Having rescued a downed American pilot, Ho decided to accompany him to safety in the hope he could parley this good deed into Allied support for the Viet Minh. Arriving in Kunming, Ho asked to meet the commanding officer of American forces in China, General Claire Chennault. The request was politely refused. But Ho stayed in Kunming to explore other avenues of support and recuperate before the long walk back to northern Vietnam.

Ho's story captured the interest of Charles Fenn, an OSS officer. Concluding that the Viet Minh was the only group capable of helping the Allies, Fenn approached Ho with the plan of establishing both a pilot rescue scheme and a radio intelligence network in northern Vietnam.

On 29 March 1945 Ho met Chennault. Before returning to Vietnam, Ho received an autographed photo of the American general and six new Colt .45 automatic pistols. These props played an important role in legitimising the Viet Minh in Vietnam as the nationalist group favoured and supported by the Allies. Ho was given the OSS codename 'Lucius' (the character in Shakespeare's *Titus Andronicus* who restores justice to Rome as a new emperor): 'Old Man Ho' was now working for the Americans.

The relationship between the Viet Minh and the Allies proved successful. American operatives became permanent features at Viet Minh headquarters. Archimedes Patti, the new American OSS officer responsible for Indochina, advocated an expansion of the relationship to include more sensitive intelligence gatherings. The Americans provided the Viet Minh with 25 boxes of weapons, ammunition and radio equipment.

By May 1945 Patti was authorised to support Viet Minh guerrilla forces and sabotage missions in northern Vietnam. Many of these used French and Vietnamese troops of the old colonial army, although the OSS advocated using the Viet Minh. By July an OSS cadre was operating out of Ho's headquarters. These Americans sent positive signals to their headquarters in China, describing the Viet Minh as 'patriots', who deserved American 'trust and support'. The communist connections were downplayed.

# 'August Revolution'

The Pacific War ended in August 1945. With France unable to accept the Japanese surrender in Vietnam and with other Allied forces some weeks away from establishing a presence in Vietnam, there was a power vacuum in the former French colony.

This provided a perfect opportunity for the Viet Minh. With the support, if not open encouragement, of the accompanying OSS officers, Ho and the Viet Minh marched on Hanoi. By 20 August they had taken control of the government buildings. The Japanese-backed Vietnamese Government was in no position to resist. Even the Emperor appeared to support the Viet Minh, stating he would prefer to be the citizen of a free country than the king of an enslaved one. Nonetheless, Bao Dai hoped the Viet Minh might be planning a constitutional monarchy. Ho, however, demanded the Emperor's abdication, which was announced on 23 August.

The 'August Revolution' spread across Vietnam. Viet Minh groups gained control of government at all levels. In places where other nationalist groups took control (such as Saigon) allegiance to the Viet Minh was quickly proclaimed.

On 29 August 1945 the 'Provisional Government of the Democratic Republic of Vietnam' (DRV) was announced, with its capital in Hanoi. On 2 September, in front of tens of thousands of his fellow countrymen and women in Ba Dinh Square, Ho Chi Minh proclaimed Vietnam's independence. He did so by borrowing from the American Declaration of Independence – although he suggested 'all people', rather than all 'men', have 'a right to live, to be happy and free'. Following Ho's speech, a Vietnamese band played the American national anthem, *The Star Spangled Banner*.

Whether it was an attempt to secure American support, or a genuine reflection of his admiration for the United States, Ho's speech pleased the American OSS officers with whom he shared the reviewing stand that day. To the gathered crowd, the presence of the Americans soldiers, and a fly-past by American aircraft, must have seemed clear proof that the new nation had the support of the most powerful nation in the world.

In Washington, DC, however, a new American president, Harry S Truman, was confronting an international situation far different from that which Roosevelt had faced before his death in April 1945. Even as the celebrations in Hanoi continued, the United States was acquiescing to France's demands that it be allowed to resume control of its prized colony.

### Excerpts from Ho Chi Minh's Declaration of Vietnamese Independence, 2 September 1945

All men are created equal; they are endowed by their Creator with certain unalienable Rights; among these are Life, Liberty and the pursuit of Happiness.

The immortal statement was made in the Declaration of Independence of the United States of America in 1776. In a broader sense this means: All the people on the earth are equal from birth, all the peoples have a right to live, to be happy and free …

… for more than 80 years, the French imperialists, abusing the standard of Liberty, Equality and Fraternity, have violated our Fatherland and oppressed our fellow citizens …

In the field of politics, they have deprived our people of every democratic liberty.

They have enforced inhuman laws; they have set up three distinct political regimes in the North, Centre, and the South of Viet-Nam in order to wreck our national unity …

They have built more prisons than schools. They have mercilessly slain our patriots …

To weaken our race they have forced us to use opium and alcohol.

They have robbed us of our rice fields, our mines, our forests and our raw materials …

They have hampered the prospering of our national bourgeoisie; they have mercilessly exploited our workers …

Notwithstanding all this, our fellow citizens have always manifested toward the French a tolerant and humane attitude …

From the autumn of 1940, our country had in fact ceased to be a French colony and had become a Japanese possession …

The truth is we have wrested our independence from the Japanese and not from the French …

For these reasons, we, members of the Provisional Government, representing the whole Vietnamese people, declare that from now on we break off all relations of a colonial nature with France …

We are convinced that the Allied nations, which at Tehran and San Francisco have acknowledged the principles of self-determination and equality of nations, will not refuse to acknowledge the independence of Viet-Nam …

The entire Vietnamese people are determined to mobilize all their physical and mental strength, to sacrifice their lives and property in order to safeguard their independence and liberty.

# Evaluating Ho Chi Minh and Vietnamese Nationalism to 1945

During early September 1945 Ho Chi Minh must have been well satisfied with his efforts. Independence, however, had been secured because of the French absence, rather than by revolution. Many of Ho's ideas on revolution were still yet to be tested. He had long advocated the importance of the peasantry and workers for the cause of national revolution, but into 1945 the leadership of the Viet Minh was comprised mainly of young men who were the sons of scholars, bureaucrats, merchants and wealthy landowners.

Circumstance, as much as good planning, was at the centre of Ho's success. His courting of the Americans had allowed him to unite many nationalists, while many of his opponents were tarnished by their association with Japan. His ability to maintain this unity would be challenged in the years ahead: disunity remained a major problem for Vietnamese nationalists and revolutionaries after World War II.

Ho Chi Minh and the Viet Minh had the overwhelming support of the Vietnamese people in September 1945. But he had underestimated France's desire to regain its empire, as one way to lessen the humiliation of defeat in 1940 and to re-assert what was no longer true – that France was a world power. The French continued to believe Vietnamese nationalists were weak and dysfunctional. They continued to delude themselves into believing the Vietnamese had come to love the French and were content to be subjugated in their own land.

Historians have analysed Ho's relationship with the OSS to ascertain whether he was first and foremost a communist or a nationalist. Ho went to considerable lengths to secure US recognition of the Vietnamese Republic. His letters to Washington, DC, however, went unanswered. The views of OSS operatives were also overlooked, including one memorandum that proclaimed that although Ho had 'formerly favoured Communist ideals', he now saw them as 'impracticable for his country' and that the course ahead for Vietnam was 'republican nationalism'. Subsequent events cast doubt on such assertions, but such statements provide some of the Vietnam War's most intriguing 'what ifs'.

---

**POINTS TO REMEMBER**

- The Vietnamese resisted French colonialism. In its early stages, this opposition was confined to the Vietnamese elite.
- Ho Chi Minh became an important Vietnamese independence leader. He was a founder of the Vietnamese Communist Party (later re-named the Indochinese Communist Party). He concluded that French colonialism could only be overthrown by revolutionary means.
- The Indochinese Communist Party was only one of a group of nationalist groups.
- During World War II the United States and Ho Chi Minh fought against Japan. During this period Ho Chi Minh's communist connection was down-played.
- Near the end of the war in the Pacific the Vietnamese nationalist groups, lead by the Viet Minh, took control of Vietnam from the Japanese.
- Ho Chi Minh hoped for American support for Vietnamese independence.

## ACTIVITIES

1  What does early Vietnamese history suggest about the likely outcomes of foreign intervention in Indochina?

2  Evaluate the impact of French colonialism on Vietnamese nationalism to the end of World War I.

3  Write a brief outline of the life and political career of Ho Chi Minh.

4  Explain why and when Ho Chi Minh became a revolutionary.

5  Why did Ho Chi Minh return to Indochina in 1941?

6  Why was the Viet Minh formed?

7  Could a non-violent Vietnamese independence campaign have succeeded against the French?

8  One of the historical debates concerning Ho Chi Minh is whether he was a communist or a nationalist. List points under the headings 'communist' and 'nationalist'.

9  What was the relationship between the United States and Ho Chi Minh during World War II?

10  What was the significance of World War II for Vietnamese nationalism?

11  How was Ho Chi Minh able to declare Vietnamese independence in August 1945?

12  Why were the French surprised that their return to Indochina after World War II was resented by the Vietnamese?

## DOCUMENTARY EXERCISE

On the Internet, find the complete Declaration of Vietnamese Independence, 2 September 1945 and answer the following questions.

### Discussion Questions:

1  To what extent can this document be used as evidence of French behaviour towards the Vietnamese?
2  Why did Ho Chi Minh borrow from the US Declaration of Independence?
3  Is this the statement of a nationalist or a communist?

## FURTHER READING

There are a number of useful works on this period, yet these works often contradict each other. American influences on Vietnamese nationalist thought are explored in Mark Bradley's *Imagining Vietnam and America* (University of North Carolina Press, Chapel Hill, 2000). David Marr's 600-page *Vietnam 1945* (University of California Press, Berkeley, 1997) is equally good. Archimedes Patti's *Why Viet Nam?* (University of California Press, Berkeley, 1980) and Charles Fenn's *Ho Chi Minh* (Charles Scribner's Sons, New York, 1973) provide personal perspectives that challenge recent claims. The Viet Minh/OSS relationship is explored in the excellent British documentary *Uncle Ho and Uncle Sam* (BBC, 1997). Another useful documentary is *Ho Chi Minh: The Man Behind the Myth* (Reuters Television Production, 1998).

# 2

# The First Indochina War: The Defeat of France, 1945–1954

IN THIS CHAPTER YOU WILL:

- be introduced to the major themes of the First Indochina War
- be introduced to reasons why France sought to remain in Vietnam and the policies it adopted to achieve that aim
- gain an understanding of the Viet Minh's approach to expelling France from Vietnam
- gain an understanding of why the United States became involved in Vietnam
- explore the reasons for French defeat and Viet Minh victory.

## The Allied Occupation of Vietnam

Ho Chi Minh's dream of an independent Indochina faded when the British and Chinese occupied Vietnam. British General Douglas Gracey was ordered to disarm the Japanese and maintain law and order. He disliked the Viet Minh and expected France to regain civil and military control of Vietnam. Gracey released French military forces from Japanese imprisonment and rearmed them to help protect French civilians. On 22 September French troops rioted in Saigon, attacking property and shooting Vietnamese civilians as a way of seizing control of the city.

The Viet Minh responded with a general strike on 24 September. Viet Minh agents moved into a predominantly French area of the city, killing 150 people. In response, Gracey used Japanese, British and French forces to attack the Viet Minh. Ho was also under threat in Tonkin, where Chinese forces removed the Viet Minh from power and replaced them with pro-Nationalist, anti-communist, Chinese–Vietnamese.

The British, however, were more concerned with their own empire than with the return of French power in Indochina. In December 1945, after disarming the Japanese, they withdrew from southern Vietnam. French soldiers (equipped by the Americans) replaced the British. Both France and Ho wanted

China to leave northern Vietnam. Under the terms of a February 1946 agreement with France, China agreed to withdraw from Tonkin; in return, France would relinquish concessions granted in an 1890 Franco–Chinese treaty. While he had 35,000 troops under his command, French General Jacques Philippe Leclerc wanted to negotiate with the Viet Minh. Fighting the Vietnamese would be 'like ridding a dog of its fleas. We can pick them, drown them and poison them, but they will be back in a few days'. The only way the French could win, he believed, would be if the Viet Minh could be lured into a conventional battle where French training and firepower would prevail.

# Ho Chi Minh Negotiates with the French

With neither side able to prevail, France and the Viet Minh sought a negotiated settlement. The result was the Franco–Viet Minh Accords, signed in March 1946. Ho reluctantly agreed to divide Vietnam and to allow 25,000 French troops to return to the north and replace the Chinese. These French troops were expected to remain only until 1951. In return, France recognised the new independent Vietnamese state within the French Union and promised to hold free elections in the 'near future' to determine if Cochin China (southern Indochina) would eventually come under Ho's control. Ho took the calculated risk that France would not try to seize power and that a negotiated settlement could be reached. General Leclerc told Paris: 'The major problem from now on is political'.

## HISTORICAL DOCUMENT

### Ho Chi Minh Contrasts Chinese and French Colonisation of Vietnam, 1946

Don't you realise what it means if the Chinese remain? Don't you remember your history? Last time the Chinese came, they stayed a thousand years! The French are foreigners. They are weak. Colonialism is dying. The white man is finished in Asia. But if the Chinese stay now, they will never go. As for me, I prefer to sniff French shit for five years than eat Chinese shit for the rest of my life.

Having established a framework for discussions, Ho travelled to Paris in June 1946 to continue negotiations. When he arrived, however, the French Government had collapsed. There was no one with whom he could negotiate. Then the situation deteriorated even further. Violating the agreement reached in March, French-controlled southern Indochina was renamed the Republic of Cochin China and designated a separate colony in the French Union. The man responsible for this violation was Admiral Georges Thierry d'Argenlieu, who in August 1945 had been appointed French High Commissioner for Indochina. Like many of his compatriots, d'Argenlieu believed that France could only regain great power status after the debacles of World War II if it re-established its overseas empire.

The creation of a separate state in the south proved a disaster for Ho. For Ho and many other nationalists, reunification was no less significant than independence. Indeed, the two goals were inseparable. There was also a very significant practical reason for this dual emphasis: while much of northern Vietnam was poor and overpopulated, the Mekong Delta, in southern Vietnam, produced a surplus of rice.

When talks finally began they were with a new, right-wing French government that was far less inclined to negotiate. Vietnamese attempts to convince France to agree to Vietnamese independence led to a draft accord that protected France's economic prerogatives in the north and made tentative plans for a unification referendum in Cochin China in 1947. The new French Government, however, had little intention of honouring the agreement. Expecting that a military solution would be needed, the leader of the French delegation, Max Andre, told the Vietnamese: 'We only need an ordinary police operation for eight days to clean all of you out.' Ho signed the draft agreement because it would buy time for the Viet Minh to build its strength for the apparently inevitable war with France.

# Massacre at Haiphong and the Outbreak of the First Indochina War

Ho Chi Minh returned to Tonkin in October 1946. Franco–Viet Minh relations had deteriorated further over the issue of customs duties. The French believed it was their right to collect customs duties in the northern port of Haiphong. The Viet Minh, however, regarded it as their right and an important source of revenue. With both sides refusing to concede, tensions soon erupted into fighting. At d'Argenlieu's request, French Prime Minister Georges Bidault authorised the local French commander to use 'every means at' his 'disposal to seize Haiphong' and teach the Viet Minh 'a harsh lesson'. On 23 November, the French attacked guerrilla hideouts in Haiphong. Supported by aircraft and by a sustained naval bombardment, French troops swept through the city. Just two hours' notice of the attack had been given to the civilian population. Much of Haiphong was destroyed and 6,000 people were killed. Only a few Viet Minh were counted among the dead.

On 19 December 1946, Giap led the Viet Minh militia in a retaliatory attack on French interests in Hanoi. They destroyed Hanoi's power plant and assassinated several French officials. Ho and his supporters left the city and established a new headquarters at Viet Bac, near the Chinese border. This almost inaccessible rugged hill country had many caves where the Viet Minh could regroup for the struggle ahead. What became known as the 'First Indochina War' – or, to the Vietnamese, the 'French War' – had begun.

# French Strategy

France sought to deprive the Viet Minh of supplies and force them into a set-piece battle where superior French firepower would be decisive. To do so the

French needed to secure not only the Red and Mekong River Deltas (to deny the Viet Minh the supply of rice) but also to block the movement of Viet Minh troops into secure areas near – and across – the borders with Laos and China.

France constructed isolated military strong-points or 'hedgehogs', garrisoned by French troops who conducted search-and-destroy missions against the Viet Minh. To prevent these missions, the Viet Minh would be forced to attack the outpost, thereby giving the French an opportunity to fight a conventional battle, in which the French were confident their fire-power would prevail. These French outposts, however, could not be supplied from the air because France lacked sufficient aircraft; re-supply, therefore, could only be accomplished by road convoys. These convoys were ideal targets for Viet Minh ambush.

*A French outpost burns after a Viet Minh attack, 1951*

The French ability to wage war against the Viet Minh was constrained by political unrest in France, the limited economic resources available and wide-spread support for the Viet Minh in northern Vietnam. French commanders knew they must win a quick victory, so their weaknesses were not exposed. Publicly, the French remained confident. The French officer assigned the task of destroying the Viet Minh, General Etienne Valluy, believed he 'could eliminate all organised Viet Minh resistance within three months'.

The early French strategy was straightforward: kill or capture Ho Chi Minh. During late 1947 France launched several attacks against Viet Minh strongholds. Although the French killed several thousand Viet Minh, Ho and other Viet Minh commanders escaped and the promised swift victory did not materialise. Valluy's replacement, General Blaizot, made no bold predictions and during 1948–1950 no major French offensives were undertaken. The Viet Minh used the respite to rebuild their forces and launch an education and indoctrination program in northern Vietnam.

# People's War

France believed its strategy would result in the quick defeat of the Viet Minh. Conversely, Ho and Giap prepared for a protracted guerrilla war. The Viet

Minh strategy was influenced by the theory of 'People's War', developed by Chinese communist leader Mao Zedong. Fighting the Nationalist Chinese, Mao conceded he was outnumbered by his better-equipped enemy. In a conventional war, Mao's forces could be easily encircled and destroyed. The key ingredient for victory, therefore, was to sustain the morale and will-power of his forces. Spiritual power and a faith in the cause would ultimately defeat an ostensibly stronger military force.

## HISTORICAL ISSUE

### People's War

People's War had three essential principles:
1 Revolution would be conducted from bases in remote rural areas.
2 The army's role would be as much political as military. 'Political mobilisation' was a crucial activity.
3 People's War would be protracted and indeterminate in length.

The military element of People's War had three stages:
1 Stage One was the defensive stage, when the enemy would have all the strategic advantages. Consequently, it would be necessary to rely on guerrilla war and not try to hold territory against the enemy.
2 Stage Two was the strategic stalemate phase. Whilst the guerrillas would have greater spiritual resources, the enemy would be able to maintain greater material resources. It would be crucial, therefore, to focus on reducing the enemy's resources.
3 Stage Three was the strategic counter-offensive. Because guerrilla war alone can never secure victory, it would be important to wait for the strategic position of the enemy to collapse (for whatever reason). During this final stage the enemy is confronted on the battlefield in a conventional engagement and defeated. This part of the struggle was sometimes described as 'positional war'.

Believing France had insufficient military or economic resources for a long war, the Viet Minh leadership believed a guerrilla war would erode France's resolve to fight.

# Elysee Agreement

The military's failure to end the war compelled France to further explore political solutions. One approach was to foster a rival, pro-French and anti-communist nationalist movement. In 1946 the French had returned the former Emperor Bao Dai to the throne after his abdication of the previous year. While thankful for his reinstatement, the 'playboy' Bao Dai did not return to Vietnam, preferring instead to enjoy a hedonistic lifestyle in southern France.

France decided to re-cast Bao Dai as a nationalist leader. On 8 March 1949 Bao Dai signed the Elysee Agreement. This created a new independent state of Vietnam within the French Union. France would control the new nation's finances, diplomacy and defence. Bao Dai was genuinely keen to play a role in the new state, but it quickly became apparent that the new Vietnam was a new state in name only. He later remarked: 'What they call the Bao Dai solution turns out to be just a French solution.'

The Elysee Agreement failed because it was too late for France to create a viable nationalist movement. French claims that they supported Vietnamese nationalism rang hollow when they were fighting a war against Vietnamese nationalists. Because the Vietnamese fear of communism was not as strong as their antagonism toward the French, France's appeals to anti-communism failed.

# Vietnam and the Cold War

As the struggle between France and the Viet Minh continued in the late 1940s, it came to be viewed as a part of the global conflict between the USA and the USSR. In America, many feared an international communist conspiracy, led by the USSR, which was determined to conquer the world. Many Americans believed the only way to win this conflict was to fight the spread of communism, whenever and wherever it emerged. Consequently, small conflicts were usually viewed as front lines in this global struggle. Soviet support for the Viet Minh 'proved' the communists intended to conquer Indochina and then the rest of Asia. To fight worldwide communism, America needed French support.

# Escalating Conflict in Vietnam

The Chinese communist revolution had important implications for the Viet Minh. While the Nationalist Chinese had been feared in 1945, the Communist Chinese provided the Viet Minh with two great advantages. First, they now had a haven to their north where they could avoid French forces. Second, Vietnam was now bordered by a nation sympathetic to its revolutionary struggle. A Viet Minh training camp was established in southern China. Giap attacked isolated French outposts so his men could not only disrupt the French, but practice for a full-scale campaign he planned to launch during 1950. The time was at hand to move to the next phase of People's War.

## HISTORICAL DOCUMENT

### Vo Nguyen Giap Discusses the Significance of the Chinese Revolution

This great historic event, which altered events in Asia and throughout the world, exerted considerable influence on the war of liberation of the Vietnamese people. Vietnam was no longer in the grip of enemy encirclement, and was henceforth geographically linked to the socialist bloc.

Thanks in part to Chinese supplies and training, Giap had six divisions to commence his 1950 campaign. His target was his enemy's weakest point: the outposts. He aimed to destroy France's will to resist, while building the morale and skills of his own forces.

---

**HISTORICAL DOCUMENT**

### *Vo Nguyen Giap Discusses Morale*

In war it is imperative that a combat unit win its first battle, particularly its first offensive battle. The troops must know beyond doubt that they can defeat their enemy. On this certitude is built battlefield morale, which feeds on victory and is consumed by defeat.

---

The Viet Minh enjoyed success in their campaign. By October 1950, after suffering nearly 10,000 casualties, France abandoned many of its outposts. By defeating the French at Dong Khe and Cao Bang, the Viet Minh demonstrated they could also subdue larger French forces. The successes of 1950, coupled with the realisation that the French position would improve with the arrival of American aid, led Giap to open the final stage of People's War in 1951. The Viet Minh would launch a 'general counter-offensive' to drive French forces back to Hanoi and out of Vietnam.

In response to their defeats, senior French officers were relieved of command. In December 1950, General Jean de Lattre de Tassigny became Commander in Chief. An imposing and highly regarded officer, whose arrival immediately boosted French morale, de Lattre believed France needed to buy time until more American aid was forthcoming and the Vietnamese National Army (VNA) was built. France could maintain its presence in North Vietnam if it could secure the Red River Delta. A perimetre line was drawn around the valley and a series of blockhouses constructed, well serviced by strong internal lines of communication. The plan worked. The 'De Lattre Line' blunted Giap's counter-offensive. During the next 18 months the Viet Minh suffered 6,000 casualties in unsuccessful attempts to break the defensive line. Giap realised the French would have to be lured out of the Red River Delta.

Some French officials believed the tide had turned. The victory, however, was little more than a respite. In early 1952 de Lattre died of cancer. He was replaced by General Raoul Salan. By 1952, Giap had found a means of drawing the French out of their Delta sanctuary. By intensifying operations along the Laotian border, he would incite French fears of a Viet Minh invasion of Laos. It was hoped that if Salan did not react, French politicians would. Laos was the most loyal of France's Indochinese colonies. If Laos was not defended, France would lose the support of its Cambodian and Vietnamese allies.

Rather than confronting Giap head-on, Salan attacked Viet Minh strongholds near the Chinese border. Giap, however, pressed his attack and captured large areas of Laos. When it became clear the Viet Minh lacked the logistical support to sustain their offensive in Laos, Giap's forces retreated back into Vietnam – but only after cultivating the opium crop in northern Laos. (Revenue from opium was used to finance the Viet Minh war effort.) Neither side seemed capable of delivering a knock-out blow.

# Navarre Arrives

Salan's inability to break the deadlock saw him replaced in May 1953 by Lieutenant-General Henri Navarre. A veteran of two world wars, who believed he could defeat the Viet Minh within a year, Navarre nevertheless left for Hanoi confused. He had not been advised of his objectives in Vietnam, nor how he was to achieve them. Reflecting the growing French impatience and sense of despair, the only direction Prime Minister Rene Mayer had given Navarre was to urge him to find a way for the government to negotiate itself out of the conflict, without damaging French prestige. Not for the last time, questions of national credibility were entangled in the Vietnamese jungles.

What was France fighting for in Vietnam? De Lattre had suggested in 1951 that France was fighting for Vietnamese independence. But no one, least of all the Vietnamese, believed this. The Americans believed the French were fighting communism. The French were happy to embrace American rhetoric if it maintained the flow of aid. It was also argued that France was protecting an important economic resource. By the early 1950s, however, many French-owned businesses had closed and relocated off-shore. Moreover, with two-thirds of the country under Viet Minh control, France was unable to exploit its colony. Vietnam was costing the French treasury, not adding to it. The only reason to stay that made any sense was because they were there.

The bad news for Navarre continued. Arriving in Vietnam he found a general staff convinced that the war could not be won militarily. Furthermore, while American aid

**PERSONALITY**

**General Henri Navarre**

The general forever associated with French defeat in Vietnam, Henri Navarre, first fought for his country as a 19-year-old on the Western Front during World War I. After the war he was involved in counter-insurgency operations in Syria and later in the implementation of 'pacification' programs in Morocco. During World War II, he served with the French underground until the return of Free French forces. After World War II Navarre served with the combined forces of the North Atlantic Treaty Organisation (NATO) before being selected by Prime Minister Mayer to take command in Vietnam.

Navarre was said to adore cats and indeed sought to replicate their independent thinking and preference for being alone. He was supposedly 'simultaneously cordial and distant, debonair and icy'. In 1953 *Time* magazine reported there was an '18th century fragrance about him' and that he believed in 'nothing but the army'.

increased, as Navarre hoped, his ability to wage war was being undermined both at home and within Vietnam. French attempts to build a VNA were dismal failures. Many of those conscripted into the army paid their way out of service, or did not show up. While Navarre's army was professional and battle-hardened, he did not have enough troops to fulfil his mission. With the continuing problems with the VNA, he commenced the 'Jaunissement' or 'yellowing' program. Vietnamese would be directly assigned to French units.

Following the hand-over of authority in Hanoi, Salan told Navarre that the Viet Minh were preparing to enter a conventional phase of battle as their units adopted a more 'European flavour'. French hopes of destroying the

Viet Minh in a large-scale conventional battle had returned: as one of his last orders Salan commenced setting the bait he hoped would lure the Viet Minh into such an encounter.

Seduced by such a possibility, Navarre began planning 'Operation Castor'. By destroying the Viet Minh in a 'traditional' European-style battle, the French hoped to gain the ascendancy in any diplomatic negotiations that would end the conflict.

## The Battle of Dien Bien Phu

'Castor' called for the airborne reoccupation of the Dien Bien Phu valley in north-western Vietnam, near the Laotian border. Dien Bien Phu was the centre of Viet Minh opium cultivation. The French had other reasons for setting up their base there, too. By establishing an 'air–land base' in the valley, the French could send patrols into the surrounding hinterland, disrupting Viet Minh lines of communication. Navarre also believed a base would prevent another Viet Minh incursion into Laos, where the Pathet Lao, a communist-supported guerrilla force, was already challenging French authority.

Navarre believed the Viet Minh would seek to destroy the French base. Thanks in part to continued training by Chinese cadre, the Viet Minh looked to the experiences of the Korean War, where Chinese forces had used human wave attacks. If the Viet Minh used such tactics, the French were confident their superior firepower could obliterate the enemy and destroy the Viet Minh ability to wage war. Time was again the enemy of the French. Navarre worried that with a cease-fire ending the conflict in Korea, Chinese equipment and supplies previously earmarked for Korea would soon arrive in Vietnam, advantaging the Viet Minh.

The French commander at Dien Bien Phu was Colonel Christian de Castries. The aristocratic Castries had a distinguished military record. In November 1953, he supervised the construction of the French base. The surrounding mountains were thickly covered with vegetation, making it difficult to deploy artillery there. If the Viet Minh managed to drag artillery onto the mountains, the French were confident they could quickly destroy them. Colonel Charles Piroth, commander of French artillery, boasted that 'no Viet Minh cannon will be able to fire three rounds before being destroyed by my artillery'.

*Colonel Christian de Castries, French commander at Dien Bien Phu*

The French built an airstrip to resupply themselves by air from Hanoi, 350 kilometres to the east. American advisors insisted the Viet Minh could not use artillery to attack the airfield. With their air superiority, the French believed they could hold out indefinitely. The main base was placed at the centre of the valley, beyond which three artillery bases were constructed. These artillery bases were named after Castries's mistresses: 'Isabelle', 'Beatrice' and 'Gabrielle'. The base was garrisoned with 13,000 paratroopers – an insufficient force, even considering the underestimation of Viet Minh capabilities. The French estimated there were two Viet Minh divisions in the area, with minimal artillery support.

Giap understood the situation differently. He must have been surprised – and presumably pleased – by the layout of the French base. Navarre wanted his artillery to be able to fire on the Viet Minh

*Ho Chi Minh and his commanders plan the Battle of Dien Bien Phu (right, General Vo Nguyen Giap)*

human-wave assaults from several directions. However, all Giap had to do was attack the artillery bases – located outside the base perimeter – and then attack the base itself. Even more curious to Giap was the logistical problems for the French. With supply by road impossible, the Viet Minh could use artillery to prevent supply aircraft landing on the hastily constructed runway.

Giap was mindful not to repeat the mistakes of earlier engagements. Contemplating the problems facing the French, he concluded a Viet Minh victory was certain. The ground, soaked by torrential rain, reduced the effectiveness of French tanks. By attacking 'Beatrice', 'Isabelle' and 'Gabrielle' individually, he could destroy French artillery. Giap envisaged a siege in which his own artillery, supplied by the Chinese, would prevent the French from using their airfield. Both sides had an added motive for success. In January 1954, the great powers agreed that discussions about Asia, including the conflict in Indochina, should begin before the middle of the year. All sides wanted to be in a strong position when this occurred.

Implementing a tactical principle he called 'One slow, four quick', Giap consolidated his forces around Dien Bien Phu over a period of months. Four Viet Minh divisions were hidden in the surrounding mountains. Navarre underestimated Viet Minh mobility. Though poorly equipped and often marching on shoes made from discarded rubber tires, Giap's troops advanced toward Dien Bien Phu. French air attacks on the roads leading to Dien Bien Phu were ineffective. Giap had at his disposal 10,000 workers ready to repair the roads within hours of any attack. French intelligence officers reported the Viet Minh build-up; but increasing tensions between Navarre and his deputy, General René Cogny, who had reservations about the plan, ensured there was no response from the French. Indeed, this was exactly what Navarre wanted.

By early March Giap had 200,000 troops and supply workers at his disposal. The French had been confident the Viet Minh could not bring heavy artillery into positions on the mountains without being spotted and destroyed by French aircraft. However, Giap's forces had disassembled their artillery pieces, then carried them to Dien Bien Phu, where they were reassembled. On 12 March, to the surprise of the French, 150 mm artillery shells began to hit the airstrip, rendering it unsafe for aircraft. The following day Viet Minh artillery hit all three of the French artillery bases. Giap launched massive human-wave assaults. Within eight hours 'Beatrice' fell. A day later, 'Gabrielle' fell. Whilst the Viet Minh had suffered heavy losses, the French had already lost most of their artillery. Told of those losses, Piroth, the French artillery commander, suicided.

Castries moved to reinforce the southern artillery base, 'Isabella', to prevent it being overrun. Giap, however, did not attack this base. He was pleased: French troops sent to Isabella could not be used to protect the main French base. The French had lost two of their three artillery bases. But of greater concern was the fact they could not be supplied by the air. French and American pilots now had to drop supplies. Meanwhile, Giap decided to change tactics. The infantry assaults had proved too costly. Instead, the Viet Minh infantry dug in and began digging trenches and tunnels towards the French lines.

# Options for the United States

Realising it would be difficult to hold the base, the French sought more American assistance. On 20 March, General Paul Ely, the French Chief of Staff, met with President Eisenhower, Secretary of State John Foster Dulles, and Chairman of the Joint Chiefs of Staff, Admiral Arthur Radford. Even as Ely sought more American aid, he conceded that the French position at Dien Bien Phu was now untenable. Eisenhower asked Radford (who was keen to assist France) to investigate whether the United States could offer more assistance.

Radford devised a rescue plan – 'Operation Vulture' – with the aid of French and American officers in Saigon. Radford intended to use American air power to destroy Viet Minh artillery, without which the Viet Minh could not press the siege. The French could then repair the airfield and the garrison would be resupplied. If the air attacks did not lift the siege, Radford proposed using nuclear weapons.

There was, however, little support for Radford's plan. Army General Matthew Ridgway, and other members of the Chiefs of Staff, expressed opposition. Ridgway, convinced the bombing would not lift the siege, used the recent experience of the Korean War to highlight the difficulties of fighting wars in Asia, where the terrain and climate were almost always unfavourable. Conditions were even more difficult in Indochina than in Korea. Ridgway advised that seven to 10 extra divisions of troops would be needed to lift the siege at Dien Bien Phu. Eisenhower, who had commanded Allied armies in Western Europe during World War II, appreciated the weight of Ridgway's arguments.

Radford did, however, receive support from Vice-President Richard Nixon, who supported France's attempts to remain in Indochina. Reflecting prevailing Cold War rhetoric, Nixon worried the communists would 'nibble us to death all over the world in little wars'. The only solution, he suggested, was 'massive, mobile retaliatory forces'. Nixon supported the use of nuclear weapons to lift the siege.

> ## HISTORICAL DOCUMENT
>
> ### Excerpts from 'Memorandum for the Secretary of Defense', 28 August 1953
>
> **The Navarre Concept for Operations in Indochina**
>
> Based on past performances by the French, the Joint Chiefs of Staff have reservations in predicting actual results which can be expected pending additional proof by demonstration of continued French support and by further French performance in Indochina ... [A] basic requirement for military success in Indochina is one of creating a political climate in that country which will provide the incentive for natives to support the French and supply them with adequate intelligence which is vital to the successful conduct of operations in Indochina. If this is accomplished and if the Navarre concept is vigorously pursued militarily in Indochina and given wholehearted political support in France, it does offer a promise of military success sufficient to warrant appropriate additional US aid required to assist.
>
> For the Joint Chiefs of Staff:
> Arthur Radford, Chairman, Joint Chiefs of Staff

Realising that military plans are inevitably more neat and tidy than the realities of war, Eisenhower stated 'he could conceive of no greater tragedy than for the US to become involved in an all-out war in Indochina'. In private, however, he suggested he wanted to help the French. He did not want to give his political adversaries room to attack him by losing Indochina. More generally, Americans were expressing contradictory views on these matters. At the same time as they expressed continuing concerns over Communist 'advances' around the world, they did not want to see their country bogged down in another 'Korean-type' conflict. (An armistice ending the Korean War had been signed just nine months before, after three years of bloodshed.)

With his Administration divided, and lacking Congressional support, Eisenhower concluded that US intervention was conditional on NATO support and on France agreeing to make concessions on Vietnamese independence. All of this would take time – which the French defenders at Dien Bien Phu did not have. The French pressed Eisenhower for air strikes, which he refused. He did, however, despatch Secretary of State Dulles to Europe to secure NATO support.

While Dulles sought European allies for the United States, Eisenhower – who continued to have grave reservations about American intervention – tried to build American public support for intervention. At a 7 April press conference he used the metaphor of dominoes to connect the prospect of a communist victory in Vietnam to America's long-term security: 'You have a row of dominoes set up and you knock over the first one, and what will happen to the last one is the certainty that it will go over quickly ... The loss of Indochina will cause the fall of South-East Asia like a set of dominoes.'

The British did not support Eisenhower's claim that Vietnam was an essential domino. Nor did Eisenhower's rhetoric hide his own concerns regarding the practicality of military operations in Indochina. Eisenhower,

US President
Dwight Eisenhower
(left) and
Secretary of State
John Foster Dulles

moreover, was concerned about French attitudes toward American assistance. The French refused to cooperate with the Americans' Military Assistance and Advisory Group (MAAG) and criticised suggestions that a multinational force should oversee the peace process in Vietnam.

## Continuing French Failures

With diminishing prospects of American intervention, France was forced to contemplate the real possibility of defeat at Dien Bien Phu. This reflected the broader failures of French policy in Indochina. The French plan to turn the war over to the Vietnamese, and in effect have the Vietnamese act as a French colonial army, was as far away from success in 1954 as it had been in 1951 when the VNA was established. Losing thousands of men through desertion, the VNA was an ineffectual fighting force.

Meanwhile, at Dien Bien Phu, monsoon rains made resupply by air almost impossible. By late April, the Viet Minh outnumbered the French defenders 10 to one. Twenty-four hours a day, Viet Minh soldiers dug trenches towards the French outpost, forcing the French to reduce their defensive perimeter. The outpost, which originally had a circumference of 24 kilometres, was reduced to 1000 square metres.

While the Viet Minh were strengthening their position around Dien Bien Phu, the Geneva Conference opened in Switzerland. The conference bogged down from the start. The Viet Minh snubbed the representatives of the Emperor, Bao Dai. The Americans, headed by Dulles, were determined not to give the communists an inch of territory. Only the British, and to a lesser degree the Soviets, were prepared to deal with everyone.

On 6 May, Giap decided to increase the Viet Minh bargaining position by launching his final assault. After a fierce bombardment of the French garrison, Viet Minh infantry assaults commenced. The following day the base fell. The French commander, Castries, along with 10,000 French troops, was taken prisoner. The Viet Minh had won one of the decisive battles of the 20th century. Giap regrouped his forces and began moving towards Hanoi. The defeat at Dien Bien Phu toppled the French Government. Responding to French public opinion, the new Prime Minister, Pierre Mendès-France, was determined to end the war quickly. In Washington, Eisenhower realised the communists would gain control of part of Indochina. Ever the Cold War Warrior, Dulles spoke of salvaging something from South-East Asia and of forming a NATO-style regional alliance in the region.

# Evaluating the First Indochina War

Dien Bien Phu was a military defeat for France. It did not have to be the end of French rule in Vietnam. But after eight years of war, France was no longer prepared to fight to retain its colonial possession. The cost had become too great and by 1954 few people could explain why France should remain in Indochina.

Politically, but to a greater extent, militarily, the French underestimated their opponents. The 300,000 dead Viet Minh showed the seriousness of this miscalculation. The French underestimated the Viet Minh will to endure, their capabilities on the battlefield and their support amongst the Vietnamese. Giap, the school teacher-turned-general, proved the Viet Minh had the military skills and logistical capacity to fight both a guerrilla and conventional war. The French had wrongly assumed Giap's guerrillas would be unable to convert from counter insurgents to a conventional army. Underestimating the Viet Minh tenacity – and the equipment and training they had received from the Chinese – the French suffered the humiliation of defeat at the hands of an enemy they had earlier denigrated.

Many French field commanders appreciated the Viet Minh strengths. But convincing staff officers back in Hanoi – or in Paris – of the enemy's potential was often difficult. How could a rag-tag group of Asians possibly defeat a modern European army? This was one of Navarre's biggest mistakes – and it was informed by notions of European racial superiority, notions that had helped create and then sustain the French colonial enterprise.

The French generals' task in Vietnam was complicated by the chaos that characterised post-World War II French politics. A virtual revolving door of governments meant that French attitudes and policies toward Vietnam were ad hoc, ill-informed and ultimately confused. The warnings made by many French officials – including, most significantly, by the soldiers who advocated diplomatic, rather than military solutions to the conflict – were either not heard or ignored. Their words would become prophetic after Dien Bien Phu.

The First Indochina War was also significant because it increasingly drew the United States into the affairs of this emerging South-East Asian nation. Vietnam had become the latest hotspot in a Cold War the United States was determined to win. By 1954 over 70% of the war was being funded by the United States, but it had still been a war the Americans had fought by proxy. The French departure ensured the United States would no longer be able to hold Vietnam at arm's length.

**POINTS TO REMEMBER**
- The French were unable to regain full control of their Indochinese colonies after World War II.
- The 1946 Franco–Viet Minh Accords divided Indochina in two.
- The First Indochina War began in 1946, after France tried to extend its control of Vietnam.
- The French sought to win a conventional war. The Viet Minh fought a 'People's War'.
- This war became part of the global 'Cold War'. As a result, America became increasingly involved in an effort to prevent a communist victory in Indochina.
- The French were decisively defeated in a set-piece battle at Dien Bien Phu.

## ACTIVITIES

1 How did the conflict begin between France and the Viet Minh after World War II?

2 Were the Franco–Viet Minh Accords of 1946 a temporary ceasefire, or the basis for long-term peace in Indochina?

3 How did the First Indochina War start?

4 Outline French Strategy to win the war. Compare and contrast this with the 'People's War.' Make a list of the advantages and disadvantages each side had in the war. In your opinion, which were the most decisive?

5 Explain the significance of the Elysee Agreement.

6 How did Navarre plan to win the war?

7 Prepare an oral or written presentation that describes the battle of Dien Bien Phu and explains how it turned into the decisive battle of the war.

8 List evidence of why American support for the French increased during this period.

9 Was the First Indochina War a war of independence, a war of revolution or a civil war?

## Discussion Questions:

1 Why did the French want to stay in Vietnam?

2 How did the Viet Minh intend to rid Vietnam of the French?

3 Why did the United States become involved in Vietnam?

4 Why did the French lose the battle of Dien Bien Phu?

## Sample HSC Exam Questions:

1 Describe the role of the Viet Minh in Indochina in the period from 1945 to 1954.

2 Briefly describe the results of the Battle of Dien Bien Phu.

### FURTHER READING

Bernard Fall's *Hell in a Very Small Place: The Siege of Dien Bein Phu* (De Capo Press, New York, 1966, republished in 2002) and *Street Without Joy* (Stackpole, Harrison PA, 1967) are both useful. One recent and valuable study is John R. Nordell's *The Undetected Enemy: The French and American Miscalculations at Dien Bien Phu, 1953* (Texas A & M University Press, College Station, Texas, 1995). Marilyn Young's *The Vietnam Wars, 1945–1990* (Harper Perennial, New York, 1991) and Phillip Davidson *Vietnam at War: A History 1946–1975* (Oxford University Press, London, 1988) look at explanations for defeat. Régis Wargnier's *Indochine* (1992) is one of the relative handful of films exploring the relationship between Vietnam and France.

# PART 2

## THE UNITED STATES
## AND INDOCHINA

# 3

# The United States, the Cold War and Indochina

IN THIS CHAPTER YOU WILL:

- be introduced to the major issues of the Cold War that provided the context for US intervention in Vietnam
- learn about the impact of the Cold War within the United States
- be introduced to the significance of the 'fall' of China to communism in 1949
- learn why the United States attached growing significance to the struggle in Indochina.

## The Cold War

The Cold War is a term used to describe international relations between the United States and the Soviet Union and their allies in the period from 1945 to the end of the 1980s. The phrase 'Cold War' described the competition, tension and conflict short of full-scale war between the two political–military blocs. The Cold War spread to Africa, the Middle East, South America and Asia.

The World War II alliance between the Western Allies (Britain, the United States and France) and the USSR was always tenuous. Joseph Stalin, the Soviet dictator, always mistrusted the West. He believed the West had deliberately delayed opening a 'Second Front' in Europe so Soviet forces would bear the brunt of the war against Germany. There was no evidence for this, but both sides could point to evidence of hostility. Britain, France and the United States had tried to overthrow communism in Russia during 1919–1920 by direct military intervention in the Russian Civil War. On the other hand, the USSR had always promoted the ultimate aim of communism: the defeat and destruction of capitalism.

In February 1945, with the war in Europe nearly over, 'The Big Three' – Stalin, Roosevelt and Churchill – met at Yalta, in southern Russia, to resolve what was to be done in Europe after Hitler's defeat. They decided that Germany should be temporarily divided into separate zones of Allied occupation.

Berlin (the German capital) and Austria were to be similarly divided. In Eastern Europe, which had been occupied by Soviet forces, free elections were to be held and a timetable was set for the USSR to enter the war against Japan.

When the Allied leaders met again in July, Truman (who had become President after Roosevelt's death in April) did not tell Stalin that the United States intended to use the atomic bomb on Japan. On 6 August, 1945, four days after the Potsdam conference closed, the United States dropped the first atomic bomb on Japan.

*The Big Three: Churchill, Roosevelt and Stalin (Yalta, 1945)*

## HISTORICAL ISSUE

### The Atomic Bomb

The bomb appeared to be a godsend to the Americans. They could impose their will on any recalcitrant nation merely by threatening to use it ... America could retain a powerful position in Europe without having to maintain a mass army there. One of the great fears in American military circles was that, having smashed Germany, the West now had to confront the Red Army, and the only nation capable of doing so was the US.

S. Ambrose, *Rise of Globalism*, Penguin, New York, 1991.

Soviet expansion into Europe could be interpreted in a number of ways. In part, it was an ideological clash between the free world, led by the United States and the 'Communist monolith', led by the USSR. Some observers saw the Cold War as a defensive measure by the USSR: Stalin was determined that the nations of Eastern Europe would form a buffer zone against any possible attack from the West. Truman and Churchill believed the Cold War was evidence of the Soviet Union's aggressive intentions. Describing the Russian threat in March 1946, Churchill spoke of an 'iron curtain' that had descended between the 'free' nations of Western Europe and the Soviet-dominated communist nations to the East.

By the end of 1947, Bulgaria, Poland, Rumania, Hungary and Albania had communist governments all closely aligned with the Soviet Union. (Marshall Tito's communist Yugoslavia refused to enter the Soviet sphere of influence. Yugoslavia was a communist nation that defied the USSR.)

The Greek Civil War was regarded as a clear example of how the West had to stop communism. In February 1947, after Britain stated it could no longer supply aid to Turkey and Greece, Truman persuaded Congress to grant $400 million in aid. In his speech to Congress Truman articulated 'The Truman Doctrine'. The Truman Doctrine drew a clear line between the capitalist free world and the communist world and committed the United

States to assist any nation fighting against 'totalitarian regimes forced upon them against their will'.

The strategy of 'containment' was central to 'The Truman Doctrine': the United States believed it should 'contain' the expansionary USSR wherever it decided to expand. The first success of containment was the defeat of the Greek Communists in 1949. For the United States containment represented an historic shift from isolationism to the hegemonic responsibilities of a great power, which meant extending American interests around the world. It also exacerbated the rivalry with the USSR.

Truman was convinced that European economic prosperity, based on a free market system, could help stem communist advances. Wealthy nations, it was assumed, were politically stable and unlikely to become vulnerable to communist take-over. In June 1947, US Secretary of State George Marshall announced that the United States was willing to provide economic aid to all European nations. The European Recovery Program ('The Marshall Plan') of 1948 provided Western Europe with US$12.6 billion in economic aid between 1948 and 1952. In return, Western European nations agreed to buy American goods and allow US investment in their industries. Stalin, accusing the United States of using the plan to dominate Europe and assist the American economy, revived the Communist International, under the new name of Cominform. In 1949, through a new economic body, Council for Mutual Economic Assistance (COMECON) Stalin offered Soviet aid to eastern bloc countries. During the late 1940s and the 1950s, Soviet and US attention was focused primarily on Europe; subsequently, these issues would be played out in Indochina.

The Soviet rejection of the Marshall Plan was an important point in the Cold War. Equally important was the crisis over Berlin, which is often regarded as the first 'real' conflict of the Cold War. Berlin had been split into four zones of occupation. The Soviets controlled the eastern part of the city, while the Western Allies controlled West Berlin. West Berlin was surrounded by the Soviet-occupied eastern part of Germany. The Western Allies' main means of access to Berlin was by road and railway. In June 1948 Stalin ordered that these roads and railways be blockaded.

Stalin hoped to force the Western Allies out of Berlin by starving its civilian population. Determined not to give up West Berlin, the United States organised the Berlin Airlift, which moved enough goods into the city to support its 2.5 million people for the 320 days of the blockade.

The moral victory the West won by standing up to Stalin exacerbated international divisions. Apprehensive about Soviet intentions, in April 1949 the United States and Western European nations established the North Atlantic Treaty Organisation (NATO). Later in 1949, the Soviet Union detonated its first atomic bomb, much sooner than the United States had expected. The same year, Mao Zedong's communists defeated the American-backed regime of Nationalist Jiang Jieshi (Chiang Kai-Shek) in China.

The 'loss' of China – the world's most populous nation and a country that had long excited American interest – left many in the free world convinced that communism was expansionary. It was widely accepted that international communist expansion was being orchestrated by Moscow and that the United States had to confront communism wherever it appeared. During the late 1940s, this concern exacerbated fears about internal subversion, which had dramatic political consequences in 1950 when Republican Senator Joseph McCarthy claimed 205 communists were working in the US State Department.

*A US aircraft flies in supplies during the Berlin Airlift*

Many Americans believed a communist underground had infiltrated the US Government. For two years McCarthy's witchhunt excited Americans' anti-communist hysteria. Thousands of Americans were questioned about their political allegiances; while many of the accusations verged on the absurd, the anti-communist witchhunts of the late 1940s and early 1950s had a profound impact on American foreign policy and political culture. In particular, the Democratic Party was accused of being 'soft' on communism and was blamed for the 'loss' of China. Those charges helped Eisenhower win the 1952 presidential election for the Republican Party. Eventually, McCarthy went too far and was exposed as a self-serving bully. But the damage was done. Witnessing the public panic and scapegoating, a Democratic Party Senator from Texas, Lyndon Baines Johnson, warned that the McCarthy-inspired 'red scare' would be 'chickenshit compared with what might happen if we lost Vietnam'.

# Vietnam and Fears of Worldwide Communist Domination

Perceiving a worldwide communist threat, American policymakers grew increasingly concerned about the Indochinese situation. It was no longer a straightforward matter of French imperialism or Vietnamese independence. Ho Chi Minh was not a nationalist leader but a Moscow-controlled communist. Particularly after the 'loss' of China, Vietnam fitted into the dominant American understanding of expansionary communism.

This explanation of expansionary communism became known as the 'Domino Theory'. This theory was central to US foreign policy and American perceptions of the world, from the late 1940s until the 1960s. According to the Domino Theory, communist success in one state would destabilise its non-communist neighbours and precipitate their 'fall' to communism. Emerging independent states were the most vulnerable. American policymakers claimed Vietnam was a potential domino. If it fell to communism, then the next dominoes, Laos and Cambodia, would also fall. It would only be a matter of time, then, before all of South-East Asia and Central Asia would fall, threatening Australasia and the Middle East. The evidence seemed to support the theory. The British were already fighting communists in Malaya and Burma and a war was being fought against communist guerrillas in the Philippines. Politicians in Australia and New Zealand expressed deep concern about a communist victory in Indochina.

It was South-East Asia as a whole that was of vital strategic and economic interest to the United States. The region was rich in economic resources. The United States would not only lose access to these resources if South-East Asia fell to the communist, but also huge potential markets. Japan and the Philippines, crucial to the US advanced line of defence in the Pacific, would also be threatened.

The American interest in Indochina was also related to Japan's post-World War II recovery. Japan had few natural resources. Since China was now in communist control, the most accessible source of raw materials for Japan was South-East Asia. Japan's economic recovery was important for the stability of the region and to prevent communist advances in Japan. Determined, too, to promote economic growth and stability in Western Europe, American policymakers were inclined to accept French arguments that their economic recovery would be bolstered by the reacquisition of their Indochinese colonies.

Events in Asia appeared to reinforce these political, economic and strategic concerns. Until 1950 Marshall Plan aid to France was provided on the condition that it would only be used to rebuild metropolitan France. But France, perceiving its colonies as crucial to its economic reconstruction after World War II, disregarded the American instructions. Following the loss of China, and after the Soviets and Chinese granted diplomatic recognition to the Viet Minh, the US National Security Council viewed communist activity in Indochina as part of a communist conspiracy to take control of South-East Asia. The Truman Administration now accepted that American dollars should play a role in supporting France in its anti-communist struggle in Vietnam. On 8 May 1950 Truman announced direct American aid to Indochina. The United States also recognised Bao Dai's state of Vietnam as an independent member of the French Union.

As late as 1950, Ho Chi Minh had toyed with the idea of seeking American support to negotiate a deal between the Viet Minh and the French. With the American decisions of that year, however, Ho realised the United States would never support him. His former friends were now his enemies.

# The Korean War

Truman's decision was vindicated by events in Korea, which after the end of World War II had been divided into Soviet-occupied 'North Korea' and American-occupied 'South Korea'. The Yalta Conference had determined that elections would be held to determine Korea's form of government. However, neither side could agree on how the elections should be organised. Truman was convinced Korea had become a 'testing ground' in the struggle between communism and democracy. Soviet and American forces withdrew from Korea in 1949. In June 1950 the North Korean Army invaded South Korea across the 38th parallel. The United States took the opportunity to enlist the support of the United Nations.

Initially, North Korean forces made rapid progress into the South, but UN troops, a majority of whom were Americans, soon drove the

*US troops, Korea*

North Koreans back over the 38th parallel. The UN commander, American General Douglas MacArthur, convinced Truman to allow him to invade North Korea. This seriously concerned China. The Chinese feared that American and UN forces would invade Manchuria. In November 1950, 300,000 Chinese 'volunteers' attacked UN forces in North Korea. United Nations forces were then driven back into South Korea. MacArthur advised Truman to attack China, with nuclear weapons if necessary. Truman resisted that advice, but he did agree the Chinese should be driven back over the 38th parallel. He also decided to remove MacArthur from command. By June 1951 the American military objective had been achieved and negotiations commenced to reach a peace deal. After two years of tedious negotiations a deal was reached and two new countries were established on either side of the 38th parallel. Over a million Koreans had died, along with 1.5 million Chinese and over 54,000 Americans.

The Korean War was an example of the Truman Doctrine in practice in Asia. It also demonstrated that although the Americans had nuclear weapons they did not risk using them in case it started a nuclear war. The Korean War was also an example of 'war by proxy' – the Soviets backed North Korea and China, but avoided direct involvement themselves.

The United States was now convinced that the USSR intended to conquer all of Asia. In response, Truman increased aid to help the French fight in Indochina. By the end of 1950, $183 million had been committed. Also, the

US National Security Council policy paper 68 (NSC 68) advocated a massive increase in spending to meet the communist challenge.

For the rest of the 1950s the Cold War oscillated between crisis and conciliation. In November 1953, the United States exploded the first hydrogen bomb. Nine months later the USSR exploded its first H-bomb. In January 1953, President Eisenhower's Secretary of State, John Foster Dulles, articulated the concept of 'massive retaliation', whereby the US would use nuclear weapons to protect an American ally, even if the USSR attacked with non-nuclear weapons. The United States, moreover, would go to the 'brink' of nuclear war to protect its interests. Dulles also advocated 'A Policy of Boldness', by which the United States should demonstrate that 'it wants and expects liberation to occur' in communist countries: in other words, he was proposing the overthrow of communist regimes. The possibility of compromise was displayed at the Geneva Conference, convened as French forces were being defeated at Dien Bien Phu in 1954.

---

**POINTS TO REMEMBER**

- The Cold War developed amid post-war tensions between the USSR and the United States.
- The Truman Doctrine established 'containment' as the US strategy to deal with the USSR.
- The USSR saw the Marshall Plan as a direct threat to its survival.
- The Berlin Crisis was one of the first conflicts of the Cold War.
- The Domino Theory is important in understanding US involvement in Indochina.

## ACTIVITIES

1  What was the 'Cold War'? Is the term 'war' appropriate to describe this period in international relations?

2  On a map of Europe identify the countries under the influence of the USSR and the Western Allies.

3  What was the significance of the Truman Doctrine?

4  Was the Marshall Plan a threat to the USSR?

5  Why was the first conflict of the Cold War over Berlin?

6  Why were NATO and the Warsaw Pact established?

7  How did Communist victory in China affect the Cold War?

8  How did the Korean War affect the Cold War?

9  What was the significance of the 'Domino Theory' for the conflict in Indochina?

10  Was the Cold War conflict over power, conflicting ideologies or a personal conflict between American and Soviet leaders?

### Sample HSC Exam Question:

1  Assess the importance of anti-communism in shaping the policies of the United States towards Indochina between 1954 and 1979.

### FURTHER READING

Chapters 2 and 3 of William H. Chafe, *The Unfinished Journey: America Since World War II*, 5th ed. (Oxford University Press, New York, 2003) provide a useful discussion of the Cold War. See also Chapters 3 and 4 of Robert J. McMahon, ed., *Major Problems in the History of the Vietnam War* (Heath, Lexington, Mass. DC, 1995), and Stephen Ambrose and Douglas G. Brinkley, *Rise to Globalism: American Foreign Policy since 1938* (Penguin Books, New York, 1997). See also Chapters 7 and 8 of Thomas G. Paterson, J. Garry Clifford, Kenneth J. Hagan, *American Foreign Relations: A History, Since 1898*, 5th ed. (Houghton Mifflin, Boston, 1999).

# 4

# Indochina After the French: The Two Vietnams, 1954–1960

IN THIS CHAPTER YOU WILL:
- be introduced to the Geneva Conference and its consequences
- explore the emergence of separate states in North and South Vietnam
- examine life in North and South Vietnam in the 1950s
- understand the forces that gave rise to the National Liberation Front
- continue to appreciate the American position in Indochina.

## Background

Told by General Giap of the Viet Minh victory at Dien Bien Phu, Ho Chi Minh warned that rather than being the end, the decisive victory was the only the beginning. The truth of Ho's observation would be borne out within a few weeks, when the Viet Minh delegation attended the international conference called to resolve the Indochinese situation. Rather than solving problems, however, the conference divided Vietnam, assuring its emergence as the next Cold War hotspot.

## The Geneva Conference

Dien Bien Phu was a humiliating defeat that compelled France to seek a negotiated settlement on terms not of its own making. Instead of improving France's bargaining position at the Geneva Conference of May–July 1954, the battle had destroyed it. The United States encouraged France to fight on until it reversed its battlefield position and could again negotiate from a position of strength. They refused. The cost was too great.

France, however, did much better in its negotiating at Geneva and left the meeting with nominal control of approximately half of Vietnam. The meeting produced a ceasefire that instructed French forces to withdraw south of the 17th parallel, while the Viet Minh would withdraw north of this line.

The division was to be marked by a 10 kilometre wide Demilitarised Zone (DMZ) and was intended to be temporary, until the will of the Vietnamese people was ascertained through a national plebiscite. The meeting agreed that free elections would take place in July 1956, where-upon the Vietnamese would decide which side they favoured. An international commission, comprising Canada, Poland and India, would monitor compliance with the agreement.

*The Geneva Conference*

Why did the Viet Minh delegation, under the leadership of Ho's trusted lieutenant Pham Van Dong, accept an agreement that failed to recognise their control of two-thirds of the nation and ceded the richest areas of the country to their opponents? One explanation suggests that the Viet Minh position reflected pressures applied by their Russian and Chinese allies. Keen to avoid a confrontation with the United States, Russia also hoped its constructive approach might reduce France's commitment to the American-led Western alliance in Europe and stop it joining the European Defence Community (EDC). Furthermore, Russia hoped that if France remained enmeshed in the region, American involvement would remain limited.

That events in Europe and the broader Cold War were of primary importance to the USSR was demonstrated by Soviet desires to have China remain largely responsible for relations with the Vietnamese communists. China was also keen to avoid Vietnam becoming the next international hotspot so soon after the Korean War. Hearing America's veiled threats of military intervention during the discussions, China's main aim was to avoid an American military intervention in Indochina – which might subsequently threaten China.

China, claiming that peaceful co-existence was at the core of its foreign policy, wanted to concentrate its resources on domestic issues. A constructive approach at Geneva was one way to demonstrate this national outlook. Vietnamese intransigence was regarded by the Chinese as evidence of their inexperience in the 'real politik' of international relations.

A second explanation for the Viet Minh's modest outcomes at Geneva suggests that foreign pressure would have counted for little if Ho Chi Minh had not been willing to accept the outcome. After discussions with Zhou Enlai in early July 1954, Ho convinced his colleagues that such a policy was necessary and that Vietnamese living in areas 'temporarily occupied by the enemy' must be patient.

Geneva was a major defeat for American diplomacy, having 'lost' half of Vietnam, the US now believed that the peace of the world was now more threatened by expansionary communism. Eisenhower and Dulles realised Ho would win the 1956 election. British officials concurred, but sensed Vietnam could develop into a non-aligned communist state. The American position, however, remained firm and the United States refused to be bound by the agreement.

### Excerpts from the Geneva Conference Declaration, 21 July 1954

2 The Conference expresses its conviction that the execution of the provisions set out in the present Declaration … will permit Cambodia, Laos and Viet-Nam henceforth to play their part, in full independence and sovereignty, in the peaceful community of nations.

3 The Conference takes note of the declarations made by the Governments of Cambodia and of Laos of their intention to adopt measures permitting all citizens to take their place in the national community, in particular by participating in the next general elections, which, in conformity with the constitution of each of these countries, shall take place in … 1955 …

4 The Conference takes note of the clauses in the Agreement on the cessation of hostilities in Viet-Nam prohibiting the introduction into Vietnam of foreign troops and military personnel as well as all kinds of arms and munitions. The Conference also takes note of the declarations made by the Governments of Cambodia and Laos of their resolution not to request foreign aid … except for the purpose of the effective defence of their territory and, in the case of Laos, to the extent defined by the Agreements on the cessation of hostilities in Laos.

5 … no military base under the control of a foreign State may be established in the regrouping zones [in Vietnam] of the two parties, the latter having the obligation to see that the zones allotted to them shall not constitute part of any military alliance and shall not be utilized for the resumption of hostilities or in the service of an aggressive policy. The … Governments of Cambodia and Laos … will not join in any agreement with other States if this agreement includes the obligation to participate in a military alliance not in conformity with the principles of the Charter of the United Nations or, in the case of Laos, with the principles of the Agreement on the cessation of hostilities in Laos or, so long as their security is not threatened, the obligation to establish bases on Cambodian or Laotian territory for the military forces of foreign powers.

6 The Conference recognizes that the essential purpose of the Agreement relating to Viet-Nam is to settle military questions with a view to ending hostilities and that the military demarcation line is provisional and should not in any way be interpreted as constituting a political or territorial boundary …

7 The Conference declares that, so far as Viet-Nam is concerned, the settlement of political problems, effected on the basis of respect for principles of independence, unity and territorial integrity, shall permit the Vietnamese people to enjoy the fundamental freedoms, guaranteed by democratic institutions established as a result of free general elections by secret ballot … general elections shall be held in July 1956, under the supervision of an international commission composed of representatives of the Member States of the International Supervisory Commission, referred to in the Agreement on the cessation of hostilities. Consultations will be held on this subject between the competent representative authorities of the two zones from 20 July, 1955 onwards.

8 The provisions of the Agreements on the cessation of hostilities intended to ensure the protection of individuals and of property must be most strictly applied and … allow everyone in Viet-Nam to decide freely in which zone he wishes to live.

9 … [R]epresentative authorities … must not permit any individual or collective reprisals against persons who have collaborated in any way with one of the parties during the war …

10 The Conference takes note of the declaration of the Government of the French Republic to the effect that it is ready to withdraw its troops from the territory of Cambodia, Laos and Viet-Nam, at the request of the governments concerned and within periods which shall be fixed by agreement between the parties except in the cases where, by agreement between the two parties, a certain number of French troops shall remain at specified points and for a specified time.

11 … [T]he French Government will proceed from the principle of respect for the independence and sovereignty, unity and territorial integrity of Cambodia, Laos and Viet-Nam.

12 In their relations with Cambodia, Laos and Viet-Nam, each member of the Geneva Conference undertakes to respect the sovereignty, the independence, the unity and the territorial integrity of the above-mentioned States, and to refrain from any interference in their internal affairs.

### The US Response to the Geneva Declaration

The Government of the United States being resolved to devote its efforts to the strengthening of peace in accordance with the principles and purposes of the United Nations takes note of the agreements concluded at Geneva … declares … that (i) it will refrain from the threat or the use of force to disturb them, in accordance with Article 2(4) of the Charter of the United Nations dealing with the obligation of members to refrain in their international relations from the threat or use of force; and (ii) it would view any renewal of the aggression in violation of the aforesaid agreements with grave concern and as seriously threatening international peace and security.

In connection with the statement in the declaration concerning free elections in Viet-Nam my Government wishes to make clear its position.

In the case of nations now divided against their will, we shall continue to seek to achieve unity through free elections supervised by the United Nations to insure that they are conducted fairly.

The United States reiterates its traditional position that peoples are entitled to determine their own future and that it will not join in an arrangement which would hinder this.

# The French Departure

Following the Geneva protocols, France's position in Vietnam was increasingly uncertain. In June 1954, even before the end of the Geneva talks, Prime Minister Mendés-France had granted the State of Vietnam full independence. The concessions France secured, therefore, were not for itself, but for its former puppet. The irony of this arrangement was that while Bao Dai's State of Vietnam was bound by any agreements made by the French before June 1954, they were not bound by any subsequent agreements. With Bao Dai's delegation refusing to accept the Geneva protocols, their usefulness was further questioned.

France was increasingly perturbed by the level of US involvement in Vietnam. The fact that Bao Dai's government was increasingly looking to the United States further irritated France. Increasingly, French officials felt bullied by the Americans; American officials, following France's decision to not join the EDC, were increasingly sceptical that France could be relied upon in Vietnam.

Seeing an American future, the State of Vietnam (increasingly referred to as 'South Vietnam') sought further support from the United States. A major stumbling block had been the composition of Bao Dai's government. Earlier American reports suggested successive governments in Vietnam had comprised 'reactionaries, criminals' and 'assassins'.

To placate the Americans, and against his better judgement, Bao Dai appointed Ngo Dinh Diem as Prime Minister. The prominent non-communist, anti-French, nationalist accepted the position only after he was promised 'full powers, civil and military'. Diem was disliked by the French (who considered him 'not only incapable but mad'). But the Eisenhower Administration,

Ngo Dinh Diem was born in Hue in 1901. Like Ho and Giap, he attended the National Lyceé before studying law at the University of Hanoi. Because of his university training, Diem was immediately appointed to a senior bureaucratic post. Diem spent time in a US seminary during the early 1950s. There, he continued to develop contacts with prominent and influential Americans, including senior clergy, judges and politicians. He also continued to consolidate his anti-communist credentials.

Diem was regarded as reclusive, ascetic and arrogant, but driven by tremendous energy that many observers felt bordered on fanaticism.

despite reservations on the part of American officials in Vietnam, was impressed by Diem's strong anti-communist credentials. The USA believed Diem could build an independent non-communist State that would serve as a bulwark to expansionary communism. The discredited French 'Bao Dai Solution' was replaced by the new American 'Diem Solution'. By early 1955 American aid was being sent not to the French, but directly to Saigon.

Diem's appointment virtually ended American–French cooperation in Indochina. French delays in granting power to Diem, in a last-ditch attempt to build the power of his opponents, caused further friction. As the date for elections approached, France began to withdraw its forces, thus ending an important chapter in French and Vietnamese history. Events in Indochina were now being shaped by the Cold War.

## The Refugee Flow from the North

*Vietnamese refugees board an American landing craft in Haiphong during Operation Passage to Freedom, October 1954*

The Vietnamese were as convinced as many others that the division of their country might last longer than the Geneva Accords stipulated. This was especially the case among Catholics in the North, who feared oppression under communist rule. Encouraged by the Catholic Church, and assisted by the United States, approximately one million Catholics 'fled' North Vietnam.

The American media represented the exodus as proof that the Vietnamese people were 'voting with their feet'. Not reported were the false claims perpetrated by the Catholic Church and the United States that the North was building concentration camps for Catholics and that the North would soon be destroyed by an atomic attack. While the DRV prevented many Catholics from reaching the South, there were no brutal campaigns launched against the one million Catholics who remained in the North. Indeed, despite some armed resistance in the first year, Hanoi sought to protect Catholic communities, lest American propaganda be proven true.

# Diem Consolidates Power in the South

Upon assuming the Prime Ministership, Diem demanded control of the military. He was able to do so during 1955 thanks to American pressure, his own bravado and the further elevation of his personal standing in the wake of the northern refugee exodus. With some help from Bao Dai, Diem sacked senior offices, appointed loyal officers in their place and then used the army to gain control of the police. With control of the military and security forces (being rebuilt thanks to generous American funds) Diem was now able to implement his reform agenda and destroy other opponents.

The other major vested interests that opposed Diem were two large religious sects: the Cao Dai and the Hoa Hao. Their power rested not only in the number of adherents, but in their large landholdings. They had large private armies to protect their interests. Diem had some success breaking up these private armies. He had less success in reducing their influence.

Diem's main concern with the sects was their political power. But his opponents regarded religious intolerance as the motivation behind his campaign to end their influence. Senior members of the Cao Dai and Hoa Hao made representations to Bao Dai complaining about Diem's rule. With widespread complaints, Bao Dai felt compelled to act. He requested Diem's resignation. 'I can no longer lend my name and my authority,' Bao Dai claimed, 'to a man who will drag you into ruin, famine and war'.

Diem rejected Bao Dai's demand, creating a constitutional crisis. The incident provided Diem with an opportunity to rid the nation of the compliant Francophile puppet king. True independence for Vietnam could not be produced until the last vestiges of the corrupt colonial system were removed and a Republic declared.

In October 1955, Diem, therefore, decided to ask the South Vietnamese people if they wished to become a Republic with him as President, or remain a constitutional monarchy with Bao Dai as Head of State. The Americans supported Diem in his quest. They suggested the government should provide two ballot papers: green for Bao Dai and red for Diem. It was no coincidence that red signified good fortune in Vietnamese culture.

*Bao Dai's image was removed from South Vietnamese notes and coinage and replaced with Diem's image*

When the voters arrived at the polling stations they found Diem's supporters in attendance. One voter complained: 'They told us to put the red ballot into envelopes and to throw the green ones into the wastebasket. A few people, faithful to Bao Dai, disobeyed … the agents went after them, and roughed them up … They beat one of my relatives to pulp.'

Diem claimed he achieved 98.2% of the vote. In his stronghold of Saigon, he received 100% of the vote; indeed 2,000 more votes were counted than there were registered voters. Warning that such figures would be disbelieved, US advisors recommended that Diem publish a figure of around 70%. Diem refused and as the complicit American advisers had predicted, the elections were widely viewed as rigged.

Diem could now pursue the greatest danger to his government – the communists. A 'Communist Denunciation Campaign' was conducted and citizens were compelled to inform on known communists and their sympathisers. The guilty were then taken away and either 're-educated', imprisoned or executed. Many South Vietnamese were wrongfully arrested. Jails built to house opponents of the state were amongst the biggest contruction projects in South Vietnam during the 1950s.

The denunciation campaign was accompanied by land 'reform' designed to repeal earlier Viet Minh reforms. Landlords who had fled rural communities in the face of the Viet Minh were allowed to return to their communities and, with the Army's assistance, reclaim land that had been redistributed to the local peasantry. Moreover, they could demand back-rent from those peasants, for the years of lost income. Trying to recoup their losses, many landlords increased rents. South Vietnamese peasants again experienced hunger.

Aware that communist political cadres were still operating in the South, Diem's most audacious reform was to physically remove the peasantry from their influence by establishing 'Agrovilles'. These purpose-built communities were often far from the original communities (and the graves of family members) and often on poor-quality land. These forced relocations caused further social dislocation, further depleted agricultural output and contributed to an influx of alienated rural workers into South Vietnam's cities.

Frustration with the Diem regime grew. Some Vietnamese lamented the departure of the French and their replacement by the Americans. As a colonial power, the French had intervened more in day-to-day affairs. If a local official was corrupt, the people could complain to the French, who removed

## HISTORICAL DOCUMENT

### *Denouncing the Communists*

We must let the peasants know that to give shelter to a communist or to follow his advice makes them liable to the death penalty. We must behead them and shoot them as people kill mad dogs.

*Nationalist Revolution,* Diem Regime Magazine, 1959.

the official. Diem's local officials were also corrupt, but they could call on the Army for protection. The work of communist agitators was assisted by the widespread dissatisfaction.

# The 1956 Elections

With his victory and the creation of the Republic of Vietnam (RVN), Diem had created separate political states in Vietnam. The South would not support free elections in 1956. Responding to the obvious charge that he would lose a free election, Diem insisted he would win a fair election, but that a fair election could not be guaranteed in North Vietnam, despite its observance by the Control Commission.

## HISTORICAL DOCUMENT

### Diem and the South's Refusal to Hold Elections, 16 July 1956

The National Government has emphasised … the price it has paid for the defence of the unity of the country and of true democracy. We did not sign the Geneva Agreements. We are not bound in any way by these Agreements, signed against the will of the Vietnamese people. Our policy is a policy of peace, but nothing will lead us astray from our goal: the unity of our country – a unity in freedom and not in slavery.

The United States supported Diem's decision, claiming that participating in the elections would equate to the mistakes of 'appeasement' that had encouraged the rise of Nazi Germany in the 1930s and that Vietnam would be the next 'domino' to fall to communism.

Internationally, the United States had few supporters. Its closest ally, Britain, insisted the election must take place. The USA, however, had already shown it was prepared to 'go it alone' in Vietnam, because the stakes were too high.

For the International Control Commission, Diem's refusal was the latest of a series of violations of the Geneva agreement. (The other major violation was the increasing American military presence in South Vietnam.) The Commission, however, had no authority to compel the parties to act. Indeed, it was questionable as to what rights it could ever have against a nation that had not accepted the agreement. The Commission's meticulous reports over many years were characterised by 'northern observance and southern defiance'.

While the USSR protested against Diem's actions, it had long since concluded that a permanent division of the country (such as had occurred in Germany and Korea) was the most likely outcome. It continued its efforts to build a communist state in the North, and even went so far as to suggest that both North and South Vietnam be accepted to membership of the United Nations – thereby signifying an acceptance of the US position that the 17th parallel was a national boundary.

# Communist Consolidation in the North

Fearing French betrayal, Ho Chi Minh did not come out of hiding and enter Hanoi until October 1954. The new DRV government was still technically representative of the broad communist and non-communist groups that had comprised the Viet Minh. Some of these non-communists found themselves with ministerial responsibilities. Many non-communists also held positions in the new bureaucracy. In some respects, therefore, the DRV represented Ho's vision of the first stage of revolution. However, the DRV was dominated by the Vietnam Workers' Party. All senior members of the government were communists and the government's agenda was dictated by the Workers' Party's Politburo (Political Bureau – the highest and most powerful group of policymakers in North Vietnam). Some senior members believed it was time to remove the last vestiges of the old collaboration with non-communists, and replace the 'national democratic revolution' with the 'socialist revolution'.

The DRV was guided by a September 1954 Workers' Party manifesto – 'The New Situation, the New Mission, and the New Policy of the Party' – which argued the time had come to shift the emphasis from war to peace and prepare for reunification. This required a two-pronged approach: continued political activity in the South aimed at supporting reunification; and the consolidation of power in the North.

One of the first tasks for the DRV was to organise the return of soldiers and cadres from south of the DMZ. Over 90,000 Viet Minh troops and another 45,000 political activists went north during the 300 days of open movement. To support the new policy, however, around 15,000 political activists stayed behind to work in villages and build support for the coming elections. Another 10,000 military cadre also remained in the South, with instructions from Giap to stay hidden and 'wait and see' what unfolded under the new arrangements.

While there was general agreement as to the tactics to be employed in the South, the Workers' Party was split on how it should go about consolidating power in the North. Inspired by the Chinese experience, so called 'leftists', led by powerful Party-Secretary Truong Chinh, argued it was time to deliver a true communist revolution in the North through a massive reform agenda. Moderates, and those suspicious of China, most notably Giap (a sworn enemy of Truong Chinh) opposed this approach, claiming the time was not yet opportune and that such activity might prompt US intervention.

The leftists triumphed, in part because of Truong Chinh's wide support in the Worker's Party, and because Ho's moderating influence had waned following his decision to assume the role of elder statesmen. In 1955 Ho relinquished the role of Prime Minister, but kept the more ceremonial role of President.

The leftists closely followed the Chinese model. Land reform was the central platform of Asian communist revolution and helped identify enemies of the new state. While there had already been significant land reform in areas previously under Viet Minh control, the new reforms went much further. As a precursor to these reforms, political cadres classified the inhabitants of North Vietnam.

Wealth was the new evil in North Vietnam. Landlords were singled out, as were 'wealthy' peasants. Once they were branded 'feudalists', these individuals were investigated. Their productivity for the whole community was evaluated, along with their loyalty to the DRV. Those who had supported the French or opposed the Viet Minh, were classified as 'traitors'.

Traitors were often brought to the attention of authorities by other citizens. Very quickly these denunciations became witchhunts, in which innocent as well as guilty became victims. In some cases villagers were compelled to betray one feudalist or traitor, lest suspicion be directed at them. Others betrayed friends in the hope of saving themselves. Panic and terror prevailed and tens of thousands of people were removed by the authorities – often with great brutality, and on false charges.

Included among the arrested were thousands of Viet Minh supporters, who were denied the privilege of enjoying their hard-earned freedom. Many 'Progressive landlords', who had helped the Viet Minh, were treated no differently from other landlords.

Feudalists and traitors were often tried in their own villages in impromptu Soviet-style show trials, where the verdict was never in doubt and where the guilty party was forced to admit their crimes and seek forgiveness. Once found guilty, the best one could hope for was to endure the privations of a re-education camp. For tens of thousands, however, guilt brought death. Many others were killed without trial, as the campaign fuelled a wave of violence that saw many peasants unleash revenge on brutal landlords.

The land reforms destroyed the colonial and capitalist basis of the rural economy, but rather than improving the lot of the peasant, the upheaval, coupled with the brutal denunciation campaigns, dislocated local communities and economies. With the North always having been a net importer of rice from the South, the cessation of this trade, coupled with the local upheavals, produced food shortages not seen since the painful days of Japanese occupation.

Independence had brought nothing but a reign of terror, as brutal as anything meted out by the French. By late 1955 the DRV had to contend with a new problem. Peasants were protesting against the government. The urban economies were also transformed. Many larger companies were nationalised, with their operations and profits placed under state control, and the DRV changed the Chinese education system. In Hanoi a number of intellectuals staged a counter-revolution in 1956–1957. The 'Intellectuals' Revolt' was quelled with as much ferocity as the peasants experienced in the countryside. Those not killed were subjected to 're-education'.

The backlash against the land reforms and other initiatives of the 'leftists' nearly brought the DRV to the point of collapse. In Saigon, American officials began to believe that if the election had taken place Diem might have won. When the true depth of the calamity was finally admitted by the Hanoi government and the Party, it was realised that Uncle Ho was the only man who could now save the fledgling state. Ho was considered to be above day-to-day politics and, therefore, not responsible for what had taken place.

Truong Chinh became the scapegoat for the disaster. He was stripped of the General-Secretary's position, which was given to Ho, who conceded that 'errors had been made'. Taking the opportunity to attack his erstwhile enemy, Giap also made a public apology: seeing 'enemies everywhere', the Party had made grave errors of judgement.

*A young South Vietnamese woman casts her ballot during the general elections held in the area to name a Constitutive Assembly, 7 March 1956*

Following these public statements thousands of North Vietnamese were reclassified. It was later admitted that in some provinces up to one-third of those arrested and condemned had been wrongfully convicted. Upon their release a new wave of violence flooded the country as the wrongly accused sought retribution against their accusers. Eventually, however, the situation calmed. Ho's intervention had probably saved the DRV from self-destruction.

# Background to the National Liberation Front

Chinese military aid commenced in 1950 and played an important role in securing Viet Minh victory on the battlefield. From 1956 to 1963 China supplied vast quantities of military materiel, and non-military aid, to the DRV. By 1960, 60% of foreign aid to the North came from China. The Soviet contribution was 30%.

Responding to Chinese and Soviet pressure, and wary of provoking direct American intervention, Hanoi had initially instructed southern communists to resist engaging in armed struggle. Instead, they were to adopt a policy of 'protracted seize'. But after the 1956 elections were abandoned and facing continuing oppression from Diem's regime, southern communists became impatient: if Diem's campaigns continued to be successful, they could soon be wiped out.

In 1956 Le Duan, the senior communist Party official south of the 17th parallel, issued the report 'The Path to Revolution in the South'. Suggesting that armed struggle may be needed to secure reunification, the report contended that Vietnamese reunification under communist rule required the North to more actively fight the political struggle in the South.

The Workers' Party's Eleventh Plenum accepted Le Duan's argument. More attention had to be turned to the struggle in the South. Ho suggested that given the aggressive nature of American policy, Soviet and Chinese desires for a 'peaceful road' could not be assured. Le Duan had the opportunity to reinforce this message when he headed north in 1957 to assume a position on the Politburo.

As a first step it was agreed that the North would help southern communists resist the counter-revolutionary activities of the Diem regime. In some locations armed struggle had already commenced as peasants refused to return land. So widespread had the resistance become, that by 1959 some landlords could go nowhere near their land for fear of violence.

## HISTORICAL DOCUMENT

### The Path of Revolution in the South, 1956

The present situation of division is created solely by the arbitrary US–Diem regime, so the fundamental problem is how to smash the US–Diem scheme of division and war-provocation … [T]o oppose the US–Diem regime, there is no other path for the people of the South but the path of revolution …

With an imperialist, feudalist, dictatorial, fascist government like the US–Diem regime, is it possible for a peaceful political struggle line to achieve its objectives?

The ardent aspiration of the Southern people is to maintain peace and achieve national unification. We must clearly recognize this longing for peace: the revolutionary movement in the South can mobilize and advance to success on the basis of grasping the flag of peace, in harmony with popular feelings. On the contrary, US–Diem is using fascist violence to provoke war, contrary to the will of the people and therefore must certainly be defeated …

… There are those who think that the US–Diem regime's use of violence is now aimed fundamentally at killing the leaders of the revolutionary movement to destroy the Communist Party, and that if the Communist Party is worn away to the point that it doesn't have the capacity to lead the revolution, the political struggle movement of the masses cannot develop.

This judgment is incorrect. Those who lead the revolutionary movement are determined to mingle with the masses, to protect and serve the interest of the masses and to pursue correctly the mass line. Between the masses and communists there is no distinction any more. So how can the US–Diem regime destroy the leaders of the revolutionary movement, since they cannot destroy the masses?

As the DRV debated its southern policy, Diem attacked the communist cadre in the South. Le Duan pointed out that while the chances of energising the general population in an uprising against Diem grew because of his regime's increasing unpopularity, the communists' ability to dominate a rebellion was being weakened by Diem's success in destroying the Party's organisational structure in the South. North Vietnamese reports suggested that about 90% of Party members who had stayed in the South had been killed by the late 1950s.

Against this backdrop, the North reversed policy in 1959. Hanoi would now encourage and support the southern insurgency. To assist its embattled communists in the South, tens of thousands of cadres would return home to organise opposition to Diem's regime and destroy 'soft targets'. The Workers' Party resurrected the southern branch of its Central Committee – the Central Office for South Vietnam (COSVN). Secret plans were made in May 1959 by the Central Military Committee to assist the movement of personnel and supporting materiel. This 'special trail' would circumvent the DMZ by moving through Laos and Cambodia.

As with the Viet Minh 20 years earlier, the communists sought to harness the broader dissatisfaction in the community and marshal it in one united front. Southern opponents of the Diem regime were already meeting secretly and planning a revolution.

# Establishing the National Liberation Front

On 20 December 1960 representatives from over 20 political, social, ethnic and religious (including some Catholic) groups opposed to Diem met in Tay Ninh province near the Cambodian border and founded the National Liberation Front of South Vietnam (NLF). The NLF linked itself to Vietnam's long history of resistance to foreign aggression and represented Diem as a 'stooge' of the 'American imperialists'. The stated program of the NLF reflected Ho's old notion of the first phase of revolution. Far from communist-dominated, the NLF's plans reflected a broad national democratic agenda.

---

**HISTORICAL DOCUMENT**

### Program of the National Liberation Front of South Vietnam

 I  Overthrow the camouflaged colonial regime of the American imperialists and the dictatorial power of Ngo Dinh Diem, servant of the Americans, and institute a government of national democratic union.

 II  Institute a largely liberal and democratic regime.

 III  Establish an independent and sovereign economy, and improve the living conditions of the people.

 IV  Reduce land rent; implement agrarian reform with the aim of providing land to the tillers.

 V  Develop a national and democratic culture and education.

 VI  Create a national army devoted to the defense of the Fatherland and the people.

 VII  Guarantee equality between the various minorities and between the two sexes; protect the legitimate interest of foreign citizens established in Viet-Nam and of Vietnamese citizens residing abroad.

 VIII  Promote a foreign policy of peace and neutrality.

 IX  Re-establish normal relations between the two zones, and prepare for the peaceful reunification of the country.

 X  Struggle against all aggressive war; actively defend universal peace.

---

Despite the NLF's wide base of support, Diem and the Americans regarded it as a communist front organisation. The rebels were the same communists they had already tagged with the pejorative label 'Viet Nam Cong San', the Vietnamese equivalent of 'Commies'. The foot soldiers of the NLF became known as 'Viet Cong'.

# Evaluating the Two Vietnams

Despite the political differences of their governments, life for the average North or South Vietnamese showed remarkable similarities between 1954 and 1960:

## HISTORICAL ISSUE

### Debating Point: Civil War or War of Foreign Aggression?

Was the outbreak of armed hostilities in the South the beginning of a civil war or an act of foreign aggression? Was the fighting that erupted orchestrated by Hanoi or was it the result of southerners' growing dissatisfaction with Diem's regime? Historians are divided between those who regard the southern communists and the NLF as puppets of Hanoi and those who argue they were independent and actually sought the support of the North.

If one accepts the NLF was the puppet of the North, the question then becomes: should the DRV be considered a foreign aggressor? Historians sympathetic to American intervention suggest that by 1957 even the Soviet bloc had recognised the two states of Vietnam. North Vietnam was supporting a war across what was now an international border and could, therefore, be characterised as a foreign aggressor.

Opponents to this view have two counter arguments. First, the Geneva Protocols never recognised such a national division between North and South Vietnam and such a division only emerged because of US intransigence. (Diem would never have been able to resist international pressure if the United States had insisted the 1956 elections be held.) Second, during the late 1950s it was southerners, rather than northerners, who were fighting Diem. Cadres who went South to assist in this struggle were almost exclusively southerners who had gone North after 1954.

Finally, many historians who continue to see Vietnamese history during the 1950s as a nationalist struggle suggest that Vietnam was the victim of external aggression, but that the aggressor was the United States. The USA was providing enormous financial aid to a regime that would not otherwise have survived. Indeed, the United States had assumed a position in South Vietnam little different from that previously held by the French. Were the Americans, driven by Cold War priorities, asserting a 'neo-colonial' agenda in Vietnam?

### Discussion Question:

Summarise the historical debate 'Civil war or war of foreign aggression?' How does this debate help your understanding of the nature of the conflict in Indochina?

- life was characterised by fear, instability and hunger
- life was dominated by denunciation, execution, re-education and land reform
- dissent was not tolerated
- both governments sought support from their superpower supporters.

There was one important distinction between the two Vietnams. Approximately one million people who might have remained critics or opponents of the northern regime had fled the DRV, while many opponents of the Diem regime remained below the DMZ. By 1960 the South's internal security problems continued to grow despite (or because of) Diem's repression. In the North, internal security problems were reduced after the 'Campaign for the Rectification of Errors' and the successful end to food shortages. Those changes enabled the DRV to become increasingly involved in activities in South Vietnam.

The Eisenhower administration had hoped Diem would embrace American solutions to Vietnam's problems. But Diem was no more likely to be a lackey to the United States than he had been a puppet of the Japanese or French. American officials filed hopeful reports from Saigon claiming Diem was producing a 'miracle' in South Vietnam. But after 1957 his authoritarian style was making enemies. Even before the establishment of the NLF, the forces marshalled against Diem grew dramatically. In the year before the formation of the NLF over 1,200 of Diem's bureaucrats had been murdered. Of greater concern for the leader was restlessness amongst his military, elements of which attempted a coup in 1960 that was only thwarted when Diem tricked the plotters and crushed the rebellion with loyal troops.

The coup also failed because the United States refused to support a change of government. The USA was increasingly unhappy with Diem's performance. Secretary of State Dulles concluded that the chances of building a viable South under Diem were no greater than 10%. Yet American officials believed they had no choice but to support Diem and increase American aid.

## POINTS TO REMEMBER

- The Geneva Conference partitioned Indochina into two regions: this division was intended to be temporary.
- The 1956 elections were not held.
- Both North and South Vietnam struggled to consolidate power. Each was characterised by fear, instability, hunger and repression. Each sought the support of superpowers. Eventually, the North was able to ease its internal security problems more effectively than the South.
- Working in cooperation with the NLF, North Vietnam was politically and militarily involved in the South.
- The United States was unhappy with the performance of the Diem regime, but felt compelled to support it and increase aid to South Vietnam.

# ACTIVITIES

1 Have students role-play the 1954 Geneva Peace Conference, in groups.
   Individuals represent the views of:
   a Government of Saigon
   b Viet Minh
   c Government of Hanoi
   d People's Republic of China
   e France
   f USA
   Students should present the historical views of the representatives.

2 Essay: Geneva Accords
   To what extent did the Geneva Accords reflect the aspirations of the Vietnamese,
   compared to the interests of the great powers? Did the Accords establish a
   strong framework for a peaceful resolution to the conflict in Indochina?
   You should refer to the excerpts from the document.

3 Why did French involvement in South Vietnam end in 1955?

4 What was the significance of the movement of refugees from North Vietnam to
   South Vietnam?

5 What were some of the problems faced by Diem as he sought to consolidate
   power in the South?

6 Why did Diem not support the elections set for 1956?

7 How did the Communists consolidate power in the North? How successful were
   they compared to the government in the South?

8 Why was the NLF established in 1959? Look at the document 'Program of
   National Liberation Front of South Vietnam'. Which parts of this program are
   communist and which parts are nationalist/democratic?

9 What evidence is there of increasing US support for South Vietnam during this
   period?

## Sample HSC Exam Questions:

1 Evaluate the view that North Vietnam's determination to spread communism in
   Indochina caused the failure of the Geneva Peace Agreement by the 1960s.

2 What were the consequences of the 1954 Geneva Accords in Indochina up to
   1960?

3 What was the impact of EITHER Ngo Dinh Diem OR Ho Chi Minh on Vietnam in
   the period after 1945?

## FURTHER READING

Peter Lowe's *The Vietnam War* (Manchester University Press, Manchester, 1998) and Ilya V. Gaiduk's
*The Soviet Union and the Vietnam War* (Ivan R. Dee, Chicago, 1996) provide very useful information.
Jean Lacouture's *Ho Chi Minh* (Penguin, London, 1968) and Marilyn B. Young, *The Vietnam War* (Harper
Perennial, New York, 1991) are also informative. See also William Duiker's 'Hanoi's Strategy in the South',
in Jayne Werner and Luu Doan Huynh, eds., *The Vietnam War: Vietnamese and American Perspectives*
(ME Sharpe, Armonk, NY, 1993) and Anthony T. Bouscaren, ed., *All Quiet on the Eastern Front: The Death of
South Vietnam* (Devin-Adair Co., Old Greenwich, CT, 1977).

# 5

# Going to War: The United States and Indochina, 1960–1968

## IN THIS CHAPTER YOU WILL:

- learn about the expanding US commitment to South Vietnam during the presidency of John F. Kennedy
- be introduced to the crises in Vietnam during 1961–1965
- trace the 'process' by which the US committed air power, then ground forces, to South Vietnam
- be introduced to the factors responsible for the escalating US commitment to Vietnam.

## Background

When John F. Kennedy was inaugurated President in January 1961 the United States was already deeply enmeshed in Indochina. The USA had provided over $1 billion in aid to Diem's regime, 900 American advisors were training South Vietnamese forces and American experts were working to develop South Vietnam's agricultural output and infrastructure. Eight years later, there were nearly 543,000 Americans in Vietnam, fighting an unwinnable war. This chapter traces that expanding American commitment, by which the United States sought to apply a military solution to what were essentially 'political' problems in South Vietnam.

## JFK: Confronting a Global Communist Challenge

In 1960 John F. Kennedy confronted Richard Nixon in the presidential election. Kennedy, a member of the Democratic Party, had served in the US House of Representatives from 1947–1953 and then in the Senate since 1953. In 1956 he declared that South Vietnam was 'the cornerstone of the free world in South-East Asia'. The US commitment to South Vietnam, he asserted, was 'a test of American responsibility and determination'. During the 1960 election campaign Kennedy and Nixon argued over who was best equipped to lead the United States in its Cold War struggle against the Soviet Union. Nixon, pointing to his eight years as Vice-President, asserted that Kennedy was too inexperienced to stand up to the Russians. Kennedy claimed that during the Eisenhower years the Soviets had established an ascendancy over the United States in the area of nuclear weapons. Kennedy suggested that because Nixon had been Eisenhower's Vice-President, he was partly responsible for this alleged 'missile gap'.

*John F. Kennedy takes the oath of office, January 1961*

The presidential election held in November 1960 was very close. Partly because Kennedy's election victory was so narrow, he believed he had to confront – vigorously and confidently – communist 'challenges' anywhere around the world. Kennedy's intention was summed up in his Inauguration Speech, when he suggested there could be no compromise or negotiation:

> Let every nation know that we shall pay any price, bear any burden, meet any hardship, support any friend, oppose any foe, to assure the survival and the success of liberty.

# The Kennedy Approach

During the early 1960s the Cold War intensified. Through a series of crises, Kennedy relied less on the traditional mechanisms of foreign policy-making – primarily the Departments of State and Defence – than he did upon his own small circle of trusted advisors. The emphasis was on 'getting the job done' and a high value was attached to 'innovation'.

Kennedy embraced a direct, military response to the communist challenge. All of these themes – the 'can do' spirit, the emphasis on America's sense of moral mission and the belief that American forces could use specific methods to combat communist guerrilla forces – were evident when America went to war in Vietnam. Kennedy believed that small groups of highly-trained 'counter-insurgency' experts were best-placed to tackle communist guerrilla forces. Elite 'special forces', such as the Green Berets, could win the 'hearts and minds' of people in nations threatened by communist insurgency.

Within the US military, not everyone was convinced that Kennedy's emphasis on unconventional warfare – and his conviction that a 'flexible response', whereby US military power could be applied gradually, as each situation determined – was the appropriate means of confronting communism.

In 1961, General Lyman L. Lemnitzer urged Kennedy to tackle the Viet Cong head-on. The United States, he suggested, should 'grind up the Viet Cong with 40,000 American ground troops'. Rather than trying to win the hearts of the Vietnamese, Lemnitzer advocated a more direct approach: 'grab 'em by the balls, and their hearts and minds will follow'. That phrase came to symbolise the American commitment in Vietnam from the mid-1960s. But before the United States committed large numbers of troops to Vietnam, Kennedy faced a challenge elsewhere in Indochina.

# Crisis in Laos

When outgoing President Dwight Eisenhower briefed Kennedy, he did not mention Vietnam. Instead, he described Laos as 'the most important problem facing' the United States. 'You might have to go in there and fight it out,' warned Eisenhower, perhaps 'unilaterally'.

The crisis in Laos had been developing for several years. For much of the 1950s, two half-brothers had vied for control of the country. Prince Souphanouvong, an admirer of Ho Chi Minh, led the Pathet Lao, which had been at the forefront of the Laotian struggle to evict the French. Souvanna Phouma was similarly committed to independence, but he rejected Souphanouvong's revolutionary rhetoric. After the Geneva agreements of 1954, the two men joined a coalition government. As the 1950s progressed, however, the United States expressed growing opposition to the coalition and supported efforts to oust Souphanouvong and the Pathet Lao. From 1954 to 1959 the United States – primarily through the CIA – spent $300 million in a secret war against the Pathet Lao.

Eventually, US officials concluded Souvanna Phouma would have to be replaced, partly because he was incompetent, but also because he believed that long-term stability in Laos could only be achieved through the estab-lishment of a coalition government that included the Pathet Lao. In response, the United States supported General Phoumi Nosavan, who was a fervent opponent of communism, but who was tainted by his association with the French. In 1959 he took control of Laos.

Souvanna Phouma and Souphanouvong then joined in a guerrilla war against Nosavan and his CIA backers. By 1960, it appeared that the Laotian 'domino' might tumble. Eisenhower's position was clear: 'We cannot let Laos fall to the communists, even if we have to fight.' When Kennedy took office in January 1961 the situation was at a crisis point, as Souvanna Phouma and Souphanouvong's forces gained control of increasing areas of Laos. The 'fall' of Laos appeared imminent.

Kennedy's options – political and military – were limited. He decided on a diplomatic, rather than military solution, particularly since American intervention could provoke Laos's neighbour, China. In May 1961 an inter-national conference began in Geneva to resolve the Laotian situation. Negotiations proceeded slowly, but in July 1962 an agreement was signed. Laos was to be a neutral nation and could enter no military alliances. No foreign military bases could be established in Laos. The government was to be a coalition of neutralists, right-wingers and the Pathet Lao. Souvanna Phouma was to be Premier.

None of the parties kept to the agreement. The CIA continued to operate in Laos, supporting a Lao mercenary army fighting the Pathet Lao and attacking North Vietnamese supply routes in the eastern part of the country. The CIA also expanded 'Air America', a commercial airline used to support anticommunist forces in Laos. North Vietnam continued to support the Pathet Lao and used Laos as a conduit to move men and supplies to South Vietnam. Until 1975, Laos was the scene of an ongoing struggle between these various forces.

# The Deepening Crisis in Vietnam

Following the 1962 agreements relating to Laos, a number of pro-American Asian leaders expressed reservations about US guarantees of protection. The United States felt compelled to act to restore confidence and trust, and support for Diem was an obvious first step.

Kennedy had been distracted by the crisis in Laos, but he understood the deeper significance of the unfolding drama in Vietnam. Keeping in mind the multiple threats the United States confronted around the world, Kennedy noted: 'This is the worst one we've got.' Two months after Kennedy's inauguration, intelligence officers warned him that Diem's government faced 'an extremely critical period'. Appointing a special task force on Vietnam, Kennedy ordered 500 Green Berets to Vietnam, authorised secret missions against North Vietnam and sent Vice-President Lyndon Johnson on a factfinding mission to South-East Asia.

Johnson reported that Diem had to be supported. Diem, Johnson stated, was the 'George Washington of Vietnam' and the 'Winston Churchill of South-East Asia'. Yet whilst Kennedy's administration agreed the communists had to be confronted in Vietnam, there was disagreement regarding the best means of doing so. Secretary of State Dean Rusk was adamant that the

PERSONALITY

Robert McNamara

Robert McNamara was a key figure in the Kennedy Administration, playing a major role in determining America's Vietnam policy. As Kennedy's Secretary of Defense, McNamara was one of a number of relatively young men to manage the business of government, informally labelled the 'best and the brightest'.

McNamara had an underlying faith in the power of quantitative analysis and a conviction that American power, properly applied, could subdue any adversary. McNamara's work ethic, and his ability to recall facts and figures, dazzled many of his peers.

After Kennedy was assassinated, McNamara remained as Secretary of Defense. During the mid-1960s he began to have doubts about US policy in Vietnam and began advocating alternative strategies and limiting the US commitment. As the years passed, and as American 'progress' in the war proved false, McNamara's reputation dimmed. Gradually, Johnson lost faith in McNamara, who in early 1968 resigned – probably with Johnson's encouragement – as Secretary of Defense. He then became head of the World Bank and remained silent on the topic of Vietnam until 1995 when he published his memoirs, entitled *In Retrospect: The Tragedy and Lessons of Vietnam* (Vintage Books, New York, 1996). Later, a documentary was made about McNamara's time as Secretary of Defense: *The Fog of War* is a valuable source for anyone interested in understanding America's Vietnam experiences.

United States had to engage the communist challenge in Vietnam – it was part of America's global mission. He advocated escalation. Secretary of Defense, Robert McNamara, also exuded optimism. McNamara was confident the United States could prevail. 'North Vietnam will never beat us,' he declared, 'they can't even make ice cubes'.

George Ball, Under Secretary of State for Economic Affairs, counselled caution. He had been watching the situation in Indochina since the early 1950s. He had also served as counsel to the French Embassy in Washington. He understood, therefore, that Vietnam was not to be underestimated. It would be extremely difficult, he warned, to create a government in South Vietnam that was sympathetic to the United States and that also enjoyed popular support.

## HISTORICAL DOCUMENT

### George Ball and John Kennedy Discuss the Possibilities of US Escalation in Vietnam

In 1961, George Ball warned President Kennedy that introducing American troops into South Vietnam would produce its own momentum, which would prove almost impossible to resist.

**George Ball:** Within five years there will be 300,000 American troops fighting in Vietnam.

**John F. Kennedy:** George, you're crazier than hell.

Kennedy was uncertain how to proceed. Until his assassination in November 1963, he expressed doubts about the feasibility of large-scale intervention in Vietnam. But he was also determined to prevent the 'fall' of the South Vietnamese 'domino'. The policy he followed, therefore, was a kind of tentative escalation. On the one hand, the military chiefs were always asking for more – in May, 1961, for example, just after Kennedy had dispatched 500 Green Berets to Vietnam, military advisors stated that with 13,000 troops they could wipe out the Viet Cong. Kennedy refused to make that commitment, at least immediately. But he was acutely conscious that countries around the world were watching his response to the crisis in Vietnam, 'as a measure of the administration's intentions and determination'. Accordingly, while he resisted the demands of military advisors to dramatically increase the number of American 'advisors' – many of whom were increasingly being drawn into the day-to-day fighting across South Vietnam – he did incrementally increase the US commitment.

By late 1962 there were 11,300 Americans in South Vietnam, advising the South Vietnamese armed forces and flying missions with or for the South Vietnamese Air Force. American military chiefs claimed progress was being made against the Viet Cong. General Paul Harkins, commander of US forces in South Vietnam, reported to Kennedy in early 1963 that before the year was over it would be possible to begin withdrawing American troops. By 1965, Harkins claimed, all Americans could be withdrawn.

**HISTORICAL DOCUMENT**

*John F. Kennedy on Demands that He Commit American Troops to Vietnam*

They want a force of American troops. They say it is necessary in order to restore confidence and maintain morale. But ... [t]he troops will march in; the bands will play; the crowds will cheer; and in four days everyone will have forgotten. Then we will be told we have to send more troops. It's like taking a drink. The effect wears off, and you have to have another.

Much of the American effort during the early 1960s was devoted to 'nation building'. In a tacit admission that 'South Vietnam' was a nation in name only, the United States devoted considerable resources to helping the Vietnamese build the machinery of government. American advisors would assist with the administration of the South Vietnamese Government. A better medical service and improved educational facilities would help win support amongst the South Vietnamese.

The Americans were confident they were doing things better than the French had done. Most significantly, unlike France, the United States was not a colonial power. Of course, to many Vietnamese, the Americans were colonists, similarly intent upon exploitation and control.

# Ngo Dinh Diem: A Difficult Ally

Whilst Americans convinced themselves they were on the verge of vanquishing the Viet Cong, the reality was very different. The war was being won by the North Vietnamese Army (formally known as the People's Army Vietnam or PAVN) and the Viet Cong (formally known as the People's Liberation Armed Forces or PLAF). Even with increased US assistance, the South Vietnamese Army (the Army of the Republic of Vietnam or ARVN) was incapable of defeating its enemies. Indeed, US assistance made it easier for Diem's opponents to portray him as a tool of the US Government. The American way of war — which was increasingly also the South Vietnamese way of war — made it more difficult for Diem's government to win popular support. Bombings by the South Vietnamese Air Force, with American assistance, killed thousands of South Vietnamese civilians. The Strategic Hamlet program, which forced peasants from their ancestral lands, caused further resentment toward Diem and the United States.

Thousands of South Vietnamese joined the Viet Cong, often armed with American weapons that had been turned over by people supposedly loyal to Diem's government. Growing numbers of PAVN troops were also infiltrating the South. For those who looked closely, South Vietnam faced an increasingly bleak future.

At the same time as Diem appeared to be an American lackey, he was proving a most difficult ally for the United States. Vast quantities of US aid and military supplies were being stolen by corrupt South Vietnamese officials. Diem paid little attention to his American advisors and refused to implement the land-reform programs that might have won support amongst the peasant majority of South Vietnam. In effect, he was an American puppet who refused to admit that he could not stand without US support.

By mid-1963 American optimism was waning. Despite the presence of 15,000 American 'advisors' in Vietnam, the latest of a succession of fact-finding missions concluded the war would 'probably last longer than we would like' and would 'cost more in terms of both lives and money' than had earlier been anticipated. There was a vast discrepancy between the Pentagon's reports of progress and battlefield success and journalists' reports of failure and the looming collapse of South Vietnam. American aid had not made Diem's government more efficient. American aid had not helped Diem win popular support.

## The Overthrow of Diem

US policy continued to be characterised by confusion. Henry Cabot Lodge, the new US Ambassador to Vietnam, arrived in a nation that appeared to be falling apart. Diem had promised Lodge's predecessor, Frederick Nolting, that he would not initiate any new repressive measures against the Buddhists. Instead, on the eve of Lodge's arrival, Diem ordered South Vietnamese forces to assault the Buddhists. Diem then blamed ARVN generals for ordering the attack. Lodge concluded that Diem's regime was doomed.

In September, Kennedy dispatched another fact-finding mission to Vietnam. The State Department's Joseph Mendenhall reported that Saigon was in a state of virtual chaos. US Marine General Victor Krulak, in Vietnam at the same time as Mendenhall, reported the war was going well and faced no serious problems. Kennedy's response was succinct: 'You two did visit the same country, didn't you?'

In Vietnam, although many officers owed their positions to Diem, there was growing discontent within the armed forces. A contingent of officers approached Lodge, enquiring whether the United States would support a coup against Diem. After receiving approval – over the telephone – from Kennedy, State Department officials told Lodge that if Diem refused to change his policies the United States would 'give them direct support in any interim period of breakdown' of the 'central government mechanism'. In effect, the USA was approving the overthrow of Diem. Lodge was authorised to announce the suspension of aid to Diem's government and do what he could to 'enhance the chance of a successful coup'.

On 1 November 1963, elements of the ARVN attacked forces loyal to Diem and surrounded the presidential palace. As the situation deteriorated and as Diem's personal safety was threatened, he phoned Lodge. Lodge, having assisted in initiating the coup, did not intend to stop it. He told Diem that since it was 4.30am in Washington, he could not provide any official response from the US Government. Yet he expressed concern for Diem's safety, promising:

'If I can do anything for your physical safety, please call me.' Diem concluded by stating he was 'trying to re-establish order'. But in the early hours of 2 November he and his brother Nhu were captured and murdered.

Despite countenancing the coup, Kennedy was shocked to learn of Diem's death. The key questions then became: who would succeed Diem and what steps would be taken to build popular support for the South Vietnamese 'nation'? Until mid-1965, there was a succession of short-lived governments in Saigon, none of which enjoyed majority support throughout South Vietnam and none of which proved capable of defeating the PLAF and PAVN.

Diem's demise did not signal a dramatic shift in US policy toward South Vietnam. According to US rhetoric and policy, South Vietnam remained a crucial barrier against communism. Yet in the weeks after the coup, Kennedy re-examined his options. On one hand, he appeared to be moving toward reducing the US commitment, even announcing that 1,000 US troops (who were still officially in South Vietnam as 'advisors') would be withdrawn. At the same time, however, Kennedy did not plan to 'cut and run'. Rather, he would at least see the war through until he won re-election in 1964. Kennedy's solution to the Vietnam 'problem' must remain speculative, for he was assassinated on 22 November 1963.

---

**HISTORICAL DEBATE**

### The Unanswered Question: If Kennedy Had Lived

The question of John F. Kennedy's intentions with regard to Vietnam have fascinated historians. Some have argued that if Kennedy had not been assassinated in November 1963, the United States would have avoided the 'tragedy' of Vietnam. According to this line of thinking – which many Americans, including filmmaker Oliver Stone, share – Kennedy would not have escalated the US commitment in the same way as his successor, Lyndon Johnson. There is some evidence that Kennedy understood the risks of large-scale intervention. Late in his presidency he did signal that some US troops would be withdrawn from Vietnam. And in an oft-quoted September 1963 television interview, Kennedy stated:

I don't think that unless a greater effort is made by the Government to win popular support that the war can be won out there. In the final analysis, it is their war. They are the ones who have to win it or lose it. We can help them, we can give them equipment, we can send our men out there as advisers, but they have to win it – the people of Viet-Nam – against the Communists.

Yet there is also compelling evidence that Kennedy would not have withdrawn US forces. Theodore Sorenson, one of the President's closest advisors, argued that Kennedy felt very strongly 'that for better or worse, enthusiastic or unenthusiastic, we had to stay there until we left on terms other than a retreat or abandonment of our commitment'. Secretary of State, Rusk, and Kennedy's brother, Robert, agreed that the President would have maintained a US presence in Vietnam and would not have accepted a communist victory there. Perhaps most significantly, Kennedy would have faced the same Cold War imperatives that drove his successor's Vietnam policies.

---

# Lyndon Johnson Takes Charge

Upon Kennedy's death, Vice-President Lyndon Johnson took over in the White House. Johnson was a very different person from Kennedy. Yet despite their differences, the two men shared a common view of the world: neither was prepared to accept the political damage within the United States that

Lyndon Johnson
(left) and Vice
President Hubert
Humphrey

might follow communist victories – anywhere in the world.

With a new government in South Vietnam and a new President in the White House there was an opportunity to reassess policies. The United Nations, the NLF (National Liberation Front) and France proposed the establishment of a coalition government in South Vietnam. Johnson, however, was not prepared to compromise. There would be no 'Communist take-over,' he insisted, in Vietnam. Confident that the United States could bring progress to Vietnam, he was motivated also by the knowledge that if he appeared 'soft' on communism, his political opponents in the United States would criticise him endlessly. Johnson was under no illusions regarding the difficulties his administration faced in Vietnam. 'It's just the biggest damn mess I ever saw,' he stated in May 1964. Withdrawal, however, was not an option. In August, an opportunity would arise to win public support for an increased American effort in Indochina.

These issues were in the forefront of Johnson's mind during 1964, as he fought an election campaign. Johnson played a more careful game: at the same time as plans were being formulated to expand American involvement in Vietnam, he promised the electorate that he was 'not about to send American boys 9 or 10,000 miles away from home to do what Asian boys ought to be doing for themselves'.

## PERSONALITY

### Lyndon Johnson

Lyndon Johnson was a complex and, in some respects, tragic figure. After a long career in the US Senate (from where in 1954 he helped persuade Dwight Eisenhower against intervening to assist the French in Indochina) Johnson became Vice-President in 1961. On becoming President, Johnson's priority was to address the social and racial problems confronting the United States. But he was soon drawn into what he called – in his colourful way – 'that bitch of a war' in Vietnam.

Amongst the range of factors that impelled Johnson to expand the American commitment in Vietnam was his determination to not let Ho Chi Minh gain the ascendancy. Johnson perceived the conflict in Vietnam in very personal terms. By the end of his presidency Johnson was a deeply tormented individual. In 1968 he decided against seeking re-election. He died in 1973.

## 'Crisis' in the Gulf of Tonkin?

While Johnson spoke of peace, the USA supported covert South Vietnamese raids against North Vietnam. To support those activities, the United States stationed a number of warships in the South China Sea and specifically in the Gulf of Tonkin. On 2 August 1964, North Vietnamese torpedo boats attacked the *Maddox*, an American destroyer that was gathering electronic intelligence off the North Vietnamese coast. The *Maddox* was not damaged, but to demonstrate that the United States would not be intimidated, the Navy ordered another destroyer, the *C. Turner Joy*, to the area. On the night of 4 August, the two vessels opened fire on what were believed to be North Vietnamese warships. Subsequent investigations revealed the second attack had almost certainly not taken place.

Johnson responded in two ways to the incidents in the Gulf of Tonkin. First, he addressed the American people, announcing that the United States would retaliate against what he described as the 'unprovoked' attack in the Gulf of Tonkin. (He neglected to mention what the American warships were doing in the region.) Second, Johnson asked Congress to pass a resolution granting him the authority to respond to aggressive actions against the United States. After a short debate, the bill was passed, with only two Senators voting against granting Johnson the powers he sought.

On 2 August 1964, while conducting electronic surveillance along the North Vietnamese coast, the US destroyer Maddox *was attacked by North Vietnamese vessels*

Johnson's critics later argued that he had proposed the Gulf of Tonkin Resolution in order to escalate the war in Vietnam. Constitutionally, it was Congress, not the President, who had the power to make war. Johnson did consider the Resolution to be almost a declaration of war. But it should be noted he had already ordered retaliatory air strikes against North Vietnam.

## HISTORICAL DOCUMENT

### The Gulf of Tonkin Resolution, August 1964

[T]he Congress approves and supports the determination of the President, as Commander in Chief, to take all necessary measures to repel any armed attack against the forces of the United States and to prevent further aggression.

Section 2. The United States regards as vital to its national interest and to world peace the maintenance of international peace and security in Southeast Asia. Consonant with the Constitution of the United States and the Charter of the United Nations and in accordance with its obligations under the Southeast Asia Collective Defense Treaty, the United States is, therefore, prepared, as the President determines, to take all necessary steps, including the use of armed force, to assist any member or protocol state of the Southeast Asia Collective Defense Treaty requesting assistance in defense of its freedom.

Section 3. This resolution shall expire when the President shall determine that the peace and security of the area is reasonably assured by international conditions created by action of the United Nations or otherwise, except that it may be terminated earlier by concurrent resolution of the Congress.

Johnson also sought the Resolution as a means of demonstrating to North Vietnam that the United States was determined to defend South Vietnam, whatever the cost. In part, Johnson was motivated by domestic political concerns: by appearing to 'stand tough' against the North Vietnamese,

## DOCUMENTARY EXERCISE

The Gulf of Tonkin Resolution has been described as a 'blank cheque' enabling the US president to do whatever he needed, with whatever force, in Indochina. Is there any evidence to support this contention in the document? What powers does it give the US president to deal with armed attack against US forces? Is this significant and why?

while promising Americans he had no intention of deploying ground troops to Vietnam, he hoped to defuse any political advantage that Barry Goldwater, his opponent in the Presidential election, might have derived from the issue.

In the closing months of 1964, Johnson's delicate balancing act – where he sought to appear tough, while talking peace – appeared to work, at least in political terms. Johnson won the November election by a landslide, polling over 61% of the vote. Having already used US air power to 'punish' North Vietnam for its alleged aggression in the Tonkin Gulf, and with the election won, Johnson could use the Gulf of Tonkin Resolution to expand America's commitment in Indochina

## An Expanding War: 'Rolling Thunder'

By early 1965 the PAVN and PLAF controlled nearly half of South Vietnam and the ARVN showed few signs of reversing or even stabilising the situation. Then, in February 1965, Viet Cong forces attacked the American airbase at Pleiku, in the Central Highlands of South Vietnam. Eight Americans were killed and a further 126 wounded. Not only was South Vietnam now on the verge of collapse, but the PLAF and PAVN had the audacity to attack Americans.

Despite evidence that the experiment in nation building in South Vietnam was failing and despite warnings that even limited US military involvement in Vietnam could lead to an open-ended commitment, Johnson's response to the Pleiku attack was immediate: US aircraft were again dispatched to bomb North Vietnam. The next month, Johnson initiated Operation 'Rolling Thunder', a sustained bombing campaign by US aircraft against North Vietnam.

Besides 'punishing' North Vietnam and impeding the flow of men and materiel into South Vietnam, Johnson and his advisors hoped Rolling Thunder would force Hanoi to the negotiating table. Johnson believed that if enough pressure was applied on North Vietnam, it would yield to the weight of American power. During the Vietnam War more bombs were dropped on Vietnam than the US dropped during World War II. Despite massive destruction and suffering, however, North Vietnam did not buckle. In the face of continued communist advances in South Vietnam, the United States was forced to consider additional measures.

## An Expanding War: The US Commits Ground Troops

In March 1965, the same month that Rolling Thunder was launched, the new US Army Commander in South Vietnam, General William C. Westmoreland, requested the deployment of US combat troops. The time had come for Johnson to make a decision: would he commit American ground troops to the defense of South Vietnam?

General Maxwell Taylor, who had been instrumental in formulating Kennedy's strategy of 'flexible response', and who in 1965 was US Ambassador to South Vietnam, argued against introducing combat troops. Along with his concern that the South Vietnamese Government would be asking the United States to perform an ever-increasing military role, Taylor doubted whether US troops could win the war.

---

### HISTORICAL DOCUMENT

**Maxwell Taylor Cautions Against the Deployment of US Ground Troops to South Vietnam, February 1965**

[O]ne may be very sure that the GVN [Government of Vietnam] will seek to unload other ground force tasks upon us ... [A] white-faced soldier, armed and equipped as he is [is] not a suitable guerrilla fighter for Asian forests and jungles. [The] French tried ... and failed; I doubt that US forces could do much better ... Finally there would be the ever present question of how [a] foreign soldier would distinguish between VC and friendly Vietnamese farmer[s] ... I am convinced that we should adhere to our past policy of keeping ground forces out of [a] direct counterinsurgency role.

---

Johnson, however, was not convinced by the arguments of Taylor, or others. Although there was ample evidence that ARVN/US forces were not winning the war, Johnson was determined to stand up to what he perceived as an almost personal affront from North Vietnam. Convinced that apparent weakness in the face of aggression would give confidence to would-be-aggressors elsewhere, Johnson dispatched two battalions of Marines to South Vietnam. Their role was to protect American air-bases in South Vietnam.

In April 1965, Johnson announced that the United States was ready to negotiate with North Vietnam and promised that as soon as the war was won the USA would join a vast effort to rebuild Indochina. But he also warned that the United States had a 'promise to keep'. The 'central lesson of our time,' he asserted, was 'that the appetite of aggression is never satisfied'. He did not mention that in private, military advisors and intelligence analysts were conceding the war was going badly.

# The Illusion of Progress and Continued Escalation

The commitment of two Marine battalions in March 1965 did not turn the tide of battle in South Vietnam. In June, Westmoreland requested the deployment of an additional 34 battalions of troops. Westmoreland was confident that America's well-equipped and highly trained soldiers would be victorious. Undeterred by the earlier French failures in Indochina, Westmoreland declared 'We're going to out-guerrilla the guerrilla and out-ambush the ambush'.

US forces would prevail, Westmoreland declared, 'because we're smarter, we have greater mobility and firepower, we have endurance and more to fight for … and we've got more guts'.

Westmoreland's request forced Johnson to make a decision: would the war in Vietnam become an 'American war'? (South Vietnamese had similar concerns: they worried that an American escalation would reflect poorly on the capabilities of the South Vietnamese armed forces and could lead to American dominance.) As on earlier occasions, some advisors argued against an expanded US commitment. The most significant – but ultimately ineffectual – critic of an expanded American commitment was George Ball (Under Secretary of State for Economic Affairs). Cautioning against what would effectively be a new war, which would involve the USA 'directly against' the Viet Cong, Ball worried that the United States was committing itself to a struggle it might not win. Referring to a CIA report that emphasised Hanoi's determination to win the war, regardless of the costs, National Security Advisor McGeorge Bundy warned that even 'with 500,000 Americans' in South Vietnam, the United States 'may not be able to fight the war successfully'. Bundy was particularly concerned that a further American commitment would make it more difficult to withdraw from South Vietnam, should that become necessary.

---

### HISTORICAL DOCUMENT

#### George Ball Warns Against the Deployment of Additional American Troops to Vietnam, 1965

When we have put enough Americans on the ground in South Viet Nam to give the appearance of a white man's war, the distinction [between Americans and the French] will have less and less practical effect … Yet the more forces we deploy in South Vietnam – particularly in combat roles – the harder we shall find it to extricate ourselves without unacceptable costs as the war goes badly.

---

Johnson had serious reservations about committing troops. Yet while he worried about 'starting something that in two or three years we simply can't finish', he was even more concerned about the implications of being labelled a president who had 'lost a war'. In July 1965, he agreed to step up the bombing campaign and to dispatch an additional 50,000 troops to Vietnam – with another 50,000 to be sent later. A steady, incremental escalation, Johnson hoped, would persuade North Vietnam to negotiate an end to the war.

Just as Ball and others had feared, Johnson's July decision was tantamount to an open-ended commitment. A pattern emerged, by which Westmoreland and other military chiefs would request additional troops and after some brief discussion, Johnson and his advisors would agree to the additional deployment.

Through the entire 'process' of escalation, there was no formal declaration of war by the United States. And although Johnson and others portrayed the expanding American commitment as a carefully calibrated policy designed to bring maximum pressure to bear on North Vietnam, the escalation was more ad hoc.

| American troops in Vietnam, 1960–1972 | |
| --- | --- |
| 1960 | 900 |
| 1961 | 3,200 |
| 1962 | 11,300 |
| 1963 | 16,300 |
| 1964 | 23,300 |
| 1965 | 184,300 |
| 1966 | 385,300 |
| 1967 | 485,600 |
| 1968 | 536,100 |
| 1969 | 475,200 |
| 1970 | 334,600 |
| 1971 | 156,800 |
| 1972 | 24,200 |

For Johnson, each stage of the escalation brought new risks, both to the United States and to himself politically. He had gone to war partly to deflect potential criticisms that he was 'soft' on communism. And there was a steady stream of reports from Vietnam suggesting 'progress' was being made. But the eventual inability of US forces to win the war exposed Johnson to criticism that he had entered the war in the wrong way – he was told he should have gone in with a massive display of force from the outset – and that he was not letting US military chiefs fight the way they wanted.

## HISTORICAL ISSUE

### Many Flags: Australia and America's Other Allies in Vietnam

One of the imperatives that drove Johnson through the period of escalation was a belief that the United States had to demonstrate to its allies that it would defend them if the need arose. In return, he expected them to support and contribute to the American effort in Vietnam. American policymakers assumed that the Southeast Asian Treaty Organisation (SEATO) – formed after the 1954 Geneva Accords – was the apparatus through which the war could be internationalised. In mid-1965 Johnson sought to persuade America's allies to participate in the struggle in Indochina. The British and French refused, urging Johnson to seek a negotiated settlement. French President Charles de Gaulle stated that the United States could 'not win this war'.

Some nations, however, did support the United States in Vietnam. The major contribution came from the Republic of Korea. At the height of its deployment in 1968, South Korea had over 50,000 troops in Vietnam – where they earned a reputation for fighting the war in the most vigorous manner.

Unlike Britain and France, Australia accepted it had obligations to Vietnam, under both the SEATO agreement and the 1951 Australian, New Zealand and US Treaty (ANZUS). In 1962 Australia dispatched a 30-man Training Team to Vietnam. In April 1965 the first combat troops were deployed. At the peak of the Australian deployment, nearly 8,000 troops were serving in South Vietnam.

New Zealand also dispatched a small contingent of troops to Vietnam. The Philippines committed small numbers of troops to Vietnam as well. Thailand made a more substantial contribution: besides committing 11,000 troops in 1967, thousands of Thai 'volunteers' participated in the war in Laos, fighting against North Vietnamese and Pathet Lao forces.

Each escalation made a withdrawal more difficult: having committed hundreds of thousands of troops, and having suffered tens of thousands of casualties, the United States could not suddenly decide that South Vietnam was not worth defending.

*Lyndon Johnson visited Australia in October 1966. Many Australians welcomed his visit; some opponents of the war took a different view*

# Conclusion: The Illusion of Progress and Continued Escalation

At each stage of the war, North Vietnam and the Viet Cong were able to match the American escalation. Having committed massive American forces to Vietnam, Johnson faced a dilemma: 'I feel like a hitchhiker in a hailstorm on a Texas highway,' he complained, 'I can't run, I can't hide, and I can't make it stop'. Despite public pronouncements of 'progress' in Vietnam, there were growing doubts about America's ability to prevail in Indochina. Just how many lives should the United States expend in defending the Vietnamese 'domino'? If the United States was to withdraw, how could it do so while preserving American credibility? It had entered a quagmire from which it could not easily extricate itself. Having been confident of victory, the United States learned to respect the Vietnamese way of war.

## POINTS TO REMEMBER

- By 1961 the Cold War was becoming more intense. It affected US policy in Vietnam.
- President Kennedy and his small circle of advisors believed they could win a war in Indochina.
- The Americans supported the overthrow of the Diem regime.
- The Gulf of Tonkin incident resulted in Congress passing the Gulf of Tonkin Resolution, which legally empowered the US president to wage war. In effect this gave President Johnson the power to escalate the war in Vietnam. The President could wage war without a formal declaration.
- Operation Rolling Thunder unleashed a US aerial bombing campaign designed to force Hanoi to negotiate. In 1965 the USA committed combat troops to Vietnam.
- There was evidence that despite the American escalation it was not winning the war.

## ACTIVITIES

**1** What was the impact of President Kennedy's change to the means of managing foreign policy?

**2** What was the impact of the crisis in Laos for the conflict in Indochina?

**3** Explain why the Kennedy administration was confident it could win a military confrontation in Indochina.

**4** Was Ngo Dinh Diem a help or a hindrance to the American goal of destroying the communist threat in Vietnam?

**5** Was the overthrow of Diem evidence that a South Vietnamese state existed without any sense of nationalism from the people in the South?

**6** Why did the United States support the coup to oust Diem? Do you think a nation should support the overthrow of the leader of a nation with which it has friendly relations?

**7** Do you think President Johnson's reasons for escalating the war was his fear of being branded as 'soft' on communism by his political opponents in the United States?

**8** What was the Gulf of Tonkin incident?

**9** How did the Americans escalate their involvement in the war?

**10** Did the US commitment to Vietnam change during the Johnson administration or was it just following on from President Kennedy's position on the war?

**11** Do you support President Kennedy's view that Vietnam was a test of American responsibility and determination?

## Sample HSC Exam Questions:

**1** Discuss the significance of the 1964 Gulf of Tonkin incident in the growth of US intervention in Vietnam in the period 1954–1968.

**2** What was the role of Ngo Dinh Diem in Vietnamese politics up to 1963?

### FURTHER READING

William H. Chafe's *The Unfinished Journey: America Since World War II*, 5th ed. (Oxford University Press, New York, 2003) and Loren Baritz's *Backfire: A History of How American Culture Led Us into Vietnam and Made Us Fight the Way We Did* (Johns Hopkins University Press, Baltimore, Md., 1998) are useful. Stanley Karnow's *Vietnam: A History* (Penguin, New York, 1997) provides a detailed account of the issues reviewed in this chapter. Marilyn B. Young, *The Vietnam War* (Harper Perennial, New York, 1991) also does a fine job of detailing America's road to war. David Halberstam's *The Making of a Quagmire* (Bodley Head, London, 1965) and George Herring, *America's Longest War: The United States and Vietnam 1950–1975*, 2nd ed. (Knopf, New York, 1986) are also valuable resources.

# PART 3

## THE SECOND
## INDOCHINA WAR

# The Vietnamese Way of War

IN THIS CHAPTER YOU WILL:
- be introduced to the ways Hanoi and the NLF (National Liberation Front) fought the war in South Vietnam
- examine how and why North Vietnamese/NLF strategy changed in response to new developments in South Vietnam, which culminated in the American commitment to a ground war
- explore the tactics employed by the People's Army of Vietnam (PAVN) and the People's Liberation Armed Forces (PLAF) in their fight against the ARVN (Army of the Republic of Vietnam) and the US military.

## Background

From 1954 to 1959 Hanoi dispensed with 'People's War' as the main strategy for reuniting Vietnam. During a period in which the superpowers were seeking more peaceful resolution of their differences, and US interest in Indochina was increasing, the DRV (Democratic Republic of Vietnam – North Vietnam) used political means to achieve reunification. In the South, however, increasing repression compelled Diem's opponents to resort to armed struggle. In 1959 Hanoi accepted that violence was necessary to stop the oppression and overthrow Diem. During the 1960s new strategies were formulated, influenced by the North's ambitions, the South's failures and increasing US involvement.

## Early Strategy 1959–1963

Hanoi's decisions of 1959 and 1960 intensified military activity in the South. But the new military approach continued to be informed by political considerations. In supporting (and ultimately controlling) an armed struggle in the South, Hanoi was influenced by the experiences of the First Indochina War and the Geneva Conference. These shaped the strategy employed; the Viet Minh's battlefield history influenced tactics.

Geneva's legacy was the relationship between battlefield success and diplomatic negotiation. In 1954 Viet Minh battlefield success had not delivered the expected bargaining power at the conference table. After Geneva it was argued that even greater military defeats should have been inflicted upon France before diplomatic resolution had been considered. While negotiations were still regarded as the key to a final victory, the Northern leadership now insisted it would need more than a few battlefield victories before sitting at any negotiating table. The enemy would need to be devastated in the field. Given the strength of the Army of the Republic of Vietnam (ARVN) a protracted war was regarded as inevitable.

There was also no doubt that 'People's War' was the only appropriate military strategy for the struggle in the South. Thanks to its American backers, the ARVN had grown into a sizeable modern force that had successfully suppressed Diem's enemies. This army could not be engaged in conventional battle until it had been weakened and the Viet Cong position strengthened.

# The People's Liberation Armed Forces (PLAF)

Reflecting the People's War strategy and a desire not to be seen to contravene the Geneva Accords, Hanoi decided against committing the PAVN to the struggle. Instead, following the Chinese example from the Korean War, 'volunteers', many of whom had gone North after 1954, went South as the 'Autumn Cadres' – ready to exploit the coming political harvest.

To assist the integration of these new cadres and better organise the southern resistance, Hanoi first established the People's Liberation Army (PLA) in 1960. In 1961 it was reconstituted as the People's Liberation Armed Forces (PLAF). The creation of the PLAF revealed that the North had assumed a leadership role in the southern struggle that contradicted continuing public assertions that the insurrection was the work of southerners. The PLAF was commanded by a PAVN General, Nguyen Chi Thanh.

## Recruitment

Many young South Vietnam men grew up knowing that one day they would be called on to fight in the war that wracked their country in either the ARVN or the PLAF. PLAF cadres served as recruiters. Unlike the ARVN, which had an impersonal conscription system, the PLAF relied on volunteers to maintain popular support.

## Organisation

When a young man joined the PLAF he was agreeing to fight for the 'duration' of the conflict. The PLAF was divided into three main types of battle units:

1  **The Main Force:** these units were well led, well trained and aggressive. These 'hard hats' (so-called because they wore the pith helmet in battle) only performed combat duties.
2  **The Regional Force:** these units were primarily involved in guerrilla

operations in their local region. These smaller units usually fought in the ubiquitous 'Calico Noir', the so-called 'Black Pyjamas'.

3   **The Local Force:** these were the archetypal 'farmers by day, soldiers by night'. Their primary role was intelligence gathering or support as porters, scouts and guides, or as snipers and setting booby traps.

---

**HISTORICAL DOCUMENT**

### Extract from the PLAF Oath of Honour

1   I swear I am prepared to sacrifice all for Vietnam. I will fight to my last breath against imperialism, colonialism, Vietnamese traitors, and aggression in order to make Vietnam independent, democratic and united.

2   I swear to obey absolutely all orders from my commanders ...

3   I swear to fight firmly for the people without complaint ... I will go forward in combat without fear, will never retreat regardless of suffering involved.

4   I swear to learn to fight better and shape myself into a true revolutionary soldier battling the invading American imperialists and their servants ...

5   I swear to preserve organization secrecy ...

6   I swear if taken by the enemy I will not reveal any information even under inhuman torture ...

---

## Indoctrination

As in the PAVN, the PLAF leadership emphasised the importance of 'political training'. Cadres inculcated the reasons for fighting the war and extolled the virtues of communism. Americans typically dismissed such activities as communist 'indoctrination'. Americans often regarded 'brainwashing' as the only possible reason the Vietnamese would reject US assistance and support communism. The organisation of PLAF units into 'three-man cells', with each member responsible for the next man, was designed to maintain morale and ensure political commitment to the revolutionary cause. As well as an oath of honour, PLAF soldiers were bound by an 'Oath of Discipline'. The most important clauses of the oath related to the treatment of civilians, whose support was considered vital.

## The Destruction of Oppression

The Hanoi-backed guerrilla war against Diem began with a program known as the 'Destruction of Oppression'. Individuals and institutions that supported Diem in isolated rural areas would be destroyed. This goal was to arrest the destruction wreaked by GVN security forces and bring areas under communist influence. After the GVN was driven from a community it was declared 'liberated'. These areas then served as bases for the wider guerrilla war and as sources for tax collection to help fund the war.

**HISTORICAL DOCUMENT**

### PLAF Oath of Discipline

1  I will obey the orders from my superiors under all circumstances.

2  I will never take anything from the people, not even a needle or thread.

3  I will not put group property to my own use.

4  I will return that which is borrowed, make restitution for things damaged.

5  I will be polite to people, respect and love them.

6  I will be fair and just in buying and selling.

7  When staying in people's houses I will treat them as I would my own house.

8  I will follow the slogan: All things of the people and for the people.

9  I will keep unit secrets absolutely and will never disclose information even to closest friends or relatives.

10  I will encourage the people to struggle and support the Revolution.

11  I will be alert to spies and will report all suspicious persons to my superiors.

12  I will remain close to the people and maintain their affection and love.

These efforts were directed initially at 'soft targets' in communities whose former support of the Viet Minh and dissatisfaction with the Diem regime was known. In some cases assassinations might be necessary. Kidnapping for ransom was a popular tactic that discouraged individuals from supporting the regime and raised funds.

So successful were PLAF attacks on soft targets that the program was quickly extended to the actual agents of oppression – the ARVN and the police. Attacks included laying mines on roads frequented by the ARVN, assassination of ARVN officers and attacks on ARVN installations.

# Responding to the Strategic Hamlet Program

Along with the security campaign against its opponents, Diem's most impor-tant defensive initiative was the Strategic Hamlet Program. Knowing that People's War relied on winning the support of the people, Diem hoped that physically removing people from their villages would reduce the opportunities for communist 'indoctrination'. Diem's brother Ngo oversaw an escalation of the old 'Agroville' scheme into the 'Strategic Hamlet Program'.

The Strategic Hamlet Program constituted a broad 'pacification' program that involved more than fortifying new residential communities against attack. Realising the Strategic Hamlet Program put its strategy at risk, the North used a variety of techniques to overcome it. In hamlets where NLF sympathisers or members already existed, proselytising could continue, if on a more covert footing. In such cases, when the gates to the hamlet were closed each night, the enemy were already within. To show residents that the RVN was unable to guarantee their safety even when it placed them behind barbed wire, hamlets that supported Diem were subjected to regular surprise attack.

The Strategic Hamlets enjoyed some success in 'protecting' communities from PLAF infiltration or attack. Ultimately, however, they failed. Often the schemes delivered sympathisers to the PLAF. Early Strategic Hamlets were often located many kilometres from the old established villages. While some villagers could continue to toil their old land, others were forced to work new land that was often of poor quality. And relocation brought social dislocation. A common complaint was that the family had been moved so far from their home village that they were unable to play their important familial role of ancestor veneration by tending family graves and shrines.

# Diem's Demise and the 'Third Phase'

PLAF successes played their part in destabilising Diem's presidency and bringing about the November 1963 coup. Following Diem's murder, Hanoi was compelled to consider its next step. Was the destabilisation in the South sufficiently advanced that the Second Phase of Revolution (a mix of guerrilla

## HISTORICAL ISSUE

### The Battle of Ap Bac

In early January 1963 the ARVN moved to destroy a NLF radio transmitter in the hamlet of Ap Bac, 60 kilometres south-west of Saigon. In a first for the PLAF, the Viet Cong 514th Battalion of about 320 men, along with approximately 30 local guerrillas, held its ground, rather than fleeing in the face of elements of the 7th ARVN Division (2,000 men under overall command of an American, Colonel John Paul Vann), which was supported by armoured personnel carriers, artillery and American helicopters. Expecting defeat, the PLAF commander noted in his diary 'Better to fight and die than run and be slaughtered'. With great fire discipline, the PLAF forces allowed the first three waves of helicopters to land ARVN troops before they engaged their enemy. Using a canal system that criss-crossed the area, the PLAF had ample cover to move around their enemy and escape the superior ARVN firepower.

At the end of the battle the PLAF guerrillas, without the advantage of armour, artillery or helicopters, had destroyed a conventional military force four times their size. Sixty-one ARVN soldiers and three American advisers were killed. Ap Bac was a major tactical and propaganda victory for the NLF/PLAF. It proved that the American-backed ARVN could be defeated in conventional battle. After the battles, posters appeared over South Vietnam, extolling the victory and predicting the demise of Diem. Journalists and historians asserted that the American failure to understand what had transpired at Ap Bac was a mistake that would cost the United States dearly.

### EXERCISE:

Evaluate the significance of the Battle of Ap Bac.

and conventional warfare) or perhaps even the Third – and final – Phase (conventional warfare and a popular revolt) should be implemented? COSVN reports claimed the coup had revealed the inherent weakness in the regime and suggested the time was ripe for a 'General Offensive and Uprising' (Phase 3). The PLAF was already capable of fighting large unit battles, as evidenced by the victory at Ap Bac in January 1963.

Opponents to such a plan offered a variety of perspectives. Some pointed to the success of their communist colleagues in Laos. Never having engaged in full-scale conventional warfare or secured a general uprising, the Laotian guerrillas had compelled the United States to agree to a negotiated settlement. Could continued guerilla activity in South Vietnam secure the same goal? Others questioned whether the United States sought a negotiated settlement. A dramatic increase in PLAF military activity might provoke greater US intervention. Unlike Laos, which bordered China and therefore presented broader geo-political problems, the United States would be more likely to consider military solutions in South Vietnam. Others suggested that because the South Vietnamese regime would soon collapse, the North need only pursue its political efforts to reunite the country.

The Politburo was split on how to respond. Despite their continuing estrangement, Truong Chinh and Giap agreed that guerrilla warfare should continue, because the situation did not warrant the next phase. Giap believed that any military increase would increase American involvement. New Lao Dong General Secretary, Le Duan, and Nguyen Chi Thanh, felt otherwise: A quick victory was possible and the opportunity had to be seized.

Ho Chi Minh split the deadlock. The Ninth Plenum of the Lao Dong, held in December 1963, agreed that the collapse of Diem's regime meant that the time was right for all-out military activity against the ARVN. The PLAF was already capable of Phase 2 engagements and this capability could be quickly expanded. Time, however, was of the essence. ARVN forces must be destroyed before the United States could increase its forces and escalate the conflict. Given the widely accepted view that the United States could not be defeated, the plan relied on the USA being presented with such a significant defeat and a successful 'general uprising' against Diem that it would question its ability to subdue the PLAF. It would, therefore, be compelled to seek a negotiated settlement – a settlement the North would this time dominate, given its overwhelming battlefield position.

Having adopted this position, the North denied its most valuable resource to the NLF. Supplies, cadres and volunteers for the PLAF would continue to flow South. However, the PAVN would not be utilised. This decision reflected

| RVN estimates of PAVN cadres and soldiers entering South Vietnam, 1959–1966 | |
|---|---|
| 1959 | 300 |
| 1960 | 2,700 |
| 1961 | 13,600 |
| 1962 | 12,300 |
| 1963 | 7,450 |
| 1964 | 13,000 |
| 1965 | 33,300 |

continuing concerns within the Politburo about US and international reactions. If the next phase of war was still considered a predominantly southern affair, the US reaction might come too late. Hanoi, moreover, claimed it, and not the South, was upholding the Geneva Accords.

## The Sino–Soviet Rift

The decision to increase military activity, but not commit the PAVN, was informed by the assumption that neither Moscow nor Beijing would welcome an expanded war. Hanoi tried to placate Chinese concerns by insisting it would do nothing to provoke an American invasion of the North (such as sending the PAVN south), which might in turn threaten China's southern border. Denials of PAVN involvement in the war in the South, therefore, were directed as much at China and the USSR as the United States.

The Sino–Soviet rift fuelled tensions within North Vietnam's leadership. While some Party officials appeared to criticise Vietnam's northern neighbour, many officials leaned towards the Chinese position. China had remained more committed than the USSR to the Vietnamese cause during the late 1950s. China claimed the Soviet position on Vietnam was a clear case of 'cowardice'. Chinese examples, moreover, remained the most useful strategic and tactical approaches to war in the South.

Despite their broader differences, China and the USSR had similar views on the Vietnamese conflict. Neither wanted to see the conflict escalate. After Khrushchev lost power in October 1964, Soviet rhetoric hardened. Whilst this did not immediately translate into greater practical support, the Soviets did try to orchestrate a united communist position on Vietnam in February 1965. Despite holding the same basic position, China refused to be involved.

Soviet rhetoric gave aid and comfort to the pro-Soviet members of the Hanoi leadership. In December 1966 Le Duan stated that the Vietnamese experience was very different from China's. He claimed that the workers (the Soviet model) rather than the peasants (the Chinese model) would deliver freedom to Vietnam. Such public alignment, however, was rare: for most of the 1960s Hanoi 'mastered the art of tightrope walking' in maintaining the support of both the USSR and China, although the support was never as great as North Vietnam sought.

## The General Offensive, 1964–1965

If the PLAF was to mount a 'General Offensive' without the direct support of PAVN units, its numbers would need to increase dramatically. In 1964 the PLAF volunteer recruitment system was revised. The age limit for volunteers was increased from 30 to 40. Recruiters used confrontational language and techniques, often aimed at shaming individuals into service. Female recruiters were used to encourage young men to compare their service to the nation alongside the women in uniform standing in front of them.

In many 'liberated' areas volunteer recruitment was abandoned. A community was now expected to provide a specific number of recruits for service with Regional or Main Force units, while all men aged 18 to 35 would be available for Local Forces. By 1967, 66% of ex-Viet Cong soldiers surveyed claimed they had been 'drafted', rather than volunteered. Some claimed that after refusing to serve they had been tied-up and taken away.

With 13,000 volunteers from the North infiltrating south during 1964 (nearly twice the figure of 1963) and with the rapid expansion of Local Forces, the PLAF enjoyed significant success through 1964. The number of assassinations and kidnappings decreased in favour of more large-scale military operations. Increasingly, the PLAF was standing and fighting the ARVN – and winning. Large areas of rural Vietnam had been 'liberated' and functioned under NLF administration. As part of the plan to prepare urban South Vietnamese for the 'General Uprising', PLAF forces used assassination and kidnapping as tactics in South Vietnam's cities.

So successful were these attacks through 1964 that plans were made to lure the remaining ARVN units out of cities and major towns. This would allow the PLAF to destroy the ARVN and assist the urban uprising. The French press reported that the PLAF already controlled some Saigon suburbs. Victory seemed near for the PLAF.

The new year began well for the PLAF. Its forces had grown substantially and inflicted heavy casualties on South Vietnamese (and American) forces. After defeating ARVN forces in the northern province of Quangngai, in late May 1965, Radio Liberation carried a report by NFL military commentator Truong Son suggesting the PLAF was about to embark on the final phase of the war. Because the ARVN had lost not only its offensive, but defensive spirit, the PLAF could now engage in 'battles of annihilation'. Furthermore, in a veiled threat to the United States, he suggested the PLAF was now capable of wiping out an 'entire task force'.

Having destroyed several ARVN battalions, by June 1965, the PLAF claimed that more than half the total rural area of the country and more than three million of South Vietnam's 14 million citizens had been 'liberated'. Another

*A Vietnamese women weeps over the body of her husband*

5.4 million South Vietnamese were in contested areas with the GVN exercising secure control over just 4.4 million people. It was estimated that the PLAF territorial gains had delivered up to one million new eligible males for war service.

# Targeting the Americans

Despite its battlefield success, the Northern leadership remained convinced that full-scale US military intervention remained unlikely. If, therefore, PLAF activity in Vietnam remained at its current level and America's allies continued to express dismay with US policy in Indochina, the United States could not be 'provoked' into greater intervention.

To further ensure that the re-elected Johnson Administration did not contemplate escalation, Ho Chi Minh and other North Vietnamese leaders again raised the prospect of a negotiated settlement. The three key terms of Hanoi's position – a coalition government in the South with NLF membership, American withdrawal from Vietnam and eventual reunification under Hanoi – remained unacceptable to the United States. And Washington rejected efforts by United Nations Secretary General U Thant to arrange a deal. But the North Vietnamese peace feelers did appear to have the desired effect of ensuring PLAF battlefield victories against the ARVN did not provoke a dramatic American escalation.

In South Vietnam, Hanoi's desire to not provoke the USA manifested itself in a COSVN directive to avoid direct engagement with US forces or major attacks on their installations. The problem for the PLAF, however, was that the ARVN was increasingly reliant on the mobility and support provided by the American military. Neutralising these American support forces and their bases became a necessary precondition to ARVN defeat.

In November 1964 the Viet Cong launched a mortar attack on the US airbase at Bien Hoa, north of Saigon. Major attacks on US bases continued during early 1965. In February, the PLAF attacked American bases at Pleiku, in the Central Highlands. This attack and increasing concerns about the safety of the US coastal base at Da Nang triggered the dispatch of the first US combat troops sent to Vietnam to support the 30,000 Americans already 'in-country'.

While the attacks on US bases led to combat troops being sent to Vietnam, they did not immediately trigger the feared US escalation. The continuing success of the PLAF in annihilating the ARVN was the key. American predictions were similar to those being made by North Vietnam. PLAF victory was imminent unless the USA acted by committing its own combat forces to the ground war in Vietnam. It was here that Hanoi misread US resolve.

# Sending the PAVN South

Despite his support of the military solution in South Vietnam, Le Duan understood that any dramatic American escalation could destroy the PLAF's chances of success. He calculated that if the United States decided to play a direct combat role in Vietnam, and increase its forces to 100,000, the PLAF would be unable to inflict a 'mortal blow'.

Hanoi's leaders were surprised by the speed of the US military build-up once Lyndon Johnson decided to commit to a ground war in Vietnam. By May American forces totalled 54,000 and were beginning to do more than defend their bases. Hanoi and its southern allies had to consider a new strategy to counter the US intervention.

Given PLAF casualties (35,000 in 1965) and concerns about its ability to secure a quick victory, some of Hanoi's leaders contended the PLAF should withdraw from the 'Big Unit War' and resume guerrilla operations – a return to Phase One of People's War. Others pointed to the continuing success of the PLAF in destroying the ARVN and argued that victory was close: US involvement in the war was increasing and assuming a direct combat role; but the Americans would be constrained by the imminent destruction of the ARVN and the ensuing general uprising.

*US pilot taken prisoner in the Vietnam War*

The Politburo decided the gamble had to be taken. The PLAF would take on the Americans and the ARVN in the 'Big Unit War'. The question then became in what ways could Hanoi improve the PLAF's chances of success?

In the field, the answer was bold but straightforward: Although some PAVN personnel already served in the South, the PAVN was now to be fully committed to the war. Despite Hanoi's denials, PAVN units began heading South to match the American escalation.

It was hoped that PAVN intervention would bring a number of advantages. In direct contradiction to American assumptions, Hanoi believed it had an 'inexhaustible source of manpower'. There were approximately four million men aged between 19 and 49 in North Vietnam, two million of whom were

## HISTORICAL ISSUE

### Even the Women Must Fight

Vietnamese tradition had long embraced the notion of women as fighters. Many 'long haired warriors' fought for the Viet Minh against the French. Following the American escalation, the DRV created the 'Three Responsibilities Movement' to mobilise women. North Vietnamese women were expected to manage the family in the absence of a husband or son, work to support the fighters at the front and, if necessary, perform military support or even combat roles.

Hanoi ensured that despite women's participation in the war effort, industrial output was maintained at pre-war levels notwithstanding the consequent social dislocation and American bombing. Approximately 200,000 women became 'long haired warriors' and joined the PAVN or PLAF. A small, but not inconsiderable, number of women served in combat units, fighting and dying with their male comrades. It has been suggested that Vietnamese women's participation in the war made the difference between defeat and victory.

classified fit for military service. Even without resorting to this pool, each year approximately 170,000 North Vietnamese males turned 18 and became eligible for conscription. Even with various draft deferments, over 100,000 young men would enter the PAVN each year. Hanoi believed the PAVN and the PLAF could counter the US escalation, regardless of its eventual scale.

The greatest danger in the decision to send the PAVN south was that it could be used by the Americans and the RVN as the trigger to launch an invasion of North Vietnam. While American pronouncements discounted this possibility, Hanoi saw the threat and the general widening of the war as an opportunity to secure direct involvement by China and the USSR. Despite their ongoing animosity, Moscow and Beijing increased their support of Vietnam. In the case of China, in April 1965 Ho Chi Minh persuaded Mao Zedong to provide support troops and an agreement to protect North Vietnam's territorial integrity. This allowed Hanoi to send more PAVN units south. Subsequent meetings also established the conditions by which China would become directly involved in the war – if the United States invaded or supported an ARVN invasion of the North. Yet China's fundamental position remained that it did not wish to become directly involved in the conflict.

By June 1965, Chinese anti-aircraft, engineer, logistics and mine sweeping units were in North Vietnam. The presence of these support troops concerned many senior North Vietnamese leaders who feared the price of such support would be Chinese domination.

# The Anti-American War of Resistance for National Salvation

In South Vietnam, the PLAF shifted its main focus from the ARVN to the Americans. ARVN units were still destroyed when possible. But the arriving American forces had to be neutralised before they consolidated their position. With 75,000 Americans in Vietnam by July, the first major assault was a planned attack on the American Marine Corps base at Chu Lai, near Da Nang, in August 1965. The attack, however, was a disaster for the PLAF. Forewarned by a Viet Cong deserter, the Americans launched a pre-emptive assault (Operation Starlite) on the gathering PLAF forces. Approximately 700 PLAF troops were killed. This was an ominous sign for the PAVN and PLAF.

The PAVN/PLAF also sought to gain a better appreciation of American tactics. These lessons were often learned by PAVN/PLAF generals with the lives of their men. The Battle of the Ia Drang Valley in early November 1965 culminated in an American 'victory', but provided the PAVN/PLAF with a better appreciation of American military doctrine and tactics. While the tenacious American victory showed the power of air mobility and fire support, it also provided an invaluable guide to American tactics. The lessons learned were applied a few days later at the Battle of Landing Zone (LZ) Albany when the PAVN adopted the new tactic of 'grabbing the belt buckle'. The PAVN closed quickly on the enemy and reached so close to their defensive lines that the use of artillery or air support became dangerous to the American defenders.

Near Plei Mei, on 17 November 1965, the 66th PAVN Regiment ambushed an American battalion that was unable to secure reinforcements or fire support. The US battalion suffered 60% casualties. These November battles left the PAVN and PLAF leadership confident that while US forces were technologically superior, they were tactically inferior. When denied their overpowering fire support, American infantry units were regarded as no match for the PAVN or PLAF.

## HISTORICAL ISSUE

### The Ho Chi Minh Trail

The United States expended considerable resources attempting to prevent the infiltration of men and materiel from North to South. The DMZ and sea routes were effectively cut off. The PAVN was then forced to rely on the series of trails that had been built through Laos during the late 1950s.

The instructions for those building the Ho Chi Minh Trail were clear: 'It must not be allowed to become a beaten path – that is, not a single footprint, cigarette butt, or broken twig may be left on it after the men's passing.' Infiltration of men and materiel down the trail began in June 1959.

The journey down the trail normally took two months. Goods were moved on the backs of PAVN soldiers or on heavily laden bicycles in numbers between five and 500 men. The difficulty lay in transporting 15 tons of supplies (which PAVN commanders believed was necessary to sustain the war) from one end of the Trail to the other, when it was subject to frequent American air attack. Deprivation and hardship characterised the journey, with soldiers not only fearing American B-52 bombers, but also being exposed to sickness from raw food (as fires would betray the Trail's position to the Americans), disease (especially malaria), snakebites and even bear or tiger attacks. Many young PAVN soldiers were from urban backgrounds and had their first encounter with the jungle during their journey down the trail. Up to 60,000 infiltrators moved down the trail each year.

For field commanders in the South, the trickle of goods down the trail allowed the war to be fought. Even if the US bombers destroyed nine out of 10 boxes of ammunition, that one box allowed the fight to go on. While American logistics in the Vietnam War were breathtaking because of the sheer scale of the endeavour, the PAVN's logistical efforts were equally remarkable, given the impediments they overcame.

Mobility in defence was essential to avoid US airpower. For the PAVN and PLAF forces detection by the Americans frequently equated to death.

Giap's offensive planning continued to be underpinned by the principle of 'One slow, four quick'. Hitting the enemy and running before he was able to bring firepower to bear was often a safer option than 'grabbing the belt'.

The safest of all offensive operations was the ambush, which became the stock in trade of PAVN/PLAF forces. It was an appropriate response to the enemy's perceived need to protect territory, communities and lines of communication. These tasks tied down large numbers of American soldiers in security operations, when they might otherwise have been available for offensive operations. American mobility made ambushes possible.

Other tactics used to blunt American advantages included conducting operations at night or in bad weather, thereby limiting the air and artillery

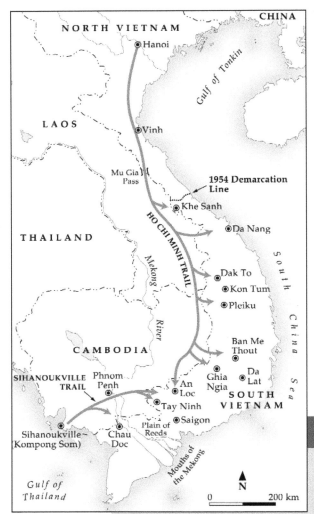

*Ho Chi Minh Trail and PAVN/PLAF supply routes*

support the enemy could utilise. So consistent were the PAVN/PLAF forces in using the cover of darkness, American GIs suggested that while they might own the day, 'Charlie owns the Night'. PAVN/PLAF forces also refrained from using radio communications, because the Americans could track and target such transmissions. Instead, runners or field telephones were used to pass information.

# 'Rightist Ideology' and the PAVN

By the end of 1965, US forces in Vietnam numbered almost 200,000. For Le Duan, this dramatic increase meant a quick victory would not be forthcoming. Some Hanoi civilian and military leaders, however, did not accept that the Americans could not be beaten: such claims were 'defeatist' talk by sections of an Army that was influenced by 'rightist ideology'.

## HISTORICAL ISSUE

### The Tunnels of Cu Chi

One way to avoid the need to be always on the move, while also avoiding the Americans, was to hide underground. In NLF-controlled villages, tunnel systems were dug to conceal PLAF fighters and stores.

The most famous the tunnel system was the Cu Chi tunnels in Hau Nghia province, 30 kilometres north of Saigon. Originally dug by the Viet Minh during the 1940s, they were rapidly expanded during the 1960s. The Cu Chi tunnels were a place to hide and a base for operations. The complex included stores, barracks, schools, conference rooms, hospitals and even munitions factories. Over 300 kilometres of tunnels were constructed. Life underground was far from pleasant. At Cu Chi a person might not see the light of day for weeks. Snakes, rats and the risk of a tunnel collapse compounded the horrors.

Aware that a major PLAF headquarters was in Hau Nghia province, almost 8,000 American and ARVN troops launched 'Operation Crimp' in January 1966. Despite regular patrols and the destruction of most of the villages in the area, the tunnels were not discovered. The Americans subsequently built a major base at Cu Chi, unaware it was above a major PLAF headquarters. Indeed, some sniper tunnels were actually extended into the American base.

*A long table in the Cu Chi tunnels*

## HISTORICAL ISSUE

### Booby Traps and Mines

As they had been against the French, booby traps and mines were part of the PAVN/PLAF arsenal. Because US and ARVN forces paid close attention to protecting lines of communication, mines (often stolen from American and ARVN minefields) were a relatively inexpensive way to inflict casualties on the enemy.

Booby traps were used for both offensive and defensive purposes. They might be placed on a trail used by enemy troops or used to protect an arms cache or a line of communication used by PAVN/PLAF forces. The most infamous was the 'punji stick' trap: a series of sharpened sticks covered with excrement. The trauma, and infection from the excrement, left the enemy soldier requiring hospitalisation. The major problem with mines and booby traps was that they did not discriminate: mines on South Vietnam's highways often killed civilians, rather than Americans soldiers.

## HISTORICAL ISSUE

### Constructing the Enemy

To boost morale and battlefield confidence, PLAF and PAVN soldiers were trained to hold little regard for their enemy. The ARVN was described as weak and poorly led. They would rarely stand and fight.

They were also told that Americans were better fighters than the ARVN, but not as good as the French. They relied too heavily on their superior firepower. If the ability to draw on this firepower was removed, it was argued, American units could be easily defeated. The Americans were considered unsuited to the climate and unable to adapt to the jungle environment in which many PLAF units operated. It was assumed American morale would soon collapse.

PLAF/PAVN training also demonised the Americans. Soldiers were told that US forces routinely killed prisoners, usually after horrendous torture that frequently involved disembowelment. These claims were intended to discourage battlefield surrender and defections. Another perception was that American were cannibals and ate Vietnamese children. An even more outrageous claim, that reflected Vietnamese racial intolerance of African–Americans, was that captured Vietnamese were placed in a machine that turned them into black Americans for service in the US Army.

Rightist ideology was believed to be manifested in 'passive thinking', a tendency to 'fear difficulties and hardships'. Consequently, soldiers would 'fail to resolutely fulfil their tasks'. In 1965 senior Party member Le Duc Tho spoke critically of the 'influence of bourgeois ideology' in the Army, claiming it was plagued by 'individualism, peacekeeping, thoughts of enjoyment and so forth'. The PAVN's inability to destroy the American forces was blamed on 'rightist ideology'.

# The Village War, 1965–1967

The guerrilla war continued in South Vietnam's villages and was expanded after 1965 because the United States attempted to project its military power into previously 'liberated' areas.

The US commitment to a ground war allegedly provided irrefutable evidence of its imperialistic tendencies. The ARVN and the GVN were described as American 'puppets'. Recruiters had a new argument for joining the PLAF and resisting the enemy: it was the Americans who were now prolonging the war. Many PLAF recruits accepted that if the Americans left, the Vietnamese would be able to settle their differences themselves. One captured PLAF soldier noted: 'It is my opinion that if the Americans hadn't come to South Vietnam, the differences between North and South Vietnam could have been settled by different and more peaceful means.' 'I only see that the people are suffering hardships,' said another PLAF prisoner. 'Now I only want to know what can be done to make the Americans go back to their country so that both [Vietnamese] governments can come to an agreement to relieve people's suffering.'

A characteristic of the PLAF approach to the Village War after 1965 was the increased use of what MACV and the RVN called 'terror tactics'. One reason for the renewed use of such tactics was the PLAF's loss of territorial control in many areas. With the Americans and ARVN exercising control during the daylight hours, opportunities for informers to betray the PLAF increased. The 'conspiracy of silence' had to continue and so terror tactics were used to ensure a community's compliance.

American and RVN propaganda emphasised these terror tactics and the seemingly senseless destruction of community assets. 'The Viet Cong are Terrorists', insisted one RVN campaign. To the Americans the terror tactics made sense: why else would the Vietnamese not support the American effort?

To counter RVN/US advances into formerly 'liberated areas', the PLAF expanded its activities in areas that had been brought under ARVN control. In January 1967 at Long My, in Chuong Thien, ARVN forces discovered two

| PLAF Terror Attacks on South Vietnamese Civilians (1962–1966) | | | | |
|---|---|---|---|---|
| Year | Killed | Wounded | Kidnapped | Total |
| 1962 | 1,719 | 6,458 | 9,688 | 17,865 |
| 1963 | 2,073 | 8,375 | 7,252 | 17,710 |
| 1964 | 1,611 | 2,324 | 6,710 | 10,645 |
| 1965 | 2,032 | 2,125 | 6,929 | 11,086 |
| 1966 | 2,613 | 5,690 | 3,700 | 12,003 |

trenches that held 79 dead bodies. Survivors of the massacre suggested the victims were pro-RVN villagers who had been forced into a 'VC Concentration Camp'.

In response to American and RVN allegations, the NLF denied using terror tactics and claimed those killed were supporters of the puppet regime – and therefore 'legitimate' targets. Whether by intention or accident, however, PLAF terror tactics killed an ever-increasing number of South Vietnamese civilians who were not 'legitimate' targets.

# Summing up the Vietnamese Way of War

Hanoi's strategy in Vietnam went through three major phases between 1960 and 1967. Following Diem's murder and PLAF success, the guerrilla war aimed at destroying the oppression gave way to the 'General Offensive'. The ARVN was saved from total annihilation in 1964–1965 by the US military. Johnson's decision to commit to a ground war in 1965 denied the PLAF the widely expected quick victory. While the addition of the PAVN enabled Hanoi and NLF to stand up to the Americans and engage in 'Big Unit' engagements, war had again become a tool of diplomacy after a period when it had appeared the military solution alone would reunite the country.

PLAF, and later PAVN, tactics were a combination of approaches used earlier against France, along with a response to the new American way of war. US mobility and firepower compelled PAVN/PLAF leaders to mesh proven tactics with new approaches.

Accepting that both sides saw the American phase of the conflict as a war of attrition, the US military was much more successful from late 1965 to late 1967. US actions into 1967 led to huge PAVN/PLAF losses. Although thousands of Americans returned home in 'body bags', many more PAVN/ PLAF soldiers were killed. Yet PAVN and PLAF losses were insufficient to force Hanoi to seriously consider negotiations. Thanks to a young population, the mobilisation of women and Chinese guarantees, thousands of PAVN soldiers were available to be sent down the Ho Chi Minh Trail.

*POINTS TO REMEMBER*
- The North Vietnamese decided to fight a 'People's War' in South Vietnam. To do this they established the People's Liberation Army (PLA) in 1960, which was reconstituted as the People's Liberation Armed Forces (PLAF) in 1961. It was organised to fight a long, protracted war.
- South Vietnam tried to counter the 'People's War' strategy by the Strategic Hamlet program.
- The Battle of Ap Bac demonstrated that the ARVN could be defeated in conventional battle by VC guerrillas. It also showed that PLAF units could fight large-unit battles.
- The PLAF's General Offensive (1964–1965) was so successful against the ARVN that it encouraged many people to believe a decisive victory was close.
- Attacks on American installations led to an escalation of American military personnel. This encouraged the North Vietnamese to commit PAVN forces to the fighting in the South.
- The PLAF used 'terror tactics' as one of its approaches to fighting the Village War after 1965.

## ACTIVITIES

**1** Early Strategy 1959–1963: How did political considerations influence Northern military strategy in the South during this period?

**2** How did the PLAF apply the principles of the 'People's War' strategy in South Vietnam? You should consider: Recruitment, organisation, indoctrination, Oath of Honour and Discipline, and 'The Destruction of Oppression'.

**3** Evaluate the effectiveness of the Strategic Hamlet as a strategy to defeat 'People's War'.

**4** To what extent did the PLAF strategy undermine Diem's rule?

**5** Do you think the PLAF general offensive of 1964–1965 had any real chance of success without the PAVN? Was it realistic to assume the United States would not intervene in force?

**6** How did the North Vietnamese react to the escalation of American forces?

**7** How did the PAVN and the PLAF react to American military tactics?

**8** How did the failure to achieve a victory in 1965 create divisions within the North Vietnamese Politburo?

**9** Were the Americans justified to label the Viet Cong as 'Terrorists'?

**10** Essay: How did the North Vietnamese fight the war in the south?

**11** The Ho Chi Minh Trail has been described as 'the key to General Giap's war'. Justify this evaluation.

### Sample HSC Exam Question:

**1** Describe the role of EITHER the Viet Minh between 1945 and 1954 OR the Viet Cong between 1960 and 1969.

### FURTHER READING

Qiang Zhai's *China and the Vietnam Wars, 1950–1975* (University of North Carolina Press, Chapel Hill, 2000) is based on previously-unexamined Chinese archives and highlights tensions between China and North Vietnam. Michael Lee Lanning and Dan Cragg's *Inside the VC and the NVA* (Ivy Books, New York, 1992) is full of interesting insights. The late Douglas Pike's *PAVN: People's Army of Vietnam* (Presidio Press, New York, 1986) is a detailed analysis of the PAVN. John Prados, *The Blood Road: The Ho Chi Minh Trail and the Vietnam War* (John Wiley & Son, New York, 1998) is an excellent introduction to the logistical miracle of the North's war in the South. Sandra Taylor's *Vietnamese Women at War* (Kansas University Press, Lawrence, 1999) and Karen Gottschang's *Even the Women Must Fight* (John Wiley & Sons, New York, 1998) suggest that female participation made the difference between victory and defeat for the DRV/NLF.

# The American Way of War

IN THIS CHAPTER YOU WILL:
- learn about the strategies and tactics used by the United States and its allies in Vietnam
- be introduced to Australian methods of waging war
- explore the experiences of 'ordinary' soldiers
- consider whether alternative American strategies might have won the war.

## Background

Americans went to war in Vietnam confident of victory. With their well-equipped, highly trained armed forces, they assumed that PLAF and PAVN would yield to superior firepower. By the late 1960s, however, those assumptions were in tatters, as the United States failed to subdue an enemy that some Americans had earlier derided as 'a rag–tag 3rd rate military force'. The underlying problem confronting the United States and its allies in South Vietnam was that a military response to what were fundamentally 'political' problems was probably doomed from the outset. This confusing and bitterly fought civil war was often waged as a guerrilla war, where there were no front lines and where the distinction between enemy and ally was often ambiguous.

## American Forces in Vietnam

Over 2.7 million Americans served in Vietnam during the 1960s and 1970s. Three-quarters of that group were volunteers. Particularly during the early stages of American intervention, many men volunteered for patriotic reasons. Yet it should not be assumed that a majority of those who served were enthusiastic participants in the war. Many men enlisted in the hope that by so doing they would avoid being sent to Vietnam – or that if they were sent they would be assigned to a non-combat role. For working-class Americans, military service could be an opportunity and a chance to escape grinding poverty.

**HISTORICAL DOCUMENT**

### Ron Kovic Recalls the Appeal of Patriotism

In the last month of school, the Marine recruiters came and spoke to my senior class ... They told us that day that the Marine Corps built men – body, mind, and spirit. And that we could serve our country like the young president [John F. Kennedy] had asked us to do ... I stayed up most of the night before I left, watching the late movie. Then 'The Star Spangled Banner' played. I remember standing up and feeling very patriotic, chills running up and down my spine. I put my hand over my heart and stood rigid at attention.

From *Born on the Fourth of July* (Corgi Books, London, 1976)

The Federal Government's 'Selective Service' system drafted men between the ages of 18 and 26. Men could avoid the draft if they qualified for one of several categories for exemptions or deferments:
• hardship deferments – for men whose contribution was necessary to keep their family fed and clothed
• student deferments – many young men stayed in college to avoid the draft (in 1967 and 1971 the rules were changed to make student deferment more difficult)
• occupational exemptions – doctors, scientists, engineers and men in other 'priority' occupations
• enlisting in the National Guard, the Coast Guard or the Reserves.

Some men avoided the draft by deliberately failing their medical examinations, by appealing against the decisions of their local draft boards or by moving to a different county or state. For every man drafted, seven men gained exemptions.

In general, better-educated and middle-class men were more likely to avoid the draft than working-class Americans. Approximately 80% of the enlisted men in the US Army and Marines were from working-class and poor families. Once in the military, a college graduate had a 40% chance of being deployed to Vietnam; high-school graduates had 65%; and for those who did not complete high-school the figure was 70%.

The average age of American servicemen in Vietnam was 19 – seven years younger than their World War II counterparts. The youthfulness of American forces in Vietnam meant they were less able to cope with the stresses of military service – and less able to re-adjust to civilian life after they returned from Vietnam.

As the conflict in Vietnam continued, as the demand from the military for recruits increased and as better-educated Americans avoided the draft, the standards required of recruits declined. Increasingly, military commanders complained that the men they were receiving were neither physically nor emotionally equipped for service. This problem, which in practice translated into less-effective fighting forces, was compounded as the war continued and the nation's original motives for going to war were discredited, reflecting Americans' deeper disillusionment with US politics, society and culture.

## HISTORICAL ISSUE

### America's Logistical Miracle

During 1965, as the US escalation accelerated, military commanders realised South Vietnamese infrastructure – including harbours, airports and transport systems – was inadequate. Over the next two years the United States built the infrastructure to support their vast military forces. Six new ports were constructed, along with four million square yards of airfields and 2,800 kilometres of roads.

By 1967, over 850,000 tons of supplies arrived per month. Soldiers were consuming 10 million field rations, 80,000 tons of ammunition and 80 million gallons of fuel each month.

*US Marines storm ashore from a landing craft during reinforcement of key Da Nang airbase*

# Waging a 'Limited War'

The United States believed it could win in Vietnam by fighting a 'limited war', with no formal declaration of war against North Vietnam, which meant applying forces according to the circumstances of each conflict. In the case of Vietnam, limited war:
* would be less likely to provoke Chinese intervention
* would make a call-up of American Reserve forces unnecessary, limiting political damage in the USA arising from the war
* would be, it was assumed, sufficient to defeat the PLAF and PAVN.

But the hope of forcing the enemy to the negotiating table proved illusory, as North Vietnam and the NLF not only survived, but matched the American escalation.

The concept of limited war was the subject of some criticism during the 1960s and has been used by some commentators to explain why American forces were unable to defeat their opponent. But by 1968 the USA had committed a large proportion of its available troops to Indochina.

**Secret War: Americans and North Vietnamese in Laos**

Both the USA and North Vietnam ignored the Geneva Accords of 1962, which had designated Laos a neutral nation. Americans devoted considerable resources to closing down the Ho Chi Minh Trail in Laos and Cambodia.

Much of the American effort in Laos took the form of an air-war against the Ho Chi Minh Trail. But the United States also utilised forces drawn largely from the Hmong minority in Laos, led by Vang Pao, to engage the North Vietnamese in Laos. In addition, small numbers of American Special Forces also operated inside Laos, where they monitored PAVN traffic along the Ho Chi Minh Trail and called in air strikes against enemy forces.

*US Military Regions in South Vietnam. The USA divided South Vietnam into four 'Military Regions,' from I Corps, which began at the DMZ, to IV Corps, in the south*

# Westmoreland's Strategy

When US ground forces began arriving in Vietnam in significant numbers from mid–1965, they were confronted with two tasks:

1  Establish a number of 'enclaves' along the South Vietnamese coast-line to provide security in the event of a major ARVN collapse.
2  Tackle enemy forces.

The enclaves established did provide security but Westmoreland regarded the strategy as too passive: it was necessary to take the fight to the enemy. Westmoreland planned a three-stage strategy:

1  US troops would construct logistical facilities and protect their bases and respond to PAVN/PLAF aggression as it occurred.
2  US troops would advance into the more remote areas of South Vietnam to wipe out enemy sanctuaries and inflict heavy casualties.
3  American forces would then launch major operations against Main Force enemy units.

In mid–August 1965, US intelligence indicated that a major North Vietnamese force was threatening the US 'enclave' at Chu Lai, 90 kilometres south of Da Nang. US Marines launched 'Operation Starlite'. On paper, Starlite was a major success for US forces. For the loss of 45 Marines killed, approximately 700 enemy troops were killed. But on closer examination, just one enemy weapon

was recovered for every six bodies discovered, suggesting that large numbers of unarmed civilians had been killed and counted as enemy casualties. Moreover, within a few weeks of Starlite, enemy troops returned to Chu Lai.

In November 1965, troops were deployed into the Ia Drang Valley and engaged in a ferocious two-day battle – made famous in the film, *We Were Soldiers*. US casualties numbered 79 killed; 634 enemy soldiers were confirmed killed, with a similar number probably removed from the battlefield by their comrades (a Vietnamese practice that infuriated Americans, who were obsessed with achieving a high 'body count'). But the results were ambiguous. The enemy had effectively chosen the time and place of the battle. Although PAVN forces eventually withdrew, the USA had no intention of permanently establishing a presence on the ground they had just 'won'. Also, as US forces withdrew, one of their battalions was ambushed, killing a further 151 Americans.

The battles of 1965 established a pattern that remained common for the duration of the war. American forces were able to inflict enormous casualties on their adversaries, but those losses did not deter enemy commanders. Ongoing guerrilla war eventually exhausted American patience.

# American Flair in Technology and Firepower

**PERSONALITY**

**General William C. Westmoreland**

A graduate of the West Point Military Academy, William C. Westmoreland first saw service during World War II. In 1964 Westmoreland replaced General Paul Harkins as Commander of the US Military Assistance Command in Vietnam. From 1965 to 1967 Westmoreland played a key role in the American escalation in Vietnam, by requesting additional US forces and adopting the contentious strategy of attrition.

In late 1967 Johnson ordered Westmoreland to visit the United States, where the General provided a measured, but optimistic assessment of the war. 'We have reached an important point,' he stated, 'where the end begins to come into view'. Declaring that he believed the USA could soon commence cutting back the level of American forces, he asserted that the ARVN could assume more responsibility for fighting the war. Westmoreland's optimism was misplaced: in January 1968 enemy forces launched the Tet Offensive, prompting Westmoreland to request that additional troops be sent to Vietnam. Soon after, he was recalled to the United States and 'kicked upstairs' to the position of Chief of Staff of the Army. He retired in 1972. In 1976 he published *A Soldier Reports*, wherein he defended his conduct of the war. Westmoreland died in 2005.

As the world's wealthiest nation, the USA had access to an almost unlimited array of high-technology weapons. This was a stark contrast to their enemies, who necessarily relied more on ingenuity and guile to fight the war. The Vietnam War was, thus, a clash of *cultures*, as well as armies.

Technology, however, had its limits. For combat soldiers, no weapon is more significant than their rifle. Developed at enormous cost, the M16 was indeed an impressive weapon – light and able to fire hundreds of rounds in rapid succession. Yet early versions of M16 were prone to jamming and it requiring constant cleaning. By contrast, the enemy's counterpart, various versions of the Russian-designed AK47, was a simpler weapon, more reliable and required less maintenance. The latest technology was not always the best. Significantly, the Viet Cong often relied on weapons scrounged from the battlefield, yet they did not always take M16 rifles from dead Americans.

The failings of the M16 symbolise the larger failings of the American way of war. US forces (and their allies) had at their disposal a vast array of weapons and firepower. But each of those weapons systems required careful maintenance – which entailed the deployment of large numbers of non-combat support units. Frequently, too, massive firepower was applied with little regard for the civilians who might be on the receiving end.

## Search and Destroy

The major American method of engaging the enemy was via search-and-destroy missions. In practice, search and destroy meant US troops were used to locate and pursue enemy units, who were then to be overwhelmed by superior American firepower. The American emphasis on seeking out the enemy meant that the task of protecting the South Vietnamese population was often neglected.

### HISTORICAL ISSUE

*Air-mobility: The Helicopter*

American commanders' faith in search and destroy was predicated on their ability to deploy troops quickly to the battlefield. The major means of doing so was by helicopter, and special 'air-mobile' units were established, which carefully coordinated the deployment and support of troops. But almost all infantry units used helicopters during the war, and for many veterans the sound of an approaching helicopter evokes vivid images of the war.

Helicopters were also used for many other tasks, from fire support to medical evacuation. Helicopters were also used as 'gun-ships' to rain fire down on enemy forces and 'soften-up' targets prior to the deployment of American or Allied forces.

For search-and-destroy missions, small units were often used as 'bait' to lure the PAVN and PLAF to battle. In theory, additional American forces, backed by air power and artillery, would then be brought to bear against the enemy. However, American units were often the victims of ambush. Then, when additional American forces were brought to bear, the enemy would melt away.

Search and destroy was the subject of considerable criticism within the United States, partly because the tactic was not working and also because

### HISTORICAL ISSUE

*Agent Orange*

American soldiers and their commanders expressed frustration that PAVN/PLAF troops could often find refuge in the jungle. One solution was to spray the jungles with herbicide, to kill the vegetation – and thereby deny cover to the enemy. The US launched 'Operation Ranch Hand', which between 1962 and 1971 led to 19 million gallons of Agent Orange and other herbicides being sprayed over Vietnam (and Laos). These chemicals were purportedly non-toxic to humans, but there is considerable evidence that the health of Vietnamese and Americans was very adversely affected by exposure to Agent Orange.

Vietnamese civilians caught up in the fighting frequently became casualties.

The notion of search and destroy appeared to contradict US objectives of winning support amongst the Vietnamese and 'nation-building', so the phrase was dropped in 1968. But the tactic continued, under the guise of 'reconnaissance-in-force' or 'pre-emptive operations'. During 1969 and 1970 South Vietnamese forces assumed increasing responsibility for these operations.

# Winning Hearts and Minds? Pacification

The process of winning the support (the 'hearts and minds') of the South Vietnamese and extending the reach of the GVN was known as 'pacification': a wide-ranging program, based around the principles of improving conditions for South Vietnamese villagers and giving them confidence that the GVN could protect them from the NLF. For Americans, the phrase described all 'non-military' aspects of the conflict. This entailed ambitious programs, such as seeking to redistribute land, and more specific programs, such as the provision of medical supplies and food to peasants.

During the late 1950s, the South Vietnamese and Americans had initiated the 'Agroville' program. But the communities that had been built to protect peasants from the NLF proved ineffectual, largely because the ARVN was incapable of protecting the communities and because peasants resented being removed from their ancestral lands. The Strategic Hamlet Program, launched in 1961, was intended to protect villages, by surrounding them with barbed wire and fortifications, as well as villagers, who were to be armed and trained to defend their communities. However, the Strategic Hamlets were unpopular amongst the villagers and the program was abandoned in 1963.

From late 1963, new attempts were made to put effective rural pacification programs into operation. Nevertheless, when US combat troops arrived in Vietnam in 1965, the NLF was effectively functioning as an alternate government throughout much of South Vietnam and much of the responsibility for pacification fell on the shoulders of the ARVN.

In 1966 the GVN agreed to establish Revolutionary Development (RD) teams to live amongst villagers and provide security and education and assist with development. But the RD program failed. GVN cadre were too few in number, were insufficiently trained and were distrusted by villagers. The ARVN, moreover, was unable to defend the villages. During 1966 and 1967, the PLAF made a particular effort to undermine the RD scheme, by kidnapping and killing hundreds of RD workers.

Pacification faced three fundamental difficulties:
1  The villagers were rarely treated with decency and respect.
2  Until the GVN made serious efforts to reform the system of land ownership, it would remain estranged from the peasant majority.
3  Programs were 'imposed' upon the villagers without consultation with the rural population.

In April 1967, MACV (Military Assistance Command Vietnam – the successor to MAAG) assumed responsibility for pacification efforts. Yet, ultimately, the refusal of successive South Vietnamese governments to enact democratic reforms and redistribute land ensured the GVN never won the affection or support of the peasants who comprised the majority of the South Vietnamese population.

# The Tour of Duty

Americans who served in Vietnam usually served a 'tour of duty'. For those in the Army, this meant a 12-month deployment to Vietnam; for Marines, the tour of duty was generally 13 months. This was a different system to that which had been used in previous wars, where men enlisted, or were drafted, for the duration of the conflict. Westmoreland hoped the 12- or 13-month deployment would improve his troops' morale, because they knew they were to spend a specific period 'in country', rather than confront an open-ended deployment.

## HISTORICAL DOCUMENT

### William C. Westmoreland Defends the One-Year Tour of Duty

Although it posed problems of continuity ... In keeping with my belief that it was going to be a long war, the one-year tour gave a man a goal. That was good for morale. It was also advisable from the standpoint of health, and it spread the burden of a long war over a broader spectrum of both Army regulars and American draftees. I hoped it would extend the nation's staying power by forestalling public pressure to 'bring the boys home'

The tour-of-duty system meant American servicemen arrived in Vietnam as individuals, rather than as part of a unit. Many Americans commented on the difficulties with the system. The one-year service system meant that soldiers often focussed less on winning the war, than they did on their own survival. It also robbed the American military of many men who had gained the experience that would have made the Army and Marines into more efficient fighting forces.

*The body of an American soldier is removed from the battlefield*

# The Grunt's Life: Tedium and Terror

It is difficult to generalise about Americans' experiences in Vietnam. Arriving in Vietnam was usually a shocking and alienating experience. Most of the young men who served had not previously travelled abroad. The sounds, sights and smells could be overwhelming. Upon arrival many Americans expressed surprise at being transported around in buses in which the windows were protected by wire mesh. Asking what the mesh was for, one soldier recalled being told: 'It's the gooks, man, the gooks ... The gooks will throw grenades through the window.'

Much of the grunt's life – 'grunt' was the phrase used to describe combat soldiers – was spent patrolling, a tedious and dangerous task. The terrain and climate could be overwhelming and Americans found it difficult to distinguish friend from foe. The enemy was both everywhere – and nowhere. The Vietnamese civilian who smiled at them one day might the next day engage them in combat or not warn them that the road leading out of the village was mined. Many Vietnamese were sympathetic to the NLF; many others were indifferent about the conflict and sought to be left alone to tend their crops.

## HISTORICAL ISSUE

### American Encounters with the Vietnamese

Few Americans had any real knowledge of, or appreciation for, Vietnam. The Vietnamese remained a mysterious, often hostile 'other', who could not be trusted:

> Too many of us forgot that Vietnamese were people. We didn't treat them like people after a while.

Americans' underlying contempt for the Vietnamese could turn into senseless acts of violence:

> I made a bet ... that I could sink a sampan with a rock. So we got radioed by a river patrol boat that there was a sampan headed our way who was probably a gunrunner. So while the helicopter pilot hovered overhead, I hooked up in my harness and leaned out. I had a good eight- or ten-pound rock. I dropped it and it went through the little boat and the boat sunk. Little Vietnamese guys are yelling and cursing ... and swimming.

Of course, not all troops were affected by what one American labelled 'crypto-racism', which transformed the Vietnamese into alien enemies, who could legitimately be treated as 'savages'. Some Americans did establish friendships with Vietnamese, whom they treated with respect and dignity. Some Americans established close, if often short-term relationships with Vietnamese women. And many Americans took advantage of the Vietnamese prostitutes who plied their trade in cities like Saigon and Da Nang, as well as in 'shanty towns' that sprang up adjacent to American bases.

Only occasionally was the Vietnam War fought in major engagements, on set battlefields. More often it was fought in the villages and rice paddies. Consequently, many Americans became casualties not in major firefights, but in skirmishes, with an invisible enemy who refused to fight on the Americans' terms. Tens of thousands of Americans were killed or wounded by snipers, booby-traps or land mines. All the while there was the suspicion that the Vietnamese villagers had known what was about to happen.

## HISTORICAL ISSUE

***Philip Caputo Discusses the Nature of War***

Philip Caputo's patriotism and optimism wilted when he arrived in Vietnam in 1965 as part of the first contingent deployment of Marines. In *A Rumour of War* (MacMillan, London, 1977) Caputo chronicled his growing disillusionment at the conduct of the war. Having dreamed of emulating the heroic figures depicted in American popular culture, Caputo was frustrated by the nature of the war and dismayed by its 'savagery'. There were no:

> Normandies or Gettysburgs for us, no epic clashes that decided the fates of armies or nations. The war was mostly a matter of enduring weeks of expectant waiting and, at random intervals, of conducting vicious manhunts through jungles and swamps, where snipers harassed us constantly and booby traps cut us down one by one ... Whether committed in the name of principles or out of vengeance, atrocities were as common to the Vietnamese battlefields, as shell craters and barbed wire ... [T]he comradeship that was the war's only redeeming quality caused some of its worst crimes.

Caputo returned to Vietnam in 1975 to cover the 'fall' of Saigon for the Chicago *Tribune*. He was, thus, 'part of the first American combat unit sent to the war' then 'among the last Americans to be evacuated'.

# REMFs

Not all Americans who served in Vietnam were combat soldiers. A much larger majority were members of the group derided by combat soldiers as 'REMFs' ('Rear-echelon mother-fuckers'). In December 1967, there were 473,200 Americans in South Vietnam, over 75% of whom were in non-combat roles.

Although the Vietnam War was in many respects a 'war without front lines', the experiences of soldiers who spent their days on patrol, where the risk of death was ever-present, were fundamentally different from those of the hundreds of thousands of Americans who worked as clerks, cooks, maintenance personnel and the myriad other tasks necessary to support the minority of combat troops. For these men – and the 11,000 American women who served in Vietnam – the tour of duty was vastly different from the brutalities and bloodshed to which combat soldiers were exposed:

> We rode to work in air-conditioned buses, we worked in air-conditioned offices. Our barracks had hot and cold running showers and flush toilets ... There was a movie every night. We drank beer. You could eat all you wanted.

## HISTORICAL ISSUE

***R & R***

American military personnel were entitled to 'Rest and Recuperation' ('R & R') leave, outside the war zone. Servicemen and women could be transported to one of a number of 'liberty' towns throughout the Asia–Pacific region. Many married men flew to Hawaii to meet up with their spouses. Other popular destinations included Hong Kong, Tokyo and Singapore. Many Americans spent their R & R in Australia. Within Vietnam, the military established R & R resorts at China Beach and at Vung Tau.

# The Ally: The Army of the Republic of Vietnam

Many Americans claim the ARVN was uninterested in fighting the enemy, that it was riddled with corruption and that its failings symbolised a deeper South Vietnamese apathy toward the war. There are elements of truth in those charges. But the ARVN was also a convenient scapegoat for the deeper failings of US policy in Indochina.

Some ARVN units were very poor. Some, possibly a majority, evaded combat whenever they could. Desertion rates were high, particularly in infantry units. Other units fought bravely, however, and during the Tet Offensive and again in 1972 and 1975 some ARVN units distinguished themselves in combat.

Although ARVN officers had opportunities to enrich themselves through corrupt means, 'ordinary' South Vietnamese soldiers had a miserable existence. Paid a pittance, soldiers typically had to supplement their military income to feed their family. And unlike the American one-year tour of duty, most ARVN soldiers were in 'for the duration' or until killed or incapacitated.

**HISTORICAL DEBATE**

## The ARVN: An Unworthy Ally?

'Marvin the ARVN' was roundly criticised by many Americans (and Australians) during the Vietnam War. The first two quotes are from American veterans; the final quotation, from Australian combat cameraman, Neil Davis, provides a different interpretation of the ARVN's role in the conflict.

**Dan Vandenberg** (US 25th Infantry Division):
They were a joke. I despised the whole lot of them. They were all cowards.

**John Pancrazio** (US advisor serving with South Vietnamese militia unit):
The majority of the armed forces could have more easily been called armed farces! They were very poor fighters, with the exception of the Rangers, and were much more eager to avoid combat than engage in it.

**Neil Davis:**
[T]hey [ARVN troops] did the bulk of the fighting ... [T]he South Vietnamese army lost at least 50% more men from 1965 to 1968 than the Americans ... [O]nly in three weeks did the Americans have more soldiers killed than the South Vietnamese.

# Failed Strategy of Attrition: the Body Count Nonsense

Through 1966 and 1967, American commanders expressed faith in their strategy of attrition. The enemy, they declared, was being overwhelmed by superior American firepower. Soldiers in Vietnam knew better. American soldiers, encouraged to produce a high body count, had a saying: 'If it's dead and it's Vietnamese, it's VC'. One consequence was that dead Vietnamese civilians were often counted as enemy

*Neil Davis (third from left) with ARVN troops, 1972*

combatants, which in turn encouraged the Americans' obsession with firepower – and which in turn caused further devastation throughout Vietnam and made the task of winning Vietnamese 'hearts and minds' even more difficult.

The 'body count nonsense', Captain Colin Powell (who would later become US Secretary of State) recalled, was widely abused:

'How many did your platoon get?'

'I don't know. We saw two for sure.'

'Well if you saw two, there were probably eight, so let's say 10.'

'Counting bodies', Powell recalled, 'became a macabre statistical competition … Good commanders scored high body counts. And good commanders got promotions'.

This 'careerism' was another issue that impeded the US war effort. Rampant amongst American officers was the tendency to regard service in Vietnam as a means of securing promotion, and 'punching the ticket' in Vietnam – serving, even briefly – was a prerequisite to advancement. Officers often served with units for just a few months, which made the tasks of forging unit cohesion and maintaining morale even more problematic. As General Douglas Kinnard noted, many officers 'made a career out of their own careers rather than a career out of leading their units'. Frequently, it was experienced non-commissioned officers – corporals and sergeants – who were best equipped to lead platoons and even companies.

An even more serious problem undermining the strategy of attrition was the enemy's ability to match the US escalation. Secretary of Defense Robert McNamara and other policymakers in Washington, and commanders such as Westmoreland, miscalculated the number of enemy troops who could join the fight. They also represented erroneous casualty figures as indicative of 'progress' in the war. Perhaps most significantly, they misunderstood the underlying determination of their opponents. For Ho, Giap and millions of other Vietnamese, the task of unifying Vietnam was not negotiable. They did not have a 'breaking point', as Americans assumed. Indeed, for many Americans, the Vietnamese persistence was evidence of Vietnamese irrationality. American historian Loren Baritz has summed up this issue: 'North Vietnam finally won its war because it was willing to accept more deaths than we considered rational.'

## A Better Way? Australian Forces in Vietnam

At the peak of the war, there were three battalions of Australian troops – and associated units such as artillery, the Special Air Service and supporting elements – in Vietnam. By 1973, nearly 47,000 Australians had served in Vietnam. Over 17,000 of these men were conscripts. A total of 520 Australians were killed in Vietnam, with a further 2,400 wounded. Most Australians who served in Vietnam arrived with a particular unit and left with that same unit. This was a very different system to the individual 'tour of duty' used by the United States. The Australian system has been praised by many veterans as a significant factor contributing to the higher degree of cohesion often demonstrated by Australian forces.

Australian forces in Vietnam operated rather differently from their American counterparts. The Australians placed a greater emphasis on patrolling and generally took greater care to avoid detection by the enemy. Australian units often avoided using jungle tracks, thus minimising the risks from ambush or mines. Generally, the Australians fought a more patient war than American forces.

Of course, Australian forces made some errors in Vietnam. Attempting to secure a section of Phuoc Tuy Province, they laid 20,000 anti-personnel mines. Later, many of these mines were dug up by the PLAF and used against the Australians. Such mistakes notwithstanding, Australian units were widely praised by American commanders. Westmoreland commended the Australians as a 'thoroughly professional force'. Perhaps the highest compliment paid to the Australians came from their adversaries. Trin Duc, who had first fought as a member of the anti-Japanese resistance during World War II, described the relative dangers posed to his PLAF unit by American and Australian forces: 'Worse than the Americans were the Australians.' He noted that his unit was often able to counter the Americans' tactic of calling in air strikes and artillery support by either withdrawing from the battle or by moving very close to the American unit. 'The Australians,' however, 'were more patient than the Americans, better guerrilla fighters, better at ambushes. They liked to stay with us instead of calling in the planes. We were more afraid of their style'.

## HISTORICAL ISSUE

### The Battle of Long Tan

On 18 August 1966, while patrolling in the Long Tan rubber plantation, D Company of the 6th Battalion, Royal Australian Regiment (RAR) encountered a much larger PLAF force. PLAF commanders were keen to establish their ascendancy over the newly established Australian Task Force – which had the temerity to build its major base in territory previously controlled by the PLAF. While most of the rest of the 6th Battalion enjoyed performances from Australian stars 'Little Pattie' and Col Joye at the nearby Nui Dat base, D Company was fighting the largest engagement fought by Australians during the Vietnam War. Heavily outnumbered, and fighting in pouring rain, D Company was at risk of being overrun by the 275 PLAF Regiment. As the battle raged, the commander of D Company, Major Harry Smith, called in artillery support, which played a vital role in saving the Company. Moving to the battle in armoured personnel carriers, B company of the 6th Battalion was despatched to the aid of D Company. Eighteen Australians were killed at Long Tan. When the PLAF withdrew they left behind the bodies of 245 of their comrades.

By 1971, the Australians had effectively 'secured' Phuoc Tuy Province (an area previously regarded as favourable to the NLF and the PLAF). Enemy activity had been reduced to almost negligible levels, and it was possible to move around the Province in relative safety. It has been argued, therefore, that the Australians won 'their' war in Phuoc Tuy – unlike the wider American effort in Vietnam. Certainly Australian forces conducted a shrewd and effective military campaign. And they also understood the importance of establishing support amongst the civilian population – which by most accounts they did. Nevertheless, within a few months of the Australian withdrawal from Phuoc Tuy, the NLF and PLAF had returned and began positioning

*Australian troops with a wounded Viet Cong prisoner, after the Battle of Long Tan*

themselves as an alternate government. No matter how effectively the Australian forces had waged their military campaign, the population's support for the South Vietnamese regime was tenuous. The Australians in Phuoc Tuy could not defeat those forces committed to the overthrow of the unpopular South Vietnamese Government. Without a government in Saigon that was genuinely responsive to the needs and aspirations of the peasant majority, no military campaign – whether it was waged by American, South Vietnamese or Australian forces – could destroy completely the NLF or defeat the PLAF.

## Conclusion

One of the persistent issues surrounding the Vietnam War is that if the United States had fought the war differently, the result could have been different. Much of this discussion can be understood as the American response to losing a war: Americans were unaccustomed to defeat. On one hand, this explains why many Americans deny they were beaten in Vietnam. At the same time, however, defeat in Vietnam has led Americans to look for explanations as to why they could not overwhelm the PLAF and PAVN. American military commanders have argued that if they had been allowed to wage the war differently, they would have won. If only they had been allowed to attack enemy sanctuaries in Cambodia and Laos, US forces could have won. If only US forces had been allowed to invade North Vietnam, they could have won. If only more US forces had been deployed to Vietnam, they could have won. If only US forces had not been forced to a limited war, to 'fight with one hand tied behind their back', they could have won. If only more serious effort had been made at pacification and building support amongst the Vietnamese, the USA could have won. If only the USA had declared war on North Vietnam, they could

### HISTORICAL ISSUE

**'Vietnam' at the Movies: The Example of Platoon**

Several Hollywood 'Vietnam blockbusters' purport to 'tell it like it really was'. But most are works of fiction and need to be 'read' very carefully. Oliver Stone's 1986 *Platoon*, for example, was widely lauded as a movie that depicted accurately aspects of Americans' 'Vietnam experience'. Stone, a Vietnam veteran, certainly captured the chaos and brutality of war. But the implication of the film – that the result could have been different if the Americans had fought the war differently (i.e. the way Sergeant Elias wanted to fight the war) – is at best tenuous. Indeed, by reducing the war to conflict between Sergeants Barnes and Elias, who represent, respectively, 'redneck' and 'liberal' America, and by emphasising the war's impact on the United States, *Platoon* is representative of the wider American habit of focusing less on what America did to Vietnam, than what 'Vietnam' did to America.

have won. If only US forces had not been 'stabbed in the back' by the antiwar movement and a hostile media, the USA could have won. If only …

These arguments make it easier for those who fought the war to rationalise the war's end. But they are unhelpful in understanding that the American way of war, including the inability to understand the social and political aspects of the conflict, was one factor contributing to the US defeat. The United States never really understood the nature of the conflict in Vietnam. Primarily concerned with the military struggle, they paid little attention to the political and social factors that made millions of Vietnamese hostile to the American war effort. Loren Baritz offers a helpful way of understanding the Americans' difficulties in Vietnam:

> [T]he military's claim that we could have won the war if it had been allowed to fight it differently is pointless. We could not have fought it differently. The constraints on the tactics of the war, and the absence of a political goal to shape those tactics, were products of American culture.

Baritz, thus, emphasises the cultural chasm between Americans and Vietnamese, and American culture itself (which shaped the way the United States fought the war) as essential elements for understanding the American defeat in Vietnam.

The inability of the United States to prevail in Vietnam and Americans' inability to understand the reasons for their defeat was summed up in April 1975, when Colonel Harry M. Summers, who had won Silver and Bronze Stars in Vietnam and who later wrote at length about the errors the United States made in fighting the war, met PAVN Colonel Nguyen Dôn Tu. 'You know,' declared Summers, 'you never beat us on the battlefield'. 'That may be so,' replied Tu, 'but it is also irrelevant'.

---

### POINTS TO REMEMBER

- Americans went to war in Vietnam confident in victory.
- This war was often fought as a guerrilla war, where there were no front lines and there was no clear distinction between the enemy and an ally.
- Over 2.7 million Americans served in Vietnam.
- The average age of American servicemen in Vietnam was 19.
- The United States tried to fight a 'limited war' in Vietnam. They used superior technology and firepower to try and win. Search-and-destroy missions were used in an effort to destroy enemy forces. To help build the political unity of South Vietnam a 'pacification' program was used.
- The nature of the warfare in Vietnam began to affect the morale of the US armed forces.
- The American reliance on the 'body count' as a measure of the success of their military strategy was not reliable.

## ACTIVITIES

1 Construct a profile of the average American soldier who was sent to Vietnam.

2 Explain the advantages to the Americans of fighting a 'limited' war in Vietnam.

3 What was General Westmoreland's strategy to achieve victory? How does this compare to the French strategy in the First Indochina War?

4 Was America's faith in technology and firepower to win the war justified?

5 What were the advantages and disadvantages of search and destroy?

6 How successful was the American strategy to win the hearts and minds (pacification) of the South Vietnamese people?

7 What were the advantages and disadvantages of the American 'tour of duty' in the Vietnam War?

8 What was the nature of the war that the American soldiers fought? Did this type of warfare have an impact on the morale of the troops? In your response refer to the extract from Philip Caputo.

9 Was the ARVN an unworthy ally? Examine the quotes in the Historical Debate box. How reliable are they as evidence of the fighting capabilities of ARVN?

10 Evaluate the American strategy of attrition. Did the Australian Army's tactics offer a viable alternative?

### FURTHER READING

Gerard J. DeGroot, *A Noble Cause?: America and the Vietnam War* (Longman, Harlow, Essex, 2000) and Loren Baritz's *Backfire: A History of How American Culture Led Us into Vietnam and Made Us Fight the Way We Did* (Ballantine Books, New York, 1985) are useful. Ron Kovic, *Born on the Fourth of July* (Corgi Books, London, 1976), Frederick Downs, *The Killing Zone* (Berkeley Books, New York, 1978), Philip Caputo, *A Rumour of War* (MacMillan, London, 1977) and Tim O'Brien, *If I Die in a Combat Zone* (Granada, repr. London, 1980) offer first-hand accounts. Keith Walker, *A Piece of My Heart* (Ballantine Books, New York, 1985), William Westmoreland's, *A Soldier Reports* (Da Capo Press, New York, 1989) and Michael Herr's *Dispatches* (Picador, London, 1978) are also informative.

8

# The Tet Offensive

IN THIS CHAPTER YOU WILL:

• learn about what happened in Vietnam in late 1967 and early 1968, when PLAF–PAVN forces launched their massive assault
• gain an understanding of the impact of the Tet Offensive on American strategy and politics.

## The Context: American Optimism

By late 1967 many Americans believed the USA was winning the war in Vietnam. 'Body count' statistics indicated enemy forces were suffering horrendous losses. The American bombing campaign had inflicted massive damage on North Vietnam. Declaring that the 'crossover point' had been reached, Westmoreland asserted there was 'light at the end of the tunnel'. Within 'two years', Westmoreland claimed, it would be 'possible' to 'phase down our level of commitment and turn more of the burden' over to South Vietnamese forces. In public, American politicians also exuded confidence. Vice-President Hubert Humphrey declared there had been 'progress on every front in Vietnam' and President Lyndon Johnson asserted: 'We are making progress.'

## The Context: American Anxieties

Yet there were also worrying portents for the United States. In August 1967, a 'Hamlet Evaluation Survey' – designed to assess the loyalty of individual hamlets and villages to the government in Saigon – suggested the South Vietnamese Government exercised effective control over just 168 of 12,537 hamlets. By contrast, the NLF controlled nearly 4,000 hamlets. The bombing of North Vietnam and the Ho Chi Minh Trail had not seriously impeded the ability of PLAF/PAVN forces to wage war. While US/ARVN forces inflicted massive losses on enemy forces, the PLAF and PAVN re-grouped quickly and launched offensives elsewhere. Inevitably, American casualties were high: during 1967, American casualties averaged over 800 killed each month. To America's military and political leaders, Ho Chi Minh's refusal to bow to the logic of American force seemed not only obstinate, but irrational. As Robert McNamara (whose growing doubts about the war had been expressed in a May 1967 memo to Johnson) noted, Ho was 'a tough old S.O.B.,' who would not 'quit no matter how much bombing we do'.

Despite official optimism, therefore, by late 1967 some US politicians and strategists were expressing anxiety about the course of the war. At the end of January 1968, those private doubts were vindicated, as US and Allied forces found themselves subjected to massive attacks across South Vietnam. Clearly, Westmoreland's claim that the 'enemy's hopes are bankrupt' was wrong.

The Tet Offensive – so called because it was launched during the 'Tet' or New Year celebrations – was a turning point in the Vietnam War. Tet exposed the 'credibility gap' between what Americans were being told about the war and the reality of the conflict. This undermined the credibility of the American political and military leadership. And while some Americans concede that the Tet Offensive was a political defeat for the United States, their claims that it ended in a military victory for US and South Vietnamese forces highlights their continuing misunderstandings about the links between the political and military aspects of the conflict.

Despite his public confidence, by late 1967 Johnson was profoundly worried. The war he had not wanted to fight was distracting public attention from the pressing issues within the United States. His own popularity was waning – just as the 1968 Presidential election campaign loomed. Johnson believed he had chosen a middle course between those who advocated an even more massive US escalation of the war and those who wanted less US involvement. He hoped choosing the middle path would ensure the survival of South Vietnam, without provoking intervention from China or the USSR. Yet the United States found itself in a 'quagmire' in South Vietnam. Victory seemed as elusive as ever. So the war dragged on, with no apparent means by which the USA could extricate itself from the mess it had helped make.

In early November 1967, Johnson sought advice from 'the Wise Men', a group of highly-regarded former government and military officials. Conceding he was 'deeply concerned' about the 'deterioration of public support' for the war, Johnson asked the Wise Men whether the United States was pursuing the correct policy. The consensus of the Wise Men was clear: the US should continue the fight in Vietnam. They urged Johnson to 'visibly take command' of the war and to formulate 'a strategy that would be tolerable in cost to the American people'.

Significantly, one of the Wise Men dissented. George Ball, who in 1965 had warned against US intervention, again questioned the direction of American policy. Convinced the other Wise Men were merely telling Johnson what he wanted to hear, Ball's frustration was apparent. 'You're like a flock of buzzards sitting on a fence,' he said, 'sending young men off to be killed. You ought to be ashamed of yourselves'. But if Johnson was disinclined to contemplate a US withdrawal from Vietnam in 1965, he was even less willing to do so in 1967. Not only did his personality preclude a withdrawal – which would almost certainly be construed as a defeat, both for the USA and for Johnson personally – but to withdraw in 1967 would have meant that the thousands of Americans who had lost their lives would have died for nothing. Johnson was certain the USA had to stay in Vietnam until victory was achieved.

# North Vietnamese Plans

Concerns about the progress of the war were also evident in Hanoi. North Vietnamese leaders knew they were not about to be defeated, but they also knew the collapse of South Vietnam was more remote in 1967 than it had been in 1965. The North Vietnamese still regarded the ARVN as ineffectual and they knew the war was inflicting grievous harm to the USA; yet they also understood that the war was in many respects stalemated. Maoist philosophy suggested victory would be achieved when a general offensive precipitated a popular uprising. But in 1967 those events appeared a long way off. Accordingly, while the guerrilla war was bleeding America's will to fight, North Vietnamese leaders considered different ways of winning the war.

Advocates for a major offensive won the debate. One Party official noted:

> ... taking advantage of a time that the American imperialists are confronted with a situation in which both advance and retreat are difficult, at a time when the United States is about to elect a president, we need to inflict a decisive blow, to win a great victory, creating a great leap forward in the strategic thinking.

The Politburo identified three possible outcomes from the offensive:
1  It might end in a 'major victory' that would compel the USA to withdraw.
2  It could result in 'important victories', which although immediately decisive, would weaken the US resolve.
3  It might lead to the United States expanding its commitment in Vietnam, thereby expanding the conflict.

Concluding that the third outcome was unlikely, partly because an election was looming in the United States, the Politburo decided to launch the attack.

The offensive was timed to commence with simultaneous attacks across South Vietnam, during the Tet (Lunar New Year) holiday period. As PLAF General Van Tra explained, the intention was to 'combine attacks by military units with mass urban uprisings, attacks from within the cities with those from outside, and military activities in rural areas with those in urban centres'. North Vietnamese planners emphasised that the Tet attacks were the first phase of the wider offensive. It was assumed that in subsequent phases, reserves would be committed and a 'decisive' – as distinct from 'final' – victory would be achieved. Ever-attentive to history, North Vietnamese strategists stressed the significance of the example of Dien Bien Phu: French forces throughout Vietnam had not been completely defeated, but the victory was decisive because it shattered the French will to fight on. Hanoi hoped for a similar outcome from the 1968 offensive.

# Khe Sanh: Prelude to Tet?

By late 1967, American eyes were focused firmly on a group of Marines besieged at the strategically important Khe Sanh, 30 kilometres south of the DMZ and just 13 kilometres from the Laotian border. In late 1967, acting on intelligence reports of increased PAVN infiltration down the Ho Chi Minh Trail, Westmoreland had deployed a Marine battalion to Khe Sanh. He believed North Vietnam was intending to launch a conventional invasion of South Vietnam. Khe Sanh would be a crucial fulcrum for any PAVN assault.

*Lyndon Johnson and advisors examine a map of Khe Sanh*

With intelligence reports suggesting there were up to four PAVN divisions around Khe Sanh, during late 1967 and early 1968 Westmoreland deployed an additional 6,000 Marines, and some ARVN forces, to the base. Westmoreland hoped to lure PAVN forces into attacking Khe Sanh, where they would be pulverised by American artillery and air power.

American public and political attention focused on the 'besieged' Marines. On the surface, there were parallels between the French position at Dien Bien Phu and the Marines' situation at Khe Sanh. Johnson was apprehensive. He was also adamant: 'I don't want any damn Dinbinphoo'.

Westmoreland rejected any such comparison, asserting the difference was that the French had been inadequately supplied and were far removed from support elements, whereas US resources and reinforcements could be deployed quickly.

On 24 January 1968, a small US Special Forces base at Lang Vei, just 11 kilometres from Khe Sanh, was overrun by PAVN forces – which included tanks. US media attention now focused on Khe Sanh: when would the North Vietnamese attack? Johnson kept a keen eye on the situation at Khe Sanh, spending hours in a special room in the White House, where a 'terrain map' of the battlefield had been constructed.

## Tet '68: Shockwaves in Vietnam

As the United States was preoccupied with Khe Sanh, on 31 January PLAF forces attacked across South Vietnam. (PAVN units played a part in the Tet Offensive, but much of the fighting was done by the PLAF.) Although some US intelligence analysts had predicted a communist offensive, few Americans anticipated an attack as widespread as that which was launched. As well as attacking in rural areas, the PLAF attacked urban areas. Hoping the offensive would highlight the failures of the GVN, the PLAF urged southerners to rise up against South Vietnamese President Nguyen Van Thieu's regime.

Across South Vietnam, communist forces attacked 36 of the 44 provincial capitals, as well as 64 district capitals and dozens of military bases. In their most audacious assault, a small suicide squad of PLAF troops attacked the US Embassy in Saigon. The Embassy was not 'occupied', as some news reports charged. But it took six hours to wipe out the PLAF attackers and images of the US Embassy under attack were soon transmitted around the world.

The attack on the US Embassy was just one component of a vast offensive, in both urban and rural areas. The fighting was savage and, although in most cases the PLAF was subdued quickly, fighting continued in Saigon

### The Tet Offensive: Hue, 1968

In most cases US and ARVN forces were able to quickly recapture towns and cities occupied or attacked by the PLAF/PAVN during the Tet Offensive. The one notable exception was the ancient capital of Hue. Just 75 kilometres south of the DMZ, Hue was Vietnam's most beautiful city. It was also the site of widespread protests against Diem in 1963 and Ky in 1966 – both of which were suppressed with considerable brutality.

Those demonstrations of GVN brutality, however, were mild compared to what happened during the PAVN/PLAF occupation of Hue. Communist cadre apprehended nearly 3,000 people, including public servants, teachers and anyone connected with the US or the South Vietnamese military. Almost all were executed. A further 2,000 people disappeared, presumed murdered.

In re-conquering Hue, US and ARVN units were compelled to apply massive firepower. As one American put it, a once-beautiful city was left a 'shattered, stinking hulk, its streets choked with rubble and rotting bodies'.

The Tet Offensive

for some days, and it took nearly three weeks for US and Allied forces to liberate Hue.

Across South Vietnam, the communist attacks met a determined US/ARVN response. Indeed, the ARVN response was stronger than even its defenders anticipated. US forces, too, rallied quickly. The PLAF suffered massive casualties. Of the 84,000 troops who took part in the offensive, US sources calculated the PLAF suffered 45,000 casualties. (In the immediate aftermath of the Tet Offensive 1,100 Americans and 2,300 ARVN troops were killed.)

Meanwhile, at Khe Sanh, US/ARVN forces awaited the massive assault that Westmoreland and others had predicted. Yet while the base was subjected to heavy artillery attack and although there were bitter battles

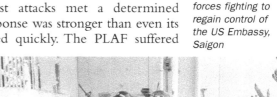

Tet, 1968: US forces fighting to regain control of the US Embassy, Saigon

in the hills surrounding Khe Sanh, the much-anticipated major attack did not eventuate. On 8 April, the 'siege' of Khe Sanh was officially lifted, when a relief force arrived, by road, at the base. The siege had lasted 77 days and claimed the lives of over 200 Marines. North Vietnamese losses, again, were much heavier: over 10,000 PAVN troops were estimated to have been killed.

On paper, therefore, Khe Sanh was a major battlefield victory for the US/ARVN forces. But was it? The answer to that question depends largely on assessing North Vietnamese intentions: did they ever intend to over-run the base?

---

**HISTORICAL DOCUMENT**

*Giap Recalls the Significance of Khe Sanh*

Khe Sanh was not that important to us. Or it was only to the extent that it was to the Americans. It was the focus of attention in the United States because their prestige was at stake, but to us it was part of the greater battle that would begin after Tet. It was only a diversion, but one to be exploited if we could cause many casualties and win a big victory.

---

## Tet '68: Shockwaves in the United States

Within the United States there was widespread shock at the scale of the enemy attacks. If the PLAF and PAVN were being beaten, as Americans had been told, how were they able to mount an offensive across South Vietnam? For Johnson, the battlefield fortunes of the United States were linked to his own political fortunes, since 1968 was an election year. His own credibility – and that of the entire military-political hierarchy in the USA – was at stake.

American doubts about their leaders grew in the immediate aftermath of the Tet Offensive. Westmoreland's claim that US/ARVN forces had inflicted a 'colossal military defeat' on the enemy and his assertion that the United States had 'never been in a better position in South Vietnam,' were greeted with scepticism. Westmoreland then called for a shift in US strategy. He sought permission to launch amphibious operations against North Vietnam and against PLAF/PAVN sanctuaries inside Laos and Cambodia. To do so would have required additional forces. Westmoreland asked Johnson for an additional 206,000 troops, which would have required the politically difficult mobilisation of reserves.

Publicly, Johnson remained determined: 'we will never buckle'. There would be 'blood, sweat and tears shed,' but 'persevere in Vietnam we will and must'. Again, Johnson felt trapped. If he refused Westmoreland's request for additional forces, the war might be lost. But if he approved it, he could lose the election. Tet had cost the PLAF dearly, but it had exposed the flaws of 'limited war,' exposed the limits of US power and highlighted the discrepancy between what Americans were being told about the war and the realities on the ground in Vietnam.

# Johnson, Public Opinion and the Media

Johnson was in a bind. His political instinct was to fight on. However, following Tet his public support dwindled further. Johnson attributed some of that decline to a hostile press.

During and after the Vietnam War, the US media was widely criticised for presenting the US war effort in negative terms. Much of the criticism of the media rested on the particular power of television. The fact that television cameramen had open access to the US war effort – many were able to film 'from the front lines' – meant that during the 1960s and 1970s Americans were exposed to the bloodshed and horrors of war – often in colour.

Yet the American media did exercise considerable restraint during the Vietnam War, only rarely showing dead or dying Americans – or Vietnamese. The views of the media, moreover, were never uniformly 'antiwar'. As with the wider American community, media views shifted over time. Nevertheless, some statements – and images – were profoundly disturbing. The image of PLAF and US forces battling in the grounds of the US Embassy in Saigon could not be easily dismissed. Nor could two other episodes, which high-lighted the contradictions in US policy:

1   On 7 February 1968 New Zealander Peter Arnett reported from the town of Ben Tre, in the Mekong. As the PLAF threatened to over-run the town, US commanders concluded the only way to repel the enemy assault was to order US artillery and aircraft to attack the town itself, which had thousands of civilians. A US Major declared: 'It became necessary to destroy the town to save it.' Such statements made it more difficult to reconcile America's stated objectives in Vietnam with the realities of the war.

2   On 1 February 1968, amidst the chaos and carnage in Saigon, a Viet Cong prisoner, Captain Nguyen Van Lam, was brought before General Nguyen Ngoc Loan, Chief of South Vietnam's national police. Associated Press photographer, Eddie Adams, and others, gathered round as they expected Loan to interrogate the prisoner. Instead, Loan drew his revolver and very deliberately shot Lam in the temple in an apparent cold-blooded execution. Yet, Loan, it was later revealed, was grief-stricken and infuriated because he had learned earlier that day that the family of one of his colleagues had been slain by the PLAF. Nonetheless,

*General Loan executes Nguyen Van Lam*

Adams's Pulitzer Prize-winning photograph further exposed the chasm between America's stated aims in Vietnam and the war as it was being fought. If America's allies – the 'good guys' – acted with such brutality, what chance did they have of building popular support and winning the war?

Johnson's belief that the press had turned against the war was not without foundation. Newspapers such as the *Wall Street Journal* and

public figures such as the widely respected CBS news anchorman Walter Cronkite were now expressing their doubts about the war.

---

**HISTORICAL DOCUMENT**

### American Media Reactions to the Tet Offensive

We think the American people should be getting ready to accept, if they haven't already, that the whole Vietnam effort may be doomed; it may be falling apart beneath our feet. The actual military situation may be making academic the philosophical arguments for the intervention in the first place

*Wall Street Journal*, 23 February 1968

We have been too often disappointed by the optimism of the American leaders, both in Vietnam and Washington, to have faith any longer in the silver linings they find in the darkest clouds ... it seems now more certain than ever before that the bloody experience of Vietnam is to end in stalemate.

*Walter Cronkite*, 27 February 1968

---

Hearing Cronkite, Johnson realised his position and his defence of the war had become untenable. 'If I've lost Cronkite,' Johnson mused, 'I've lost middle America'. After winning the 1964 Presidential election by a landslide, Johnson had almost exhausted his political capital.

# The Democratic Party and the 1968 election

Even before the Tet Offensive, Johnson faced a political challenge from within his own political party. Whilst Johnson had once dominated the Democratic Party, by 1968 many Democrats were disillusioned by his handling of the war. In November 1967 Senator Eugene McCarthy (no relation to Joseph McCarthy) announced he would challenge Johnson for the Democratic Party's Presidential nomination.

Despite his long political career, McCarthy was an unlikely politician. Introspective and gentle, McCarthy captured the attention of disillusioned liberals, as well as significant elements of the often-inchoate antiwar movement. Many college students rallied to his cause. On 12 March, he drew 42% of the vote in the New Hampshire 'primary'. As the incumbent president, Johnson had not thought it necessary to formally place himself on the ballot. But an informal campaign on his behalf meant he won 49% of the vote. Technically, this was a victory for Johnson. In reality, it was a victory for the quixotic McCarthy and the antiwar movement.

McCarthy's momentum encouraged another potential candidate. Robert Kennedy, a younger brother of the slain president, had entered the US Senate in 1966. Kennedy and Johnson disliked each other intensely. Carefully nurturing an antiwar position, through 1966 and 1967 Kennedy presented himself as the respectable voice of a 'movement' that often seemed intent on antagonising 'middle America'. In the US Senate, Kennedy attacked America's involvement in Vietnam on moral grounds.

Yet Kennedy hesitated to run for the Presidency, fearing that if he sought the presidency in 1968 it would split the Democratic Party and lead voters to conclude he was motivated by self-interest, rather than that of the nation. Kennedy also understood, prior to the Tet Offensive, that he stood little chance of defeating Johnson. But the Tet Offensive, and McCarthy's success in New Hampshire, changed the equation: Johnson was suddenly vulnerable.

On 16 March 1968, Kennedy declared his candidacy for the presidency. He represented his candidacy as an attempt to restore American confidence, morality and leadership – all of which were threatened by the war in Vietnam:

*Eugene McCarthy (left) speaking to President Lyndon Johnson*

> At stake is not simply the leadership of our party and even our country, it is our right to the moral leadership of this planet.

In the words of one historian, when Johnson heard of Kennedy's candidacy, he 'went ballistic'. He promised to destroy Kennedy, whom he described as a 'grandstanding little runt'. Publicly, Johnson remained defiant, rejecting suggestions he should halt the bombing of North Vietnam and vowing, 'We are going to win'.

# Johnson Consults the Wise Men

Yet Johnson was racked by self-doubt. Again he sought the advice of the 'Wise Men'. The briefings they received from US military commanders were less optimistic than just a few months earlier. Where before they had been led to believe the war would be over in one or two years, they were now told it might take five to 10 years. When General Earl Wheeler, Chairman of the Joint Chiefs of Staff, reported that the United States did not seek 'a classic military victory' in Vietnam, the Wise Men responded with amazement. Dean Acheson, Secretary of State during the Truman Presidency, and an architect of the Cold War, summed up the sentiment in the room: 'Then what in the name of God do we have 500,000 troops out there for? Chasing girls?'

The Wise Men also understood that the USA was confronting a financial crisis because of the war. Heavy war spending had led to a growing government deficit. Any expansion of the war in Vietnam would require increased government expenditure, which would further damage the US budget, fuel inflation and compound international fears about the strength of the American economy. American business leaders made their reservations about the war clear to Clark Clifford, who in January 1968 replaced the disillusioned McNamara as Secretary of Defense. 'These men now feel we are in a hopeless bog,' reported Clifford. It was impossible, he argued, to 'maintain public support for the war without the support of these men'.

*Lyndon Johnson addressing the nation to announce the bombing halt in Vietnam and his intention not to run for re-election*

With antiwar candidates running for the nomination of the Democratic Party, with public opinion turning against the war and feeling a virtual prisoner in the White House, Johnson addressed the nation on 31 March. He declared a bombing halt north of the 20th parallel. He invited Hanoi to begin negotiations. Then, in one of the most dramatic moments in American political history, he announced:

I have concluded that I should not permit the Presidency to become involved in the partisan divisions that are developing in this political year. With America's sons in the fields far away, with America's future under challenge right here at home, with our hopes and the world's hopes for peace in the balance every day, I do not believe that I should devote an hour or a day of my time to any personal partisan causes or to any duties other than the awesome duties of this office – the Presidency of your country. Accordingly, I shall not seek, and I will not accept, the nomination of my party for another term as your President.

Americans' surprise at Johnson's announcement was paralleled by joy in Hanoi. The war, the North Vietnamese believed, was effectively over – not militarily, but politically. Ho's prediction that the United States could not sustain a long-term war proved correct. On 3 April, Hanoi announced it would accept the American invitation to begin peace talks.

## Turmoil and Tragedy

Johnson had withdrawn from the presidential race, yet was determined that Vice-President Hubert Humphrey should win. Humphrey could count on the support of the Democrats and those against the antiwar movement. Yet, over the following months US politics was beset by turmoil and tragedy. On 4 April, Martin Luther King was assassinated. Black America was outraged and cities exploded in violence. White politicians demanded the restoration of 'law and order' on the streets. On 5 June, hours after winning the Democrats' presidential primary, Robert Kennedy was assassinated. Kennedy's death tore the heart from the antiwar movement. Eugene McCarthy's support base had been eroded. In August, the Democrats gathered in Chicago to select their presidential candidate. The Convention turned into a debacle as thousands of antiwar protesters were subjected to brutality and treated with contempt by the leaders of the Democratic Party. Amidst the violence, Humphrey was nominated as the Democrats' candidate. Given the Democrats' were widely blamed for the chaos across America and for the war in Vietnam, Humphrey faced a daunting task.

## Searching for a Negotiated Settlement

In May 1968, peace talks began in Paris. Progress proved infuriatingly slow. American negotiators first sought North Vietnamese assurances that they would respect the Demilitarised Zone and curb their attacks on South Vietnamese cities. North Vietnam agreed to the talks in part to stop the US bombing. But the North Vietnamese had no intention of de-escalating the war: rather, their whole strategy became one of fighting while negotiating.

When the delegates gathered in Paris, a disagreement broke out. The South Vietnamese delegates refused to sit at the same table as the delegates of the National Liberation Front, on the grounds that to do so would be an admission that the NLF constituted a legitimate political force. Although a compromise was eventually reached, it took six months – during which time nearly 8,000 Americans and perhaps 100,000 Vietnamese died.

When negotiations eventually began, North Vietnam demanded the United States cease all bombing raids over North Vietnam and withdraw its forces from South Vietnam. The Americans demanded that PAVN troops withdraw from South Vietnam, that North Vietnam recognise the South Vietnamese Government and that prisoners of war be exchanged.

Resolving those issues was predictably difficult. The USA had to 'sell' any agreement to South Vietnam, who demanded assurances that the USA would come to their aid if North Vietnam broke any peace treaty that might be signed. And the South Vietnamese would not recognise the NLF. The North argued the NLF should be part of a coalition government in South Vietnam. By October 1968, virtually no progress had been made on the substantive issues.

# The Return of Richard Nixon

The Democrats' woes, the stalled negotiations in Paris and the ongoing conflict in Vietnam played directly into the hands of Richard Nixon, who emerged from political oblivion after losing the 1960 presidential election, and then the 1962 election for the governorship of California, to be the leading Republican candidate for the 1968 election. At the Republicans' Convention in Miami Nixon presented himself as a unifier, who would restore 'law and order' to the United States. He also made vague references to what the media labeled a 'secret plan' to end the war in Vietnam. Nixon was evasive about details of his 'plan'. No one 'who is seeking office,' he stated, 'should give away any of his bargaining position in advance'.

As the November election approached, Democratic Party candidate Hubert Humphrey eroded Nixon's lead in the polls. Then, in October, a breakthrough appeared imminent in Paris. The United States agreed to a complete bombing halt over North Vietnam in return for North Vietnamese concessions. An agreement was reached that included plans for negotiations over the future of South Vietnam that would have included both the NLF and the South Vietnamese Government. Importantly, South Vietnamese leaders supported the deal.

On 31 October, Johnson announced he was stopping the bombing. But then Thieu reversed his decision. It emerged later that his reversal was encouraged by the intervention of Anna Chan Chennault, widow of Claire Chennault, the US general who had met Ho in 1945. Chennault, co-chairwoman of the 'Republican Women for Nixon', and a well-regarded

*October 1968: Lyndon Johnson listens to tapes sent by his son-in-law, Captain James Robb, who is serving in Vietnam*

figure in Asia, persuaded Thieu he would secure a better deal if Nixon won the election. Chennault had acted directly on behalf of the Republican Party. To improve his electoral chances, Nixon, had, in effect, worked to thwart the peace process, at the cost of American – and Vietnamese – lives.

Nixon went on to narrowly win the presidential election, securing 43.4% of the vote to Humphrey's 42.7%. Having won the election, Nixon set out to end the war with 'peace and honour'. He achieved neither.

# Assessing the Tet Offensive

It is often asserted that the Tet Offensive was a military victory, but a political and psychological defeat for the United States. The PLAF and PAVN did not defeat American and ARVN forces on the battlefield. Clearly, too, the PLAF suffered massive losses, forcing the PAVN to assume a greater role in the war. Equally clearly, the South Vietnamese people did not rise up in revolution against the Thieu regime. Yet the events of 1968 can only be considered a 'military defeat' for the NLF and North Vietnamese if one separates the military aspect of the struggle from its political aspect (as Americans often did – and do). But North Vietnamese and the NLF always viewed military action as part of a synthesis, of which each element would play a part in achieving eventual victory.

---

**HISTORICAL DOCUMENT**

*General Giap Discusses the Legacies of the Tet Offensive*

There is no such thing as a single strategy. Ours is always a synthesis, simultaneously military, political and diplomatic – which is why quite clearly, the Tet offensive had multiple objectives.

---

The Tet Offensive was a significant turning point in the Vietnam War. After Tet, it was evident that the United States had lost much of its will to continue the fight. Despite the strong performance of US/ARVN forces in 1968, after Tet the American focus was not on winning, but on withdrawing. There was also a profound irony about the events of 1968: within the United States, Tet played a key part in bringing about the downfall of the Democrats, who had probably lost the will to continue a spirited struggle in Vietnam; their Republican successors, Nixon and Kissinger, prosecuted the war vigorously for another four years.

**POINTS TO REMEMBER**

- In 1967 most Americans believed the United States was winning the war.
- The North Vietnamese believed that a major offensive could have military and political benefits.
- The Tet Offensive began on 31 January 1968. It was called Tet because it began in the Vietnamese New Year. It aimed to apply political pressure on US leaders at home and to try to ignite a popular rebellion in South Vietnam.
- The United States won a tactical victory on the battlefield. But the Offensive demonstrated to many Americans that the USA was not winning the war.
- Media coverage reflected and contributed to Americans' growing doubts about the war.
- The 1968 peace talks did not succeed.
- The Tet offensive influenced Johnson's decision to not seek re-election as president. It also helped the Republican candidate, Nixon, win the presidential elections.

# ACTIVITIES

**1** List evidence that shows that, in 1967, the South Vietnamese and the Americans were losing the war.

**2** Compare and contrast the political situation in Washington and Hanoi in late 1967.

**3** Why did Hanoi decide on a major offensive for early 1968?

**4** Was Khe Sanh the prelude to Tet and is the comparison with Dien Bien Phu justified?

**5** Briefly describe the tactical victory that the United States and South Vietnam were able to win on the battlefield.

**6** What impact did the Tet Offensive have on US politics?

**7** Essay: Why is the Tet Offensive considered a turning point for the Vietnam War?

**8** What was the impact of the media on the American public's support for the war?

**9** Why did the peace talks fail in 1968?

## Sample HSC Exam Question:

Describe the involvement of the United States in Indochina between 1954 and 1968.

### FURTHER READING

Don Oberdofer, *Tet!* (Doubleday, Garden City, NY, 1971) is a useful source. Peter Braestrup, *Big Story: How the American Press and Television Reported and Interpreted the Crisis of Tet 1968 in Vietnam and Washington* (Yale University Press, New Haven, 1983) explores media reactions to Tet. George Herring, *America's Longest War: The United States and Vietnam 1950–1975*, 2nd ed. (Knopf, New York, 1986), Marilyn B. Young's *The Vietnam War* (Harper Perennial, New York, 1991), Stanley Karnow's *Vietnam: A History* (Penguin, New York, 1997), George Donelson Moss's *Vietnam: An American Ordeal*, 4th ed., (Prentice Hall, Upper Saddle River, NJ, 2002) and James S. Olson and Randy Roberts' *Where the Domino Fell: America and Vietnam, 1945–1990* (St. Martin's Press, New York, 1991) all cover events of 1968.

# 9

# The Antiwar Movements

IN THIS CHAPTER YOU WILL:

• be introduced to the antiwar movement
• explore the movement's origins, agenda and tactics
• chart the movement's move from non-violence to militancy
• understand the debates regarding the movement's significance for the Vietnam War.

## Background

The Americanisation of the Vietnam War by Lyndon Johnson was widely supported by the American public. A number of Americans, however, opposed the war and sought to reverse national policy. This 'antiwar movement' built on existing pacifist traditions in American national life, was energised by a new political phenomena known as the 'New Left' and used protest methods developed by the African–American Civil Rights movement. As the war continued, opponents of the war came to include a broad cross-section of American society.

## Beginnings of the Antiwar Movement

The Vietnam antiwar movement emerged from the pacifist tradition in American public life and the anti-nuclear 'peace movement' of the 1950s. During the Cold War the threat of nuclear annihilation fuelled a broader peace movement. Yet the peace movement remained small and was pilloried during the McCarthy era for its alleged disloyalty.

It was from these groups that the first public protests against involvement in Vietnam were staged. In 1963 a pacifist group known as the Student Peace Union carried placards during the New York City Easter Union Parade, while other branches of the union staged small public demonstrations. In October 1963 the religious Society of Friends (the Quakers) opened a Vietnam Information Centre in Washington, DC, which circulated material critical of the Diem regime and American support. Religious and pacifist groupings remained the dominant opponents of the war into 1965.

When Diem visited the United States in 1963, students staged protests, but these demonstrations were not well orchestrated. Academic staff was more vocal in its opposition; 5,000 signed an antiwar petition in July 1964. The Gulf of Tonkin Resolution, Johnson's commitment of ground troops and the increasing realisation that the 'draft' could see American youth fighting and dying in Vietnam, saw American students play an increasingly important role in the antiwar movement.

# The New Left

The New Left was a political and cultural response to the Cold War and late industrial capitalism. Fuelled by the end of Stalinism, McCarthyism, economic prosperity and the fear of nuclear annihilation, many postwar middle-class citizens ('babyboomers'), who were being educated in America's rapidly expanding tertiary education system, identified serious problems with the society they were inheriting and felt empowered to change it. The result was a 'generational rebellion' that radical sociologist C. Wright Mills labeled the 'New Left'.

The New Left sought to modify, rather than overthrow capitalism. It sought to make capitalism more inclusive and better share the massive wealth the United States enjoyed in the postwar period. The movement also articulated the concept of 'participatory democracy'. The New Left advocated change through 'non-violent direct action'. To the students of the New Left the Vietnam War was the clearest example of what was wrong with American society in the 1960s. Furthermore, because of the draft, the war's consequences were mostly keenly felt by this generation.

# What Sort of Movement?

The New Left's engagement with the Vietnam War encouraged a debate amongst those already lobbying against the war. They confronted three major issues:

1   Who should control the antiwar movement? Should the elite control, which had characterised the movement until 1965, continue or should it be replaced by non-exclusive democratic structures?
2   What were the goals of the new antiwar movement? Did it seek to end all fighting in Vietnam; an American withdrawal; or a NLF victory or a negotiated settlement?
3   What tactics should the antiwar movement use? Should it further enhance civil rights-inspired mass action or small confrontationist stunts? As the war continued, some members of the movement advocated militant action.

The movement's failure to adequately answer these questions to the satisfaction of all remained a structural weakness it found difficult to overcome.

## 'Teach-Ins'

College and university students were at the centre of the New Left and American universities were breeding grounds for the mass antiwar movement. The Students for a Democratic Society (SDS) was a driving force of campus activism. With the assistance of sympathetic academics, SDS sought first to educate their fellow students through 'teach-ins' that set out to provide a greater understanding of the conflict and its consequences. As a reaction against Johnson's decision to deploy 3,000 Marines to Danang in March 1965, the first 'teach-in' was held at the University of Michigan on 24 March 1965. Its success led to the SDS organising a 'National Teach-In' at 122 colleges and universities on 15 May 1965.

SDS also staged the first national demonstration against the war in 1965 when 20,000 people, predominately students, travelled to Washington, DC, to protest. The gathering gained national media coverage and was followed by events at the University of California at Berkeley on 21 and 22 May, when 20,000 students and staff participated in a 36 hour 'teach-in' marathon.

---

**HISTORICAL DOCUMENT**

*The SDS Manifesto: The Port Huron Statement*

The core of the American New Left was a group formed in Michigan by students from a number of north-eastern and mid-western universities in 1961. Students for a Democratic Society (SDS) produced a manifesto that outlined their motivations and vision for the future:

We are the people of this generation, bred in at least modest comfort, housed now in universities, looking uncomfortably to the world we inherit

---

During 1966 SDS membership grew from 2,000 to 30,000 members. Off campus, the liberal peace movement, led by organisations such as the National Committee for a Sane Nuclear Policy (SANE), organised a march in New York attracting 18,000 people. On 27 November, 30,000 people marched around the White House. New liberal groups included the 'National Emergency Committee of Clergy Concerned about Vietnam', 'Catholic Peace Fellowship' and 'Another Mother for Peace'. War opposition was spreading.

Antiwar protesters were also willing to risk their own lives. In 1965, members of the Vietnam Day committee in northern California attempted to block a munitions train by laying on the railway tracks. Ethical concerns about the war were taken to the extreme in November 1965 when Norman Morrison, a Quaker, immolated himself in front of the Pentagon.

## African–American Opposition to the War

Many African–Americans were initially more concerned with their fight at home than with the fight in Vietnam. However, leaders of the

African–American community, represented by radicals such as Malcolm X, and later by liberals such as the Reverend Dr Martin Luther King, expressed opposition to the war. As racial tensions across the United States became more acute, the war's racial dimension seemed obvious: 'white people sending black people to make war on yellow people in order to defend the land they stole from the red people.' In January 1965, Malcolm X placed African–Americans on the same side as 'those little rice farmers' and predicted an American defeat. One civil rights organisation, the Student Nonviolent Coordinating Committee (SNCC) explained its opposition to the war in terms of opposition to racism.

While opposition to the war was strong within African–American communities, many blacks avoided participation in public demonstrations. This silence reflected black Americans' general disempowerment and the discrimination they faced if they spoke out.

# Congressional Opposition

US policies in Vietnam were also subject to increasing scrutiny and criticism within the US Congress. Senator J. William Fulbright of Arkansas emerged as the foremost opponent of the war. A Rhodes scholar, and close friend and ally of President Johnson, Fulbright became alarmed about the war. At the Senate Foreign Relations Committee hearings on the war in February 1966, Fulbright contended the war had started out as a war of liberation from colonial rule and then became a civil war. Witnesses attacked the government's reasons for involvement in the Vietnam War and declared that the United States should end its involvement 'as soon as possible'. Fulbright's opposition to the war was taken as a personal criticism by Johnson, who began referring to his former friend as 'Senator Halfbright'.

Lyndon Johnson has a quiet word with Senator J. William Fulbright

Despite the Senate hearings, there was still strong Congressional support for the war. In March 1966, a bill to repeal the Gulf of Tonkin Resolution was defeated by 92 votes to five. In 1967 Congress also approved another $12 billion for the war to enable Westmoreland to increase his force to 480,000. It would not be until 1969 that a Congressional subcommittee argued an American withdrawal was in the national interest.

# Draft Resistance and Civil Disobedience

Through 1966 and into 1967 the antiwar movement protested as the American build-up continued. Frustrated by their lack of success, a number of civil disobedience campaigns commenced in 1967, including draft evasion.

Draft evasion was supported by the formation of 'Resistance' in March 1967. Along with public displays where eligible men burned their draft cards or tried to close induction centres, individuals used a variety of techniques to avoid service, such as university deferments or being ruled medically unfit. Others escaped to Canada. From 1963–1973, 13,518 men were prosecuted for draft resistance.

## HISTORICAL ISSUE

### Popular Culture and the Antiwar Movement

Antiwar demonstrations became part of the youth counterculture of the 1960s. Folk-singers, some of whom expressed direct opposition to the war, spread the antiwar message. Later, rock music also reflected an antiwar sentiment.

Opposition to the war also manifested itself in forms of popular culture. The 10th-most popular television program in 1965 was *Combat!* The program was cancelled, however, at the end of the 1966 season. One of the program's stars, Vic Morrow, explained the program's demise as a consequence of the increasing criticism of the Vietnam War. Other war programs also lost popularity. By the end of 1966, *Convoy*, *McHale's Navy* and *Wackiest Ship in the Army* were also discontinued.

Some programs began to represent antiwar sentiments. The controversial *That Was the Week That Was* occasionally attacked Johnson's policies. Other programs were more subtle in their criticism of the war. *Daniel Boone* was a popular program about a legendary American frontier hero. Barry Rosenzweig instructed the writers of the program to depict the Revolutionary War by making it Vietnam with the colonials as the Viet Cong and the English as the Americans. *Star Trek* aired allegorical stories that consistently condemned war and a prime directive issued to Star Fleet captains was to not interfere in the internal affairs of any new civilisation they discovered. *Mission Impossible* stopped overthrowing foreign regimes and began attacking organised crime. Less subtle were attempts by *The Smothers Brothers*, a singing comedy team, to promote the antiwar cause on their program. They featured an interview with folk-singer Joan Baez, who referred to her husband's prison term for evading the draft. The program was cancelled in 1969, despite its high ratings.

Novelists also turned their attention to criticising the war. John Sack's *M* (1967) is regarded as one of the first antiwar novels of the Vietnam era. Other novels such as David Halberstam's *One Very Hot Day* (1967), Daniel Ford's *Incident at Muc Wa* (1967) and William Eastlake's *The Bamboo Red* (1969) explored antiwar themes. By 1968, even Marvel Comics had abandoned Cold War and Vietnam War stories.

# Declining Support for the War and Operation Chaos

During 1967 many Americans feared their country was tearing itself apart. Antiwar liberals struggled against the administration's attacks on all protesters as communist sympathisers, while the radicals' actions alarmed many Americans. SDS leader Tom Hayden and 40 other antiwar radicals met with the North Vietnamese and NLF in Czechoslovakia. Hayden also organised a trip to Hanoi in an attempt to secure the release of American POWs.

These actions were considered treasonous by many Americans. Antiwar liberals feared the radicals were more interested in a communist victory then an end to the war.

By mid-1967, support for the war had dropped below 50% for the first time; this reflected a growing sense that the war was immoral, as well as a belief that Johnson was not fighting the war effectively. Support for the war weakened further in August when Johnson asked Congress for a 10% income tax surcharge to help finance the war. By October only 28% of Americans supported Johnson. While most Americans did not identify with antiwar activists, they were tiring of the war. There was also growing evidence that the antiwar movement was gaining support in 'mainstream' American society. In 1967 over 600 business executives urged Johnson to stop the war.

Johnson reacted to the antiwar movement in a variety of ways. 'Operation Chaos', an FBI surveillance campaign, entailed spying on antiwar activists. Files on over 7,000 Americans were compiled. These people were accused, without any real evidence, of being communists under the direction of Hanoi. Johnson also tried to build support for the war through a public relations campaign. A 'Committee for Peace and Freedom in Vietnam' was established to give voice to the 'silent center' of the American public. Speakers travelled across America to argue that the war was being won.

Striving to reclaim faltering public support, Johnson, in a speech at San Antonio, Texas, on 29 September 1967, proposed to stop bombing North Vietnam if the DRV agreed to serious negotiations. Dubbed the 'San Antonio Formula' by the press, it received no response from North Vietnam.

Johnson and others sought to emphasise the radical nature of the antiwar movement by calling upon the armed forces to protect Washington from its own citizens. On 21 October, over 100,000 demonstrators took to the streets of the capital: most were peaceful, but a minority sought violence. The police and troops retaliated and arrested 647 demonstrators, while another 47 were hospitalised.

Yet while the antiwar movement continued to grow, it was still beset by tensions and divisions. The SDS was troubled by internal conflicts and student radicalism seemed to be increasing.

*Protest at the Pentagon, October 1967*

# Columbia Rebellion and the Chicago Firestorm

The Tet Offensive, with its images of graphic violence and suggestions of American failure, saw more Americans join the antiwar movement and public support decline further. On 26 April a million college students boycotted their classes. Between January and June 1968 the FBI reported 3,483 antiwar incidents on American campuses. The most significant of these incidents occurred at Columbia University (New York City) in May 1968. For months

## HISTORICAL ISSUE

### Supporting the War

While folk and rock musicians championed the antiwar cause, other voices in American popular culture championed the American endeavour in Vietnam. Staff Sergeant Barry Sadler's the *Ballad of the Green Berets* was at the top of the popular music charts for the first three months of 1966.

The song became the title theme to a cinematic effort to support the war. *The Green Berets* was a pro-war film starring John Wayne and made with the cooperation of the American military. Airing and then debunking many of the reasons for opposing the war the film was an unsophisticated example of wartime propaganda.

the campus had been wracked by antiwar demonstrations. A new target was the university administration, which was regarded as a part of the national power structure that had led the United States into war.

On the evening of 30 April the president of the university had had enough of the protests and occupations and summoned the police. Over 200 officers entered the campus to evict the students. Most students complied, but a small section barricaded themselves in buildings and threw objects at the police. Pitched battles lasted through the night and 711 students (most not from Columbia) and three academics were arrested. A temporary truce broke down in late May when over 1,000 police entered the campus and subdued the 'student rebellion'.

Following Johnson's decision to not seek re-election, the 1968 Democratic Party Convention in Chicago was an important opportunity for leaders of the antiwar movement to present their message in front of the nation's media. The planned peaceful protests, however, ended in a week of violent riots between police and protesters – the 'Chicago Firestorm'. Hundreds of people were injured, property was destroyed and 668 demonstrators were arrested, including the leaders of the protests ('Chicago Seven').

The Chicago Firestorm had wide-reaching consequences for the antiwar movement. Many Americans were appalled by the violence and the attacks against authority. The Firestorm further divided 'liberal' and 'radical' opponents of the war, with liberals suggesting protesters' behavior had hurt rather than helped the cause, by undermining the movement's moral authority. SDS leaders such as Tom Hayden rejected such criticism and vowed to cease association with the liberals. SDS rhetoric became increasingly revolutionary and was reflected by actions, such as meetings with members of the NLF, which appeared to suggest students were not against the war, simply against an American victory.

Following the Chicago Firestorm some antiwar protestors gave-up any pretense to non-violent action and advocated the use of violence as the only way to end the war, reflecting rising militancy. One group that held some of the responsibility for the Firestorm was a radical group known as the 'Weathermen'. Rejecting the New Left in favour of the Marxist–Leninism of the Old Left, the Weathermen attacked a number of ROTC buildings in 1969 and 1970 before a number blew themselves up in New York City while preparing a bomb.

# Nixon and the Moratoria

Nixon won the Presidential election in November 1968. Given his pledge to end the war, the public displeasure at the increasing militancy of the antiwar movement, the gradual decline of the New Left and the tensions between liberals and radicals, 1969 began with the antiwar movement at its lowest ebb.

## HISTORICAL ISSUE

### Vietnam Veterans Against the War

In 1967 a small group of veterans established 'Vietnam Veterans Against the War' (VVAW), which came to the fore in 1969, reflecting opposition to the war from members of the armed forces. From 1966 to the end of 1973, there were 503,926 incidents of desertion.

Its members encountered greater animosity and violence than many other antiwar groups. Opponents saw them as traitors as veterans testified not only against the war, but also against racism and atrocities committed by American troops in Vietnam. A prominent member of the group was a decorated former naval officer, John Kerry, who stated during Congressional Hearings before gathered politicians: 'How do you ask a man to be the last man to die for a mistake?' Kerry contested the 2004 US Presidential election, where his Vietnam War service and his alleged 'betrayal' of American veterans through his opposition to the war became major campaign issues.

It was claimed that the antiwar movement often took its frustrations out on the symbols of the American endeavour in Vietnam – American soldiers. (Spitting on GIs was widely reported by veterans, although recent studies have discredited such claims.) Liberal opponents of the war rejected such allegations and insisted they sought to save the lives of men and women serving in Vietnam. Veterans opposed to the war gave such a message more credence.

Following Nixon's failure to deliver on his promise to end the war, and with the radical groups disintegrating, the opportunity arose for the liberals to once again assume leadership of the movement. In April 1969 antiwar groups in New England met to consider their options. They decided on a 'Moratorium': a pause in business for the purpose of highlighting the protest against the war. This led to the establishment of the Vietnam Moratorium Committee. Its aim was to stage a 'National Protest' in Washington, DC, in October 1969. Another collective of antiwar movements, the 'New Mobilization Committee to End the War in Vietnam' ('New Mobe'), was also intent on protesting against the war.

Vietnam Moratorium Day was held on 15 October 1969. *Life* described the events as 'a display without parallel, the largest expression of public dissent ever seen in this country'. Across the country teach-ins and rallies were held. Over 100,000 protested in Boston; 250,000 in New York, 250,000 in Washington, DC, and millions more elsewhere. The event was followed by a national student strike and a 'March Against Death', where 47,000 people each carried a candle – representing the number of American deaths in Vietnam to that time – as they marched to Arlington National Cemetery. Nixon rejected the protesters' pleas, claiming he still had the support of the 'great silent majority' of American people.

The national moratoria marked the highpoint of the antiwar movement. The two great 'peace offensives' of 1969 drained the movement, financially, physically and emotionally. The VMC, along with many other groups, ceased to exist. With the US commitment in Vietnam decreasing, many Americans saw little reason to continue protesting.

## HISTORICAL ISSUE

### *The Vietnam War and Australian Film and Television*

Like their American counterparts, Australian filmmakers in the 1970s and 1980s considered the Vietnam War as a topic worthy of exploration. One Australian film (*The Odd Angry Shot*, 1978) and two mini-series (*Vietnam* and *Sword of Honour*) were made about the war and its legacies. These have common themes, centring around the loss of innocence, Australia's place in the world, its subservient relationship to the United States and the plight of young men whose country appears to have forgotten them. Questioning why they are in Vietnam, but unable to find the answers, the two lead characters in *The Odd Angry Shot* return to Sydney and deny they have fought in Vietnam.

Unlike American films, which generally distance themselves from the historical and political conditions that produced the war, the Australian mini-series explored the reasons behind the Australian commitment. The representation of the Vietnam War by Australian film and television provides the opportunity to contrast the American cinema version and provides further avenues to explore Australia's war in Vietnam.

### EXERCISE:

Compare and contrast the endings of the following Vietnam War films. What do they say about the legacy of the Vietnam War in the three countries depicted:
1  *Platoon* (United States, 1986)
2  *The Odd Angry Shot* (Australia, 1978)
3  *White Badge* (South Korea, 1994)

# 1970: Protest and Counter-Protest

In 1970, however, opponents of the war mobilised one more time, to protest against the invasion of Cambodia. The movement's swansong produced one of its greatest tragedies, when protests on the campus of Ohio's Kent State University saw members of the National Guard shoot and kill four student protesters. Nixon defended the National Guard troops: 'When dissent turns to violence, it invites tragedy.' Further tragedy occurred 10 days later when two African–American students from Jackson State College, Mississippi, were shot and killed by police officers. On 8 May over 100,000 people marched in protest through Washington.

On the same day their colleagues were marching in Washington, students from New York University and Hunter College held their own demonstration. The result was the so-called 'Hard Hat Riot' when around 200 construction workers wearing their yellow hard-hats attacked the demonstrators. The workers then marched on City Hall, demanding the Mayor raise the America flag, which was at half-mast to mourn the Kent

State dead. The workers sang the national anthem as the flag was raised. Noticing an antiwar banner at Pace College, the workers broke into a building and attacked several students.

Two weeks later, a peaceful demonstration was organised by the Building and Trades Council of Greater New York. More than 100,000 workers marched through the streets of New York, waving American flags and praising the young men who were risking their lives fighting in Vietnam. The last great public demonstration of the Vietnam War was in favour of American policy. The hard-hats demonstrated that class played a role in shaping one's position on the war in Vietnam. Opposition to the war was inversely proportionate to wealth and education. Gallup polls revealed that college-educated Americans were more likely than those with high-school education to favour a US withdrawal from Vietnam.

*Tragedy at Kent State*

Significantly, too, Nixon's troop withdrawals reduced US casualties: although Vietnamese casualities remained enormous, the faltering support for the antiwar movement suggested many Americans were more concerned about American casualties than with the underlying immorality of the conflict. In November 1972 Nixon was re-elected President in a landslide.

## HISTORICAL ISSUE

### *The Australian Antiwar Movement*

The Australian antiwar movement offers interesting comparisons and contrasts to the American experience. While the antiwar movement in Australia probably constituted a larger proportion of the population than in the United States, the local movement was very much influenced by American trends and similar events. Parallels included:

1  Conscription helped to mobilise opponents.
2  The opening of an Australian chapter of SDS.
3  An Australian Moratorium movement.
   Differences included:
1  Early antiwar demonstrations were conducted by the youth wing of the Australian Communist Party.
2  Protests never reached the heights of militancy and violence experienced in the United States.
3  The peculiar manifestations of Australian protest such as the organisation of 'Save Our Sons' (SOS), which was made up of middle-class/middle-aged women.

# Evaluating the Antiwar Movements

Historians continued to debate whether the antiwar movement helped end America's involvement in the Vietnam War. The issue has also affected American political and cultural life. During the 1960s and '70s, supporters of the movement claimed they had influenced policy; the government and its supporters claimed otherwise. By the 1980s, however, viewpoints had shifted. Conservative politicians and historians saw an opportunity to blame America's failure in Vietnam on the antiwar movement: a united America would never have suffered such a defeat if the antiwar movement, with the support of the media, had not undermined public confidence in the enterprise.

Left-wing politicians and historians rejected such claims because those arguments were associated with the broader assertion that the Democratic Party had supported the antiwar movement – and had, therefore, helped undermine the nation. These commentators suggested that the movement was the most successful antiwar movement in American history, but that it did not stop the war. It may have prevented Johnson from further escalating the war in 1968, and was a factor in Nixon's Vietnamisation Policy, but it did not force American withdrawal. Furthermore, the antiwar movement's increasingly militant agenda, and the support given to the NLF by some members of the movement, alienated 'mainstream' America. The antiwar movement, seen by some critics as a symptom of a wide national malady and decline, became unpopular at the same time as the war. To suggest the antiwar movement lost the war for the United States also raises the contentious claim that the United States could have won the war.

A recent argument suggests the antiwar movement actually prolonged the war. According to this line of reasoning, public opinion had been turning against the war, until the antiwar movement was hijacked by the radicals. Mainstream opponents of the war were pushed underground, while for some antiwar activists, the militancy produced a psychological reason for staying and seeing the war through. Another argument suggests the antiwar movement undermined America's negotiating power. People's War had always insisted on the spiritual support of the people and North Vietnam could see that in this respect its opponents came from a violently divided nation.

---

### POINTS TO REMEMBER

- It is more accurate to refer to antiwar 'movements' than to one single, cohesive movement. 'Liberals' ('moderates') and 'radicals' disagreed over tactics and goals.
- The antiwar protests reflected class and racial tensions in America.
- The mass antiwar movement began with the 'Teach-ins' at colleges and universities. Some of the movements became more radical and adopted civil disobedience as a tactic to protest.
- Liberals assumed national leadership of the movement with the Moratorium in 1969. It was the highpoint of the movement.
- Historians still debate whether the antiwar movements helped to end America's involvement in the war.

## ACTIVITIES

1  Using a timeline, briefly outline the history of the Vietnam antiwar movement.

2  To what extent can the antiwar movement be described as 'white' and 'middle class'?

3  In what ways did the antiwar movement change during the course of the war?

4  Evaluate the effect of the antiwar movement on ending the war. You should mention the opposing historical arguments about its success.

5  The Vietnam War created the largest and most publicised protest against any war in US history. Why do you think this happened?

6  Look up the American Bill of Rights on the internet (the first 10 Amendments to the Constitution) and in particular the rights of citizens to disagree with public officials. The American republic was born from protests over what were considered 'unjust' British laws. Was the antiwar movement legal and patriotic?

### FURTHER READING

Useful studies of the antiwar movement include Rhodri Jeffrey-Jones' *Peace Now!* (Yale University Press, New Haven, 1999), Melvin Small's *Antiwarriors: The Vietnam War and the Battle for America's Hearts and Minds* (Scholarly Resources, Wilmington, Del., 2002) and Adam Garfinkle's *Telltale Hearts: The Origins and Impact of the Vietnam Antiwar Movement* (St. Martins, New York, 1995). See also Gerard J. DeGroot, *A Noble Cause?: America and the Vietnam War* (Longman, Harlow, Essex, 2000) Chapter 12.

Oliver Stone's film *Born on the Fourth of July* provides insights into one soldier's journey from supporter to opponent of the war. John Wayne's *Green Berets* presents a one-dimensional and crude portrayal of the pro-war position. Mark Kitchell's *Berkeley in the 60s* (1991) offers a detailed and compelling examination of one of the 'epicentres' of antiwar activism.

# 10

# Vietnamese Home Fronts, 1960–1975

IN THIS CHAPTER YOU WILL:
- explore non-military explanations for success and failure during the Vietnam War
- gain a deeper understanding of South and North Vietnamese politics and government and how they affected war efforts
- be introduced to aspects of daily life in North and South Vietnam for average citizens
- examine specific themes, including the impact of the airwar on the North, the failure of land reform and corruption in the South.

## Background

The Vietnam War was fought not only on the battlefield. Southern and northern home fronts also played significant parts in the conflict. In both cases the boundary between the war front and the home front was often blurred. Whether it was in a southern village or a Hanoi suburb, a home front during the day might quickly become a war front at night. Examining the home front histories of North and South Vietnam helps explain the North's success and American failure.

## Confusion, Chaos and Coups in the South

From November 1963 until mid-1965, political life in the Republic of Vietnam was characterised by a succession of short-lived governments. Diem's success in removing political rivals ensured a power vacuum followed his demise.

Following Diem's assassination, the government was ruled by a military junta headed by General Duong Van Minh ('Big Minh'). The junta attempted to govern through a new apparatus, the Military Revolutionary Council (MRC). It aimed to pave the way for the eventual return of civilian and, ultimately, democratic government.

The MRC, however, was ineffective due to internal squabbling. In late January 1964 disgruntled members of the Council, led by General Nguyen Khanh, staged their first coup. Implying that Big Minh was prepared to accommodate the North, he was charged with being a 'neutralist'.

The United States took a close interest in South Vietnamese politics as instability was unacceptable to its plans. The US insisted that the deposed Minh be appointed to the ceremonial position of 'Chief of State', while Khanh became Prime Minister. Yet, infighting and instability continued. On occasions, political life appeared to be a game of pass-the-parcel. During 1964 South Vietnam had seven governments.

As political life descended into farce, the United States sought stability and a return of government to civilian hands. The first step was the formation in October 1964 of a High National Council (HNC) chaired by the aged Dr Phan Khac Suu. In November, the HNC appointed a former schoolteacher and Mayor of Saigon, Tran Van Huong, as Prime Minister. Preparations also began for the writing of a new constitution.

The HNC quickly became known as the 'High National Museum' because of the age of its members. Since Diem had virtually destroyed his generation of politicians, the HNC was filled by older men who had escaped Diem's wrath because they had already retired from public life.

Many senior South Vietnamese officers doubted the HNC and a civilian government could defeat the North. Reflecting the fact that it was a new and growing army, many senior ARVN officers were young men. They believed only their generation had the energy and determination to lead the country. Convinced Huong was weak and ineffectual, these officers (the 'Young Turks') suggested he too had 'neutralist' tendencies. In December 1964 the 'Young Turks' staged their own coup. Yet with the United States again demanding at least the appearance of stability, the Young Turks allowed Huong to remain Prime Minister.

Frustrated by yet another coup, US Ambassador General Maxwell Taylor summoned the ringleaders and insisted the United States was 'tired of coups'. American plans, he reiterated, relied on government stability. The Young Turks' guarantees to Taylor lasted only a matter of weeks. In early 1965, as the battlefield situation deteriorated, the newly formed Armed Forces Council (AFC) forced Huong to resign. General Khanh became Prime Minister.

Alarmed by Khanh's allegedly dictatorial style, his colleagues on the AFC secured his resignation (at the same time as they quelled another attempted coup, this time orchestrated by General Lam Van Phat). Attempting to meet American demands, the Young Turks appointed the civilian Phan Huy Quat as Prime Minister.

# The Emergence of Nguyen Cao Ky

Quat remained Prime Minister until June 1965 when, with the military situation deteriorating, it was agreed that the military must lead the government. Nguyen Cao Ky became Prime Minister and General Nguyen Van Thieu became Chief of State. While Ky's Cabinet was comprised mainly of civilians, the United States saw the Government of Vietnam (GVN) as a

**PERSONALITY**

**Nguyen Cao Ky**

Nguyen Cao Ky was born into a Scholar-Gentry family in the town of Son Tay near Hanoi in 1930. Educated in Hanoi, Ky grew up hating the French and admiring Ho Chi Minh. At the age of 12 he joined the Viet Minh. Later, however, Ky repudiated the Viet Minh and volunteered for service with the Vietnamese Air Force. In 1954 he flew a DC-3 from Hanoi, leaving the North, never to return. Precisely when Ky turned against Ho and the Viet Minh is not clear, but his motivation was opposition to communism.

By age 30 Ky was commanding an airbase in Saigon and assisting the CIA in flying covert operations into North Vietnam. He became an important member of the 'Young Turks' and a powerful figure within the South Vietnamese military.

Ky was Prime Minister from 1965 to 1967 and Vice President from 1967 to 1971. In his autobiography he portrayed himself as a young democrat, gallantly fighting the corruption undermining Vietnam. Ruled ineligible (by Nguyen Van Thieu) for running for President in 1971 Ky retired from public life, before returning briefly late in the war in an attempt to save the nation. As Saigon collapsed he flew a helicopter to an American aircraft carrier to begin a new life in the United States.

military government – which American officials believed was more likely to support the war.

South Vietnamese had welcomed Diem's demise. But when their situation did not improve and chaos ensued, support for the GVN collapsed further. Ky knew that as well as winning on the battlefield, he had to regain popular support for the government and his leadership returned some stability to government. Like his predecessors, however, he spent considerable energy silencing internal opposition.

In May 1966 Ky announced a decree for electoral reform. An election of a constituent assembly was scheduled for 11 September. This assembly would meet in October and begin drafting a democratic constitution. By 1967 the new constitution was in place and South Vietnam adopted a presidential system of executive government. In the ensuing election a ticket consisting of the politically astute Thieu as President and Ky as Vice-President prevailed, despite receiving only 34.8% of the vote and losing outright in Saigon, Danang and Hue. This poor result came despite the mobilisation of the ARVN to intimidate voters and opponents, the disqualification of some serious contenders, the disqualification of voters in 'insecure areas' and electoral fraud.

*Marshal Ky (left) and General Thieu (right) meet President Johnson in Hawaii, July 1966*

At a meeting scheduled for 1 October 1967, the National Assembly was to ratify the election and endorse the winners. To intimidate the members, the Assembly was surrounded by the military. The win by Thieu and Ky (both of whom maintained their military positions) was ratified by 58 votes to 43. An hour later the National Assembly was dissolved. The Johnson administration spoke of a 'victory for democracy'.

To ensure the military remained in control, the Generals formed a Military Council. This secret committee could veto military and

civil appointments, and direct policy. Part of the motivation of the Council was to act as a check on Thieu's presidency; but he quickly sidestepped the Council and became more dictatorial.

At the second presidential election in 1971, Thieu ensured through his control of a newly constituted National Assembly that rivals such as Ky were ruled ineligible for contesting the position. In the end Thieu was the only nominee in the 'one-man election'. Determined to receive a strong vote, he mobilised the Army to

*A farmer casts his vote after being wounded by a PLAF bomb*

compel citizens to perform their 'national duty'. It was claimed that 88.4% of the population voted in the election and 91.5% voted for Thieu. With echoes back to Diem's election of 1956, American officials called the election 'embarrassing', while journalists dismissed it as 'ludicrous'. Any pretence that South Vietnam was evolving into a democracy was over.

Thieu remained in office until early 1975, with his rule prompting increasing public indignation amidst claims of corruption and despotism. Ky, who had retired from political and military life, returned as the leader of the National Salvation Committee and attempted to organise a coup in early 1975. But the United States refused to back the initiative. In the end, the US forced Thieu's resignation. He was first replaced by his Vice President, the rehabilitated Tran Van Huong and then, a few days later, by Big Minh in the hope that the North Vietnamese would negotiate with the ARVN General. They refused.

*'I'm modifying democracy in order not to confuse the simple voters – I'll be the only candidate!' An Australian cartoon observes the 1971 presidential elections in South Vietnam*

# Summing up the Political Failures of the GVN

The Government of Vietnam's shortcomings contributed significantly to the overall failures of South Vietnam and the United States. The coups and instability that characterised the government and military in the two years after Diem's demise left it incapable of securing popular support. Ky and Thieu delivered a semblance of political stability, but were unable to reverse their government's poor standing amongst the disillusioned populace.

The GVN was also compromised because of its relationship with the United States. Fears that American intervention would damage the reputation of the GVN proved prophetic. South Vietnamese labeled successive US Ambassadors as the 'Governor General'. This, of course, was the old title of the senior French official in Indochina during the colonial period and reflected both North Vietnamese rhetoric and South Vietnamese reality.

The GVN's inability to secure popular support also reflected the ARVN's failures. The fact that senior generals also saw themselves as politicians did not help. Infighting and factionalism saw senior generals build their units as personal armies for purposes of protection and the exertion of power and influence. In practice, the ARVN was as much a political tool as a military organisation.

# Political Developments in the North

Unlike the turmoil in the South, North Vietnam was characterised by political stability. By contrast to many other communist states, there were no great purges in the DRV after 1954. The key to stability was the enormity of the task facing the DRV and Ho Chi Minh's leadership. Building a nation while fighting a war against a superpower left little time for internal dissent. Ho had also built a collective leadership that did not allow power to be concentrated in the hands of any one of his 'nephews'.

The DRV was also unusual in comparison to other communist governments because non-communists continued to hold important positions in the DRV. One reason why the DRV continued to have non-communists in senior positions was because Hanoi continued to consider itself as the government-in-waiting for a reunited Vietnam. Having long advocated a coalition model as the first step in reunification, the DRV could demonstrate its ability to work alongside non-communists.

Further evidence of the DRV's anticipation of reunification lay in the composition of the government, the National Assembly and the Lao Dong Party.

## HISTORICAL ISSUE

### North Vietnam: A Police State?

American propaganda maintained that one of the reasons the North Vietnamese resisted the United States was because they lived in a 'police state', which kept a close eye on citizens and did not tolerate dissent.

The DRV had in place those apparatus commonly associated with communist regimes. The People's Armed Security Force (PASF) played an internal security role in removing opponents of the regime and countering espionage activities launched by the South or the United States. Laws against 'counter-revolutionary activities' increased during the 1960s and academics' activities and writings were closely monitored. Most senior university appointments went to well-regarded Party members.

Yet, international visitors to North Vietnam during the war were surprised to find little evidence of a police or military presence. During his visit in 1970, American commentator Noam Chomsky observed that most of the police he saw on the streets were unarmed and directing traffic and that most of the soldiers he saw were relaxing on leave.

Within the government, many southerners served in senior bureaucratic and ministerial roles. Within the National Assembly, seats were reserved for southerners. Within the Party, southerners such as Pham Hung were members of the Politburo, while Le Duan's advancement to First Secretary in 1960 meant a southerner was second only to Ho Chi Minh. This contradicts claims that the North should be constructed as a foreign aggressor during the Vietnam War.

Yet despite the overall stability and the unified public face, there were tensions within the Hanoi leadership. These difficulties reflected continuing personal estrangements, disagreements regarding ideology and international patronage and debates about the best way to secure the nation's reunification.

The lightning rod for much of the dissent within the Hanoi leadership was Truong Chinh. Truong's personal animosity towards Giap continued during the 1960s. Truong also disliked Le Duan, who had taken from him (via Ho) the coveted role of Party Secretary. Predictably, Le Duan and Giap were leaders of the anti-Truong faction.

## HISTORICAL ISSUE

### The Death of Ho Chi Minh

Suffering ill health for much of his life, Ho Chi Minh died of a massive heart attack on 2 September 1969, aged 79. Contrary to his last wishes for a simple burial, a state funeral was organised, with nationwide mourning. Following Soviet tradition, Ho's body was embalmed, placed under glass and displayed in a purpose-built mausoleum in Hanoi that was completed in 1975. His body became the symbol of the Revolution and visiting the mausoleum remains a national ritual.

Disunity also reflected continuing tensions between northerners and southerners. Politburo member Le Duc Tho, for example, was noted for his personal dislike of southerners and his inability to cooperate with Le Duan. Truong Chinh also had little regard for southerners.

Yet another dimension of these rivalries was caused by the Sino–Soviet rift. While North Vietnam publicly sought to maintain a neutral position on the struggle, privately Hanoi's leaders took sides in the dispute. This saw pro-China supporters coalesce around Truong Chinh, while Le Duan, Pham Van Dong and Giap sided with the Soviet Union.

*Ho Chi Minh's mausoleum in Hanoi*

# Power Struggle After Ho's death

While Ho had done his best to keep a system of checks and balances on power, his death in 1969 precipitated instability and an internal struggle. Prior to Ho's death, power was balanced between three of his deputies: Le Duan controlled the Party;

*Pham Van Dong*

*Truong Chinh*

Truong Chinh the National Assembly; and Pham Van Dong (Ho's 'favourite nephew') the government.

Traditionally, this had translated into the Party dominating both the government and the National Assembly. After Ho's death, however, Truong Chinh sought to increase the power of the National Assembly and, hence, his own influence. His leadership of the Viet Nam Fatherland Front (the DRV equivalent of the Viet Minh Front) and the Vietnam Trade Union Federation consolidated this power.

From the mid-1960s Truong wrote and spoke of the National Assembly as the 'highest authority of state power'. He began exercising the power of the Assembly to the detriment of his opponents.

In his most blatant attack against an opponent, Truong asserted that his National Defence Council was the most important military body in the country and that both the Army and the Ministry of Defence were answerable to it. Despite Giap's position as Head of the Army and Minister of Defence, Truong structured the Council so that Giap was only the fourth-ranking member – a significant reduction in Giap's influence.

Truong sought to curtail the political influence of pro-Soviet individuals and allies of Le Duan and Giap. Representing southerners as major supporters of the two men, he took the bold step of ending direct southern representation in the National Assembly. Seen alongside actions such as demoting the status of the Committee of Reunification, Truong's commitment to reunification could be questioned.

By 1969 it was widely assumed in the West that the hardliner Truong had eclipsed Le Duan and elevated the National Assembly's influence at the expense of the Party. Moreover, supporters such as Le Duc Tho had been rewarded for their support – they now exercised more power than before.

This view of Truong's triumph remained the orthodox interpretation of North Vietnamese politics for nearly 30 years. There were, however, a number of problems with this argument. Most important, why, if the pro-Chinese faction had succeeded, did China and Vietnam go to war in 1979?

# Interpreting Power Struggles in the DRV

More recent studies, complicating the story of North Vietnamese politics during the American War, confirm that pro-Chinese and pro-Soviet factions existed within the senior echelons of the Party and government. However, factional allegiances were not as strong as previously thought and Truong Chinh did not secure as much power as was previously assumed. His bid to make the National Assembly the base of all power within the DRV failed during the early 1970s. The Lao Dong Party machine won this battle and with this victory, what Soviet diplomats of the time called the 'moderate group', regained control.

The 1972 Easter Offensive, which earlier historians had assumed was part of a tilt by Le Duan and Giap to regain power, was in fact an initiative of the pro-China faction, which was following Mao Zedong's new theory that military action alone could secure revolution. After it failed, the moderates, with their old definition of People's War, regained influence. They, however, now added a third bow to the People's War strategy: military and political approaches would be complemented by the diplomatic approach.

While this political infighting was taking place, the Hanoi leadership never aired their dirty linen in public. Even Russian and Chinese officials found it difficult to understand the machinations of political control in Hanoi. In public, the leadership presented a united front. This appearance of stability helped enable the Party and government to maintain popular support and unity, and focussed on the goal of reunification. The political stability enjoyed in North Vietnam is crucial to understanding its success in the Vietnam War.

# The Airwar Against the North

Another factor uniting the North Vietnamese – which also helps explain the North's success – was, perhaps surprisingly, the American airwar. Operations Rolling Thunder and Linebacker firmed public resolve and united the North Vietnamese. Nonetheless, the American airwar transformed daily life in North Vietnam.

From early 1965 Hanoi became the front line in the American airwar. Although the least damaged of North Vietnam's six major cities, early air attacks greatly concerned government officials, with 42% of the nation's urban population residing in the city – and as many as 15,000 people per square kilometre. In February 1965 it was decided to evacuate Hanoi. In the first instance 50,000 people, including many children and elderly people, were relocated, causing significant hardship to Hanoi's families and strain on rural communities. Many evacuees stayed away just a short time before returning to the city and their families. With the intensification of Rolling Thunder, a further evacuation was ordered in 1966. The DRV claimed that by late 1966 three-quarters of Hanoi's population was evacuated.

The American bombing campaign also damaged the North Vietnamese economy and industrial output. For those who stayed in Hanoi, life was transformed. Many people left their bombed-out homes and lived in caves. Peak-hour on city streets now lasted from 4am until 6am: the time when American aircraft did not attack. Department stores opened from 5am to 8am; factories operated between 6am and 10am, then another shift between 4.30pm and 8pm.

By the end of the war the USA had dropped 2.5 million tons of bombs on North Vietnam, more than had been dropped during World War II. By 1967 economic damage was already calculated at over US$200 million. The North's nation-building efforts in the 10 years since the Geneva Conference were almost obliterated. Claimed targets were selected to weaken the North's ability wage war, but a very liberal interpretation was taken of

*An elderly peasant woman shows the misery of having war conducted around her home in Quang Ngai Province, one of the more embattled locations in Vietnam*

what constituted a legitimate target: Rolling Thunder inflicted enormous death and destruction on the DRV.

Notwithstanding that death and destruction, as early as 1966 the CIA expressed doubts that the airwar would break the North Vietnamese will to fight or force them to the negotiating table: 'There continues to be no indication of any significant decline in North Vietnamese morale.' Even when reports in 1967 concluded that the North's ability to wage war was 'severely eroded', it did not prevent the Tet Offensive from taking place. Like the Ho Chi Minh Trail, as long as North Vietnam's economy was supplying *something* to the prosecution of the war in the South, the fight could continue. Material support from China, the Soviet Union and other communist countries became even more vital. While American bombs helped push the DRV to the negotiating table in 1968, and again in 1972, bombing did not break North Vietnam's spirit. Nor did it dramatically improve the American negotiating position.

## The Failings of the Southern Economy

Despite the American airwar's significant disruptions, North Vietnam's economy survived and delivered its people a quality of life that enabled them to prosecute the war. In the South, indiscriminate American and South Vietnamese bombing and the activities of the PLAF also damaged the South's economy, especially in rural areas. Yet it was government policy, not war damage, that really explains RVN failure.

The RVN and US failure in the war was in their inability to win popular support amongst South Vietnam's rural population: what they failed to appreciate, until it was too late, was that at the heart of peasant discontent was the perennial issue of land ownership. Little was done to address the issue of land reform until the mid-1960s, when the GVN finally realised the war was being won and lost not in the cities, but in the countryside. Rural reform was crucial because of the demise of the rural economy as a result of the war. Food production in South Vietnam began collapsing in 1965 and continued to decline until 1968. Total farm production was 23% less in 1966 than in 1963.

A 1967 study found that for 76% of tenant farmers the biggest single issue was that they did not own the land they tilled. The GVN, however, continued to sidestep the issue and sought ways to increase farm profitability under existing arrangements. It was assumed that if the peasantry could do more than subsist on their rented lands, the issue of ownership would become moot. Fair prices at market and good yields were considered essential.

Prior to 1966–1967 the South Vietnamese rural economy – with its emphasis on cash crops – reflected the legacies of its colonial past. Government agricultural policies favoured international export markets and urban consumers, rather than small-scale farmers. The GVN had done little to correct this bias because rice provided one of the few sources of export income, and cheap commodity prices in urban areas were considered vital to 'urban tranquillity'. This stability was regarded as crucial to the government's survival.

In late 1966 the GVN increased the price of rice in the cities. This had a knock-on effect for vegetables and meat prices. The result was that by 1967 many small-scale farmers' income had doubled from previous years. While some of these gains were eaten up by inflation, cost of living increases had more impact in the city than the country. The new income meant that for the first time many farmers could consider more than simple subsistence farming. They could consider surplus production to increase their prosperity.

For many farmers, however, any extra income was used to repay debts. In 1967 it was estimated that 60% of all farmers had significant debts. While some farmers could borrow money from their families, many others were forced to seek funds from less-reputable sources. Farmers could be charged as much as 60% interest. The GVN attempted to address this issue through the creation of National Agricultural Credit Office and a new Agricultural Development Bank. Money became cheaper to borrow, thus increasing farmers' prosperity.

# The Green Revolution

On the advice of American experts, the GVN also used technology to improve the rural sector. Pesticides, fertiliser and new rice strains were the key to greater yields and greater income. Again, whether a person owned or worked the land would hopefully become irrelevant.

New rice strains were also introduced from 1967. During the late 1960s thousands of farmers exploited these new rice strains. By 1970 over one quarter of the nation's rice land (rice comprised 80% of the rural economy) used the new strains.

Alongside these market reforms and technological improvements, the GVN finally accepted in March 1970 what the peasantry had long demanded. The principle of 'Land to the Tiller' was acknowledged in a new raft of legislation. Importantly, the reform's compensation packages won the landowners' approval. The NLF attempted to counter the GVN's program by intimidating and by continuing with its own program of land reform. The major advantage of the NLF program was that the program was structured to take into account local variances to permit local outcomes. The major disadvantage of NLF land reform was that no deed of ownership was ever forthcoming, so many farmers assumed, therefore, that their new land could easily be taken away.

*In Phuoc Tuy province Australian farming practices were also implemented. In the village of Tam Phuoc in July 1971 a farmer feeds his poultry using Australian methods*

When re-conquering former 'liberated' territories, the GVN had to deal once again with the consequences of communist land reform. Unlike the Diem regime, Thieu's government accepted the status quo as they found it. Land redistributions were honoured and former owners were compensated for their loss. This approach won considerable support because it not only recognised the importance of ownership, but also provided a degree of land tenure more permanent than that offered by the NLF.

The 'Green Revolution' and new government reforms precipitated a transformation of South Vietnam's rural economy. The January–February rice crop of 1971 was the largest in Vietnamese history. The surpluses freed many of the nation's farmers from the drudgery of subsistence. Agricultural investment by the farmers themselves grew dramatically as a consequence. In 1970 private citizens imported over US$15 million dollars of farm machinery. The new special rice yields became commonly known as 'Honda rice' because thousands of farmers could now afford to buy a motorcycle. With the reforms and the consequences of the Green Revolution, by the end of 1970 farmers living under GVN control were far better off financially than those living in the NLF's 'liberated zones'.

But this prosperity was temporary. Some farmers reported environmental damage from overuse of the land and the frequent use of pesticides and insecticides. 'Agricultural development' soon fell victim to corruption. Retailers supplying the new rice strains, fertilisers and pesticides increased their prices through price fixing or hoarding. In many villages the cost of farming doubled, ending the farmers' newfound prosperity and redistributing the new wealth to corrupt retailers and government officials. By 1973 many farmers were again subsistence farming, with debts and little disposable income. Betrayed again, many turned their back on the government for the last time and returned their support to the NLF.

# Corruption

The 'Green Revolution' was undermined by systemic corruption reflecting a much wider malady. South Vietnam was characterised by widespread government corruption. In 1966 Ky commenced an anti-corruption campaign. Defence Minister Nguyen Huu Ci was dismissed for corruption and a prominent Chinese businessmen involved in corrupt activities was executed by firing squad in Saigon's central market.

Such harsh penalties, however, had little effect on this systemic problem. For many South Vietnamese, corruption had become part of everyday life. Bribery – for everything from avoiding Army conscription to getting a promotion – was considered a part of the cost of living.

The American presence exacerbated corruption. Flourishing 'black markets' relied on American goods, which came via the US military's Post Exchange (PX) system, where American service personnel could purchase anything from chewing gum to a new car. Tax and duty free, the items were much cheaper than those that could be acquired by Vietnamese citizens. Some Americans sold their PX goods on the black market, where they made a handsome profit. The American PX kept the black market in operation.

The black market also fuelled inflation. For much of the war inflation hovered around 30%. It had a dramatic impact on urban salary earners, whose fixed incomes were unable to meet price increases. To find some protection against inflation, many Vietnamese tried to convert their South Vietnamese currency into American dollars. The government limited the amounts that could be exchanged legally, but the black market met the demand, further devaluing the local currency.

In rural communities government officials used corruption and extortion to line their pockets. ARVN officers also used their positions to make money. Some traded rice or opium. Others sold rice to the PLAF. Officers' corrupt behaviour was emulated by enlisted men. 'Soldiers should be so educated that they no longer oppress the people and loot their property,' pleaded one village leader.

Public indignation with corruption grew, especially when Thieu's family was engaging in corrupt conduct that raked in millions of dollars. Undeterred, Thieu launched a mass anti-corruption campaign in 1974 that saw thousands of officials dismissed. The campaign, however, was derided as a ploy to remove opponents of the regime and further reward its supporters.

# Surviving Amidst a War

Rural Vietnamese knew their villages and homes could become the front line. The aggressive manner in which the United States conducted the war forced many to leave the land and seek sanctuary in the cities. Harassment by either ARVN or PLAF troops often antagonised South Vietnamese civilians. The NLF encouraged migration to the cities, believing it would improve its support base in urban areas and that these 'refugees' would put more pressure on GVN services.

Where Hanoi's population declined during the 1960s, between 1960 and 1970 Saigon's population rose by 45% to 3.3 million. Many people sought refuge in cities such as Danang or Cam Ranh City, which had large American bases that employed thousands of Vietnamese in menial jobs. In all cases these dramatic increases put enormous pressure on infrastructure, services and unemployment rates.

# Conclusion

Civilians' experiences of war comprise an important aspect of the study of any conflict. In the case of the Vietnam War, they also help to explain the reasons for North Vietnamese success and American failure. It has often been claimed that securing the 'hearts and minds' of the Vietnamese people was the key to victory for either side. The home front history of the war challenges those American historians who suggest the United States could have won in Vietnam if not for the limitations politicians put on military activities.

**POINTS TO REMEMBER**
- South Vietnam experienced political instability following the overthrow of Diem.
- The government in South Vietnam was never able to gain the popular support of a majority of its citizens.
- The war had a dramatic impact on southern society and economics, in both urban and rural areas.
- North Vietnam was more politically stable than South Vietnam.
- The US airwar against North Vietnam was intense. They dropped massive quantities of bombs, yet this did not weaken the resolve of the population to continue the war.

# ACTIVITIES

1 Evaluate the efforts of the South Vietnamese to reform the rural economy.

2 Compare and contrast the political situation in the North and South after 1954.

3 Was the South Vietnamese Government a puppet state of the United States?

4 What were the effects of the US bombing campaign on North Vietnam?

5 Evaluate the opposing views concerning the power struggle in North Vietnam after the death of Ho Chi Minh.

6 Why was the South Vietnamese Government unable to gain the popular support of a majority of the South's rural population?

7 Was the North Vietnamese Government more concerned than the South Vietnamese Government with Vietnamese nationalism?

8 Considering the social and political history of North and South Vietnam, was America realistic to predict that it could win the war?

### FURTHER READING

W. Trullinger's *Village at War* (Stanford University Press, Stanford, CA., 1994) is an excellent study of a South Vietnamese village in the midst of war. A useful insight into the inner workings of the South Vietnamese Government is Nguyen Cao Ky's *How We Lost the Vietnam War* (Cooper Square Press, 1976; repr., New York, 2002).

# An Elusive Peace: Defeat and Victory, 1969–1975

IN THIS CHAPTER YOU WILL:
- be introduced to the ongoing struggle between US/ARVN forces and the PLAF/PAVN
- learn about the process of negotiating an end to the conflict
- explore the American withdrawal from Vietnam
- learn about the defeat of the US-backed South Vietnamese Government and the end of the war.

## The Continuing Struggle in Vietnam

In 1969, an American military victory in Vietnam seemed as elusive as ever. Nixon realised quickly that his options were limited. The 'secret plan' (which Nixon never actually revealed) had helped him win the election, but it would not help him win the war. Ho's death did not weaken North Vietnam's resolve. Against the backdrop of continuing debate within the United States regarding the war, General Creighton Abrams – who replaced Westmoreland as commander of US forces in South Vietnam in June 1968 – faced a new strategic situation. In 1968, 14,589 Americans had died in South Vietnam. Abrams knew the American public would not tolerate similar loses in 1969. Westmoreland had fought to win the war; Abrams planned to fight in a manner that would reduce American casualties.

A more pressing concern was how to remove American forces from Vietnam, while preparing South Vietnamese forces to defend their country. While Abrams was doing this, he wanted to 'kill as many of the bastards as he could'. He concluded that Westmoreland's strategy of large-unit search-and-destroy missions had proved ineffective. The PLAF and PAVN usually found out about these operations before they commenced. Westmoreland had conducted more than 1,200 battalion-size operations in 1967. In 1969 only 700 similar operations were conducted.

# Hamburger Hill

On 22 February 1969 North Vietnam launched an offensive. Whilst the PAVN/PLAF did not benefit from the surprise of their Tet 1968 offensive, 1,140 American soldiers died in three weeks of fighting. In April American troop numbers peaked at 543,000. A large-scale military action in the A Shau Valley (near the Laotian border, in north-western South Vietnam) compounded Nixon's political problems.

In May, Abrams launched 'Operation Apache Snow'. The Americans attacked Ap Bia Mountain in the A Shau Valley, where the PAVN had constructed a substantial bunker complex. Abrams 'softened up' the battlefield with B-52 strikes and heavy artillery bombardment. Before American troops attacked on 18 May, torrential rain turned the sides of the pulverised mountain into mud. After 12 separate assaults, the mountain fell to the Americans on 20 May. They found 630 dead Vietnamese troops. American troops called the battlefield 'Hamburger Hill', a description that the media exploited. 'Apache Snow' cost another 241 American lives.

*American troops at Hamburger Hill*

The American tactical victory at Hamburger Hill turned into a public-relations nightmare when Abrams abandoned Ap Bia just one week after the battle. Many saw it as a callous waste of American lives to win the ground, only to give it up. This fuelled the antiwar movement and further affected troops' morale.

# Crisis Within the US Armed Forces

There was ample evidence that American forces were suffering from a crisis of morale. The Army's desertion rate in 1966 was 14.9 men per thousand. By 1971 it was 73.5 per thousand – three times higher than the worst desertion rates of the Korean War. The AWOL (absent without leave) rates told a similar story. In 1966 the army AWOL rate was 57.2 per thousand. This increased to 176.9 per thousand in 1971.

Of more concern to the American military was the 'fragging' of officers. Fragging was a term used to describe the assassination of officers and non-commissioned officers by their own troops. Usually, a fragmentation grenade was thrown into the victim's tent, killing the victim. In 1969, there were 96 documented incidents of fragging. By 1971 this had increased to 542 documented cases.

The decline in morale was evident also in the use of drugs. A huge supply of various drugs flowed into South Vietnam from Laos, Burma and Thailand. Amphetamines came from the United States and from laboratories in Saigon. South Vietnamese officials helped maintain a cheap and constant supply of drugs. A heroin addiction could be maintained for only US$2 a day, just a 70th of the cost in the United States. The Pentagon estimated that two-thirds of American troops in Vietnam were using marijuana and three-quarters had tried heroin. Thousands of American troops returned home with the 'monkey on their backs', a term used to describe heroin addiction.

Some Pentagon officials worried about a total collapse of discipline or even a mutiny. A 1971 report, 'The Collapse of the Armed Forces', published in *The Armed Forces Journal*, noted:

> Our army that now remains in Vietnam is in a state approaching collapse, with individual units avoiding or having refused combat, murdering their officers and non-commissioned officers, drug ridden and dispirited where not near-mutinous.

*Drug use in the US Army in Vietnam reflected a crisis of morale*

# The My Lai Massacre

Nixon and his National Security Advisor Henry Kissinger soon had more concerns. In November 1969 *Life* magazine broke the story of the My Lai massacre. The story by Seymour Hersh, and the disturbing photographs accompanying the article, horrified Americans. Many civilians had died as a result of American military actions. But the killings at My Lai could not be argued away as an accident. American soldiers had massacred women, children and babies.

On 16 March 1968, Captain Ernest Medina led Charlie Company, 11th Brigade, Americal Division, into My Lai village. The troops were conducting a search-and-destroy mission in this alleged PLAF stronghold. The soldiers herded the civilians into groups and began murdering them. According to the Army's official report, the troops' actions included 'individual and group acts of murder, rape, sodomy, maiming and assault on non-combatants and the mistreatment and killing of detainees'. The massacre was halted by a US Army helicopter crew who landed their chopper between the attacking American troops and the remaining Vietnamese. Between 300 and 500 Vietnamese died.

One American war wounded was injured when he shot himself in the foot. No weapons were found. Only one American, Lieutenant William Calley, was ever convicted over the incident.

The My Lai massacre highlighted serious problems with the nature of the war being fought in Vietnam and further eroded American public support. Nixon's announcement of troop withdrawals further affected morale. Troops expressed growing doubts about America's purpose in fighting the war. And there was the more personal and immediate question: Why risk your life when the United States was withdrawing?

# US Troop Withdrawal and the Nixon (Guam) Doctrine

The Nixon (Guam) Doctrine of 27 July 1969 reflected a change in American global strategy. The change was designed to ease tensions around the world and reduce the burden of America's commitments. Nixon stated that he expected America's Asian allies to take responsibility for their own military defence. This was the beginning of Vietnamisation of the war. In a 13 November address, Nixon outlined the three main points of this policy:
1  The USA would maintain its treaty commitments.
2  The USA would provide 'a shield if a nuclear power threatened the freedom of a nation allied with the US or of a nation whose survival was considered vital to US security'.
3  In 'cases involving other types of aggression', the United States would 'furnish military and economic assistance when requested in accordance with its treaty commitments'. But the US would 'look to the nation directly threatened to assume the primary responsibility of providing the manpower for its defense'.

This was the solution to Nixon's dilemma of how to end America's involvement in the war, without an American defeat. Yet there was a contradiction in this policy: American troops were to be withdrawn, while the war was escalated. Nixon intended to secure 'Peace with Honour' through Vietnamisation, increased use of American strategic bombers and peace negotiations.

America's strategy to withdraw its troops rested on modernising South Vietnam's military forces and assigning them responsibility for running the war. This strategy was similar to Navarre's unsuccessful plans of 1953–1954. Vietnamisation of the war had been a common theme of French and American policy. However, in 1969, Nixon had little choice. He had to withdraw American troops and leave the South Vietnamese to fight the war without relying on direct American military support. However, despite huge shipments of materiel to the South Vietnamese and despite enemy weaknesses after the 1968 Tet Offensive, few people in Washington believed South Vietnam could stand alone. Nixon and Kissinger wanted to reduce American troop levels to 470,000 personnel by the end of 1969. To compensate for the reduction in the numbers of US troops, Nixon proposed to increase the use of air strikes.

# Widening the War

Abrams made increasing use of the B-52 bombers. Critics ridiculed it as 'swatting flies with a sledgehammer'. Widening the war had been one of the strategic alternatives some Americans had been pressing for some years. Since 1965, US military commanders had argued for an invasion of Laos and Cambodia, attacks across the DMZ into North Vietnam and the mining of Haiphong Harbour. In March 1969, Nixon authorised 'Operation Menu', which saw the United States launch secret B-52 raids over Cambodia. This was part of Nixon's plan to use American power to force North Vietnam to the negotiating table. He wanted to send a clear message to the North Vietnamese leaders that he could escalate the war. The bombing of Laos was also increased. The United States and South Vietnam did not have the troops to intervene directly in Laos, but they could help the Royal Laotian forces by bombing Pathet Lao and PAVN forces on the Plain of Jars.

# Kissinger's Negotiations in Paris

Kissinger began meeting secretly with Le Duc Tho, the head of the North Vietnamese delegation, on 21 February 1970. Tho could not be convinced to change the North Vietnamese demands that Nixon withdraw all American troops from Vietnam, that Thieu and Ky be removed from power, and that South Vietnamese communists, the Provisional Revolutionary Government (PRG), be allowed to participate in the government of South Vietnam. Thieu was equally stubborn. He would not talk to representatives of the PRG.

**PERSONALITY**

**Henry Kissinger**

Henry Kissinger was born in Germany in 1923. Confronting the extreme anti-Semitism of the Nazi regime he fled to the United States in 1938. During World War II, he was drafted into the Army, where he served as a translator in Intelligence units. After the war he earned a PhD from Harvard University, with a thesis on international relations in early 19th-century Europe. Kissinger worked in the Government Department at Harvard until 1967 when he undertook a diplomatic assignment from Lyndon Johnson, seeking to negotiate a ceasefire with North Vietnam. That attempt failed, but Kissinger remained a prominent figure in Washington.

During the presidential election campaign of 1968 Nixon sought Kissinger's advice on national security issues. After Nixon's victory in the November election, he appointed Kissinger to the post of National Security Advisor.

Kissinger was credited with a number of foreign policy successes. As National Security Advisor until 1973, he was instrumental in forging new US relationships with China and Russia. Kissinger also received considerable credit for forging the 1973 agreement that led to the United States withdrawal from Vietnam. For their role in brokering that agreement Kissinger and Le Duc Tho were awarded the 1973 Nobel Peace Prize.

In 1973 Kissinger was appointed Secretary of State, a position he retained after Nixon's resignation in August 1974. Kissinger was famous for his 'shuttle diplomacy': he would step in, sometimes with great fanfare, to resolve international crises. He stepped down as Secretary of State in early 1977 but remained a public and controversial figure. 'I don't see why,' Kissinger once remarked, 'we need to stand by and watch a country go communist, due to the irresponsibility of its people'.

Kissinger believed he was negotiating from a weak position. As long as American troop withdrawals proceeded, North Vietnam had little reason to compromise. Kissinger wanted to force North Vietnam into serious negotiations. To do this he proposed to reduce or slow the troop withdrawals, renew the massive strategic bombing of North Vietnam and even consider an invasion of North Vietnam. However, both Nixon and Kissinger knew Congress opposed any expansion of the war. At the same time, Kissinger, like other Americans before him, believed US power could prevail over North Vietnam. He stated in 1969: 'I refuse to believe that a little fourth-rate power like North Vietnam does not have a breaking point.'

Hanoi had already resolved to step up the war. In January 1970 Hanoi decided to support Pathet Lao guerrillas with North Vietnamese regular troops to drive the CIA-financed Hmong–Lao–Thai troops away from the Ho Chi Minh Trail inside Laos. The attack in February drove the Hmong–Lao–Thai forces westward and off the Plain of Jars. The North's supply line to the South was secured. This North Vietnamese military action forced a response from Nixon. The Joint Chiefs had been pressing the administration for military action in Cambodia and Laos. Johnson had refused because he did not want to widen the war. It now appealed to Nixon as a way of making South Vietnam more secure, if only temporarily, so the USA could proceed to withdraw more troops. Nixon had previously denied American air raids on Cambodia and Laos, but on 6 March 1970 he stated there were no American forces inside Laos and there were no plans to send forces there. Two days later Captain John Bush of the US Army was killed 16 kilometres inside Laos.

During April and May 1970 the United States, and its South Vietnamese allies, moved against Communist forces inside Cambodia. (This topic is detailed in Chapter 12.) The US invasion of Cambodia was of dubious military value and led increasing numbers of Americans to see the Indochina war as Nixon's war.

Nixon had to accelerate the withdrawal of troops. At the end of 1970, Abrams had 335,000 troops under his command. However, North Vietnam was using the Ho Chi Minh Trail to expand its forces in the South. Abrams wanted to invade Laos and cut the Trail. Nixon agreed. On 8 February 1971, the South Vietnamese invasion ('Lam Son 719') began. The objective was to cut the Ho Chi Minh Trail. ARVN troops took Tchepone on 6 March, then withdrew on 9 March. Confronting strong and determined North Vietnamese forces, the ARVN took two weeks to withdraw. Nixon claimed Vietnamisation was succeeding. But the Pentagon's assessment was that it was failing. The PAVN had successfully defended the Ho Chi Minh Trial against a strong ARVN offensive.

*ARVN troops move into Laos, February 1971*

Globally, the Vietnam War impeded Kissinger's grand plan for improving superpower relations. Kissinger, confident that he understood the realities of international relations, believed that improving US relations with both China and the USSR could play a role in ending the conflict in Vietnam. The Chinese had become more afraid of the Soviets than the United States. With a Soviet force deployed along China's northern border and with increasing numbers of North Vietnamese forces deployed along China's southern border, China was prepared to talk to Kissinger. During 1971 Kissinger met secretly with Chinese representatives. Improved American–Chinese relations would change the negotiating position of the Soviets in any negotiations about arms limitations. Kissinger named this new form of realistic international relations 'détente' (a French word meaning release from tension). He planned summit meetings in Beijing and Moscow during 1971 and 1972.

If the United States left Vietnam without 'honour' it would lose international credibility. But Nixon and Kissinger needed a settlement of the Vietnamese War for détente to have any hope of success. Nixon was anxious to force North Vietnam to an agreement in Paris. His only military option was bombing. 'Unless they deal with us,' he told Kissinger in late 1971, 'I'm going to bomb the hell out of them'. Nixon was about to play his 'madman' card.

## HISTORICAL ISSUE

### Richard Nixon, Vietnam and the 'Madman' Theory

Nixon confronted several imperatives in seeking 'peace with honour' in Vietnam.

1  It was increasingly clear the United States could not force a victory on the battlefield.
2  If he was to be re-elected in 1972, he had to withdraw American troops.
3  He could not afford to be seen to 'lose' the conflict: this would damage his own political credibility, as well as American credibility around the world.
4  South Vietnam was likely to denounce any agreement it believed enhanced the position of North Vietnam or the NLF.

In seeking a negotiated solution, Nixon enjoyed several advantages over his predecessors. Nixon was less likely to be criticised by right-wing 'hawks' within the United States: given his staunch anti-communist record, it would be difficult to describe him as being 'soft' on communists.

A second factor working to Nixon's advantage was his willingness to be described as a 'madman'. If the North Vietnamese were led to believe he would go to any lengths to end the war (including the use of atomic weapons), they would be more likely to negotiate an end to the conflict. During the peace talks Nixon allowed, and even encouraged, Kissinger to suggest to North Vietnamese negotiators that he (Nixon) was irrational and prepared to do anything to achieve his objectives in Vietnam. Kissinger was, thus, to appear the reasonable, restraining influence on the 'madman' Nixon.

North Vietnam was keen to test out the 'madman' in Washington. Concerned about the improving relations between China and America, North Vietnam decided to attack in order to force the Americans to end the war from a position of defeat. The United States had been expecting an attack, but could not predict its precise timing.

# North Vietnam's Easter Offensive, 1972

North Vietnam's offensive began on Good Friday, 30 March 1972. The remaining American military force of 95,000 included only 6,000 combat troops. Over 200,000 PLAF/PAVN forces launched a three-pronged attack. In the north, the DMZ was crossed and Quang Tri City assaulted. A second attack from the Central Highlands cut the main highway to Saigon, while a third assault threatened Saigon. If the Easter Offensive achieved only partial success it would threaten Kissinger's bargaining position with North Vietnam. The only way for the United States to support the embattled ARVN was by heavy bombing. On 6 April 'Operation Linebacker' commenced. This was the first heavy bombing of North Vietnam since 1969. The raids were initially limited to targets within 100 kilometres of the DMZ, but on 10 April the B-52s were authorised to attack targets close to Hanoi and Haiphong.

*One of the most enduring images of the war: On 9 June 1972, nine-year-old Phan Thi Kim Phuc flees the village of South Vietnamese village of Trang Bang, after being napalmed by the South Vietnamese Air Force*

During early May, the initial North Vietnamese military successes influenced the Paris peace talks. North Vietnam's negotiator, Le Duc Tho, would not allow any movement in the negotiations. He believed military victory was close. PAVN forces had taken Quang Tri City and Loc Ninh. An Loc and Hue were also threatened and an attack towards Saigon appeared imminent. Nixon was furious. He suspended the Paris peace talks and decided to put more military pressure on North Vietnam. The US Navy mined the North Vietnamese ports of Haiphong, Cam Pha, Hon Gai, Thanh Hoa and blockaded the coast. Over 100 B-52s were deployed. In March the United States flew approximately 700 sorties. This increased to 2,200 sorties by the end of May. By the end of June, PAVN forces began to withdraw from An Loc and an ARVN counterattack recaptured Quang Tri City. Having suffered over 100,000 casualties, North Vietnam could not consider a major offensive for at least three years.

The military defeat was humiliating for Vo Nguyen Giap. He had also been diagnosed with cancer. Pham Van Dong decided to replace Giap with General Van Tien Dung, the Army's Chief of Staff and a close associate of Giap's. When Dung gained control of the PAVN he faced a daunting political and military situation. The last American combat troops had left on 23 August 1972. However, with 1.1 million troops, the lavishly equipped ARVN was now the fourth-largest army in the world. South Vietnam's Navy, with 1,500 ships, was the fifth-largest in the world and with 2,000 aircraft the South Vietnamese Air Force was the fourth-largest in the world. The North Vietnamese had been hoping that the political situation in America would assist them. But the 1972 election did not unfold as they predicted. The Democrats' presidential campaign collapsed; Nixon would be re-elected.

With limited military and political options, North Vietnam concluded that a negotiated settlement to the war was the only realistic option. Dung wanted to re-open the talks, which would end 'Linebacker' and give him time to re-build the PAVN for a final assault on South Vietnam.

# Negotiations Recommence

In August 1972, Kissinger resumed talks with North Vietnam. Both sides wanted a settlement. North Vietnam wanted the 'Linebacker' raids to end; Nixon wanted a peace treaty before November to seal his re-election. In September, Kissinger agreed to the withdrawal of all American troops. In a major concession, Kissinger agreed to allow all PAVN soldiers to remain in South Vietnam, while North Vietnam dropped its demand that Thieu resign. At the end of September the basis of a deal was reached. In essence both sides agreed to a mutual ceasefire, the complete withdrawal of American troops, an end to American bombing and an exchange of prisoners of war. All PLAF, PAVN and ARVN forces were to remain in place, and both the PRG and Thieu's government were recognised as legal political entities in the South. A 'Council of National Reconciliation' was established to resolve outstanding issues.

The US State Department and the National Security Council expressed some reservations about the agreement. Kissinger, however, was more concerned about opposition from South Vietnam. Thieu saw the agreement as a sell-out. He wanted the withdrawal of all PAVN troops from South Vietnam, the recognition of the DMZ as an international border and no recognition of the PRG. However, Nixon and Kissinger were in no mood to make concessions to the South, when a treaty was so close – and when an election was looming. On 22 October the United States reduced the 'Linebacker' raids. On 26 October, after more negotiations and just over a week before the US Presidential election, Kissinger announced 'we believe peace is at hand'.

Nixon's landslide victory on 7 November gave him the mandate to put pressure on North Vietnam. North Vietnam was presented with 69 proposed changes in the treaty, all concessions to Thieu. North Vietnam countered with proposed changes of its own. Nixon then promised Thieu that if the North broke the treaty the United States would 'take swift and severe retaliatory action'. Pham Van Dong saw the division between the United States and South Vietnam as an opportunity to rebuild his military and logistical infra-structure. On 13 December Le Duc Tho suspended negotiations.

Nixon did not tolerate this delay. He wanted a peace treaty before his inauguration on 20 January 1973. He threatened the North with 'consequences' if they did not resume negotiations within 72 hours. On 18 December 'Operation Linebacker II' commenced. It was the one of the heaviest aerial assaults of the war. Over 11 days, 2,000 sorties were launched.

In January 1973 Le Duc Tho decided to resume talks. Now, the only obstacle the Americans had to a peace treaty was the South Vietnamese. In a secret 5 January message to Thieu, Nixon stated that the Americans intended to sign a treaty with or without them. Thieu had no place to manoeuvre. On 15 January Nixon halted all military action against North Vietnam.

## HISTORICAL ISSUE

### The Christmas Bombings

The massive US bombing of North Vietnam during December 1972 to January 1973 provoked outrage, both within the United States and internationally. Using huge B-52 bombers, the US Air Force concentrated its attacks on Hanoi and Haiphong, causing havoc and killing over 1,700 people. Hanoi and Haiphong were well defended by Soviet-supplied surface-to-air missile systems and North Vietnamese fighter aircraft and took out 15 B-52s; 92 American pilots and crew-members were killed or captured.

Defenders of the bombing claimed it drove North Vietnam back to the bargaining table. But the bombing caused only a temporary disruption to the North's ability to wage war. And the agreement reached in January 1973 was not substantially different from that which had been agreed upon three months earlier. The bombing was a public-relations nightmare for the United States. Senator Edward Kennedy, younger brother of John and Robert Kennedy, said the raids should 'outrage the conscience of all Americans'. Swedish Prime Minister Olaf Palme compared the bombing campaign to Nazi atrocities. Within the US Congress, critics made it clear they would cut off the funds Nixon needed to wage war. Opinion polls revealed the bombing had cut Nixon's approval rating to just 39%, the lowest rating of his presidency up to that time.

In Paris on 27 January 1973, all four parties – the United States, North Vietnam, South Vietnam and the PRG – signed the peace treaty.

The treaty came just in time for Nixon. In January, Congress voted to cut all funds for military operations in Indochina. Many in the new Congress wanted to end American involvement in the region. Political support for the war had evaporated. Nixon announced that all American troops would be out of South Vietnam within 60 days and US prisoners of war would return home.

## PERSONALITY

### Le Duc Tho

Le Duc Tho was born in 1911 in Phan Dinh Khai (Nam Ha Province). An advocate of Vietnamese nationalism, Tho was one of the founders of the Indochinese Communist Party in 1930.

The French authorities were alert to Tho's political activities and he was twice imprisoned. In 1945 he joined the Viet Minh. He was the senior Viet Minh official in southern Vietnam and during the 1960s he supervised much of the war effort from secret jungle bases.

From 1968–1973, Tho was North Vietnam's principal negotiator at the Paris peace talks. Tho refused to be intimidated by American threats and continued to insist upon a US withdrawal from Vietnam and Thieu's resignation. When an agreement was eventually reached, Tho and his negotiators had largely achieved their objectives. For his part in reaching the agreement with the United States, Tho shared the Nobel Peace Prize with Kissinger, but declined the award. Tho returned to southern Vietnam, where he worked alongside Van Tien Dung in organising the 1975 offensive that led to the fall of the South Vietnamese Government. Tho later oversaw Vietnam's invasion of Cambodia. He resigned from the Politburo in 1986 and died in 1990.

In the treaty America agreed to withdraw its remaining 24,000 military personnel. In return, all American prisoners of war would be released. To monitor the ceasefire, a four-nation International Commission of Control and Supervision was established. To support the ceasefire, all foreign military activity in Laos and Cambodia would cease. To prop up South Vietnam, America promised economic aid and military supplies. As a compromise to North Vietnamese designs to forge a united Vietnam, a 'Council of National Reconciliation and Concord' was established to resolve outstanding political issues and organise elections in South Vietnam. By the end of March all American POWs had returned home. A ceasefire was also arranged for Laos. Although a peace treaty had been signed and although the United States was able to withdraw its forces from Indochina, there were no real guarantees of South Vietnam's survival. Indeed, Kissinger expressed grave doubts about the long-term viability of South Vietnam: at best the United States had secured a 'decent interval' between its departure from Vietnam and the eventual, anticipated collapse of the Saigon regime.

## HISTORICAL ISSUE

### The POWs and MIA: Where Are They?

One of the most contentious aspects of America's tormented intervention in Vietnam has been the fate of those men who were captured by the PAVN and PLAF – and the 2,273 who were listed as 'missing in action' (MIA).

In March 1973, in accordance with the Paris agreement, 591 American POWs were released by North Vietnam. The Nixon Administration claimed all the prisoners had been returned. But many Americans were not convinced and argued that North Vietnam continued to imprison hundreds or even thousands of Americans. In 1975–1976 a Select Committee of the US House of Representatives concluded that 'no Americans are still being held alive as prisoners in Indochina'.

Yet the issue would not go away. Continued reports of 'live sightings' of Americans in camps deep in the North Vietnam and Laotian jungles encouraged an American public that remained deeply suspicious of both its own government and the Vietnamese. By the 1980s it had become a major issue in American political and cultural life and a major obstacle to the normalisation of relations between the two nations (which was further exasperated by the 1985 film *Rambo*, where a soldier returns to Vietnam to uncover government-forgotten POWs). Polls were reporting that 70% of Americans believed the US Government had left POWs behind in Vietnam and that they were still captives.

In 1995 Bill Clinton granted formal recognition to Vietnam. US and Vietnamese investigators began the laborious and difficult task of collaborating to ascertain the fate of those Americans who were still MIA. It should not be forgotten that tens of thousands of Vietnamese soldiers also went missing. Most of their bodies will never be recovered.

Nixon had solved his Vietnam problem. But during 1973 he was confronting other, equally pressing, problems. The Watergate controversy engulfed the administration, reducing its effectiveness and control over policy. The televised hearings connected the scandal to Vietnam and to Nixon's illegal actions against the antiwar movement. Congress was linked in its support of an appropriation bill to the end of the bombing in Cambodia. Then Congress passed legislation ending all American combat activities in Indochina by 15 August 1973. In July, Congress began debating a joint resolution requiring the president to advise the Congress within 48 hours of the commitment of US troops to a foreign conflict or a substantial increase in American combat troops in a foreign country. In October, Congress passed the War Powers Resolution. Nixon vetoed the legislation, but Congress overrode his veto and the resolution became law.

---

**HISTORICAL ISSUE**

*Richard Nixon, Vietnam and the Watergate Controversy*

The origins of the Watergate crisis began in June 1971 when the Pentagon Papers, official government and bureaucracy files tracing the history of US intervention in Vietnam from 1945–1968, were leaked to the press and published in the *New York Times*.

Although they did not incriminate Nixon he was outraged as they energised the antiwar movement and compounded his paranoia about government secrecy. The Nixon Administration established a clandestine group known as 'the plumbers', who were ordered to gain information on antiwar activists and political adversaries. In June 1972 there was a break-in at the office of the Democratic Party's National Committee Headquarters, based in the Watergate building in Washington, DC. There were connections between the men caught breaking in to the Watergate building and the Nixon Administration.

Although some Americans believed Nixon was 'just unlucky' to be caught doing what his predecessors had probably also done, the significant point is that because he was caught, during 1973 and early 1974 he was forced to try and cover up his own involvement: it was the cover up as much as the crime that led to Nixon's undoing. Having declared he had 'never been a quitter', that is precisely what Nixon was forced to do in August 1974.

There was a profound irony about the 1972 break-in at the Watergate: it was motivated by a desire to gain political advantage over the Democrats in the November elections. But Nixon had won the 1972 election by a landslide.

---

# Continuing Conflict in Indochina

The collapse of US political support for the Indochinese conflict coincided with the breakdown of the peace agreement. North Vietnam began infiltrating large numbers of troops and supplies into Cambodia. In late 1973, Thieu launched attacks on communists. Canada withdrew from the International Commission of Control and Supervision and was replaced by Iran. In effect, the commission was dead. In Cambodia, the Khmer Rouge was close to victory and by 1974 the Pathet Lao controlled most of northern Laos.

Yet North Vietnam was cautious about launching another offensive in South Vietnam. It feared Nixon would launch air strikes with the same intensity that had destroyed the Easter offensive. North Vietnam's leaders paid close attention to the mood of the US Congress, which in 1974 reduced aid to Vietnam to $1.1 billion, a vast decrease from the $3.2 billion allocated in 1973.

South Vietnam's economic woes further eroded support for Thieu. The peasantry remained alienated from Thieu's government, which remained more totalitarian than democratic. In effect Thieu ruled a single-party authoritarian state.

South Vietnam's political and economic problems enticed North Vietnam to plan an offensive. North Vietnam was also encouraged because political problems in the United States suggested the Americans may not be prepared to save South Vietnam. But North Vietnam decided to move slowly and cautiously. By 1974, although General Van Tien Dung had 22 infantry divisions in South Vietnam, he estimated an offensive could take years to succeed, particularly if the United States launched air strikes. Dung decided to attack Phuoc Long province, near the Cambodian border – and at one point only 65 kilometres from Saigon. The attack yielded two valuable pieces of information: the fighting capacity of the ARVN and the extent of US military intervention.

# North Vietnamese Offensive, 1974–1975

The attack began on 26 December 1974. PAVN troops moved on Phuoc Long. Thieu sent only one ARVN battalion to defend the city. Significantly, American aircraft did not appear. This encouraged the North to step up the offensive. To cut Vietnam in half, a major attack moved from the Central Highlands to the South China Sea. On 9 March 1975, PAVN forces attacked Ban Me Thuot, which fell on 12 March. Again, there were no American air strikes.

Following the fall of Ban Me Thuot, Thieu ignored his military advisers and redeployed South Vietnamese forces. The resulting enclave strategy was designed to protect the major cities, by concentrating ARVN troops in these areas. As a result the Central Highlands were evacuated. On 14 March PAVN troops attacked along Route 14 towards Pleiku and Kontum. The North Vietnamese encountered hundreds of thousands of civilians and thousands of ARVN troops fleeing the Central Highlands. PAVN artillery inflicted heavy losses, killing over 100,000 civilians and 15,000 ARVN troops.

Events in Cambodia and Laos looked equally troubling to the Americans.

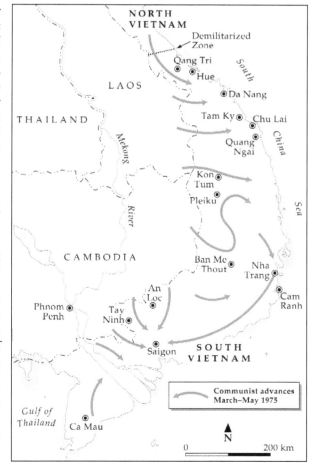

*The North Vietnamese advance, 1975*

## HISTORICAL ISSUE

### Chaos in Saigon: The Last Days of the Republic of Vietnam

During March and April 1975 Saigon was a city living on the edge. With the population growing as hundreds of thousands of refugees fled the advancing communist forces, residents knew they were living on borrowed time. Some Vietnamese hoped the United States would return. But after the US Congress denied President Ford's 10 April request for additional funds for South Vietnam, the end was nigh. Vietnamese who had collaborated with the Americans watched with growing alarm as the United States evacuated its citizens: while thousands of Vietnamese were also evacuated, tens of thousands who had served the United States for many years were abandoned to the conquering North Vietnamese. The inglorious spectacle of American helicopters taking off from the roof of the US Embassy, as anguished Vietnamese realised they would not be evacuated, became a stark symbol of the American defeat in Vietnam.

## DOCUMENTARY EXERCISE

### DID AMERICA SELL OUT SOUTH VIETNAM?

In the years following the 'fall' of Saigon, Americans and South Vietnamese have blamed each other for the debacle of early 1975. One line of argument suggests that if the US Congress had honoured the agreements signed in 1973, and continued to supply and support the South Vietnamese, the ARVN could have repelled the PAVN assault. Richard Nixon – who had plenty of reasons to criticise Congress – claimed Congress had 'betrayed' South Vietnam.

### NIXON BLAMES CONGRESS FOR THE FALL OF SOUTH VIETNAM

The war and the peace in Indochina that America had won at such cost over 12 years of sacrifice and fighting were lost within a matter of months once Congress refused to fulfil our obligation.

The American people could not be expected to continue indefinitely to support a war in which they were told victory was around the corner, but which required greater and greater effort without any obvious signs of improvement.

### Discussion Questions:

**1** Why did the US Congress refuse to increase aid to South Vietnam?

**2** Would additional US aid have ensured South Vietnam's survival?

**3** Was Nixon's criticism of the US Congress justified?

**4** Should a democratic government, in time of war, be expected to 'reveal all' to its people?

Having surrounded Phnom Penh, the Khmer Rouge was close to victory. In Laos, the Pathet Lao was advancing towards the capital, Vientiane.

In South Vietnam, the PAVN offensive gained momentum. Again surprising the South Vietnamese, Van Tien Dung attacked south from Quang Tri Province towards Hue. By the end of March Hue and Danang had fallen.

On 31 March 1975, Van Tien Dung was ordered to take Saigon. Dung moved 18 PAVN divisions towards Saigon. Thieu resigned on 21 April. He was replaced by long-term rival Duong Van Minh. On 26 April 1975, North Vietnam launched the 'Ho Chi Minh Campaign' and the remnants of the ARVN collapsed. President Ford launched 'Operation Frequent Wind', the evacuation by helicopter of 7,100 Americans and South Vietnamese from Saigon.

*An inglorious end: evacuations from the roof of the US Embassy, Saigon*

South Vietnam surrendered unconditionally on 29 April 1975. The planned two-year campaign had taken only 55 days to achieve victory. After three decades of war, the United States withdrawal enabled North Vietnam to once again try Phase Three of People's War. This time it succeeded.

*POINTS TO REMEMBER*
- By 1969 many Americans, including those serving in the armed forces, believed they could not win the war. This belief was reflected in the crisis in morale in the armed forces.
- Revelations about the My Lai massacre further eroded American support for the war.
- The Nixon Doctrine was based on the assumption that America could not win the war, but it could achieve a peaceful solution to the war.
- The failure of the North Vietnamese 1972 offensive helped to convince it to negotiate a treaty.
- A Peace Treaty was signed in 1973.
- The antiwar movement and the Watergate controversy weakened the Nixon administration. This affected the willingness of Nixon and Gerald Ford to continue to fight the war.
- In 1974–1975 North Vietnam was able to quickly defeat South Vietnam.

## ACTIVITIES

**1** Explain the significance of 'Hamburger Hill'.

**2** Why was there a crisis in morale amongst US troops during the later stages of American involvement in Vietnam? What evidence is there of this crisis in morale?

**3** What was the impact of the My Lai Massacre on American perceptions about the conduct of the war? Use the Internet to research sites and view pictures of the massacre.

**4** What were the implications of the 'Nixon (Guam) Doctrine' for American policy in Indochina?

**5** Describe Vietnamisation. What were the reasons behind it?

**6** How significant were the Pentagon Papers?

**7** Do you think America was justified in widening the war into Laos and Cambodia?

**8** Why was the United States unable to negotiate a peace treaty until 1973?

**9** How effective was Nixon's 'madman' strategy?

**10** What was the significance of the 'Easter Offensive'?

**11** What were the key points of the 1973 Paris Accords?

**12** How, after 30 years of war, was North Vietnam able to defeat South Vietnam so quickly following the US departure?

**13** Opposing Viewpoints: On the Internet, find and download President's Nixon's 3 November 1969 'Address to the Nation on the War in Vietnam' and Vietnam War Veteran John Kerry's Testimony to the Senate Foreign Relations Committee, 22 April 1971.
 **a** What did Nixon mean by the 'Silent Majority'?
 **b** What reason did Nixon give to support his argument that America could not withdraw from Vietnam?
 **c** What was Nixon's view on Vietnamisation? How did Kerry view this policy?
 **d** Did Kerry believe that American policy had been as successful in Vietnam as Nixon promised it would?
 **e** How did Nixon and Kerry differ about the necessity for fighting in Vietnam?

**14** Did the 1973 Peace Accords provide a realistic basis for long-term peace in Indochina? Was Nixon justified in describing the treaty as achieving 'peace with honour'? With reference to the document, write points for and against Nixon's statement.

**15** There have been two opposing views explaining the failure of the Paris Accords and the fall of South Vietnam.
 · One view, supported by Nixon and Kissinger, has argued that the United States won the war and that the US Congress lost the peace. By 1975 Congress had destroyed the ability of the United States to enforce the Paris Accords. Kissinger believed that Nixon 'would have bombed the hell out of them during April'.

- Others have contended that by 1973 American leaders were more concerned about American POWs and MIAs than the future of South Vietnam. Proponents of this view contend that America 'sold out' South Vietnam. Indeed, the only thing guaranteed in the Accords was the withdrawal of American troops. The issues that caused the conflict in Indochina were not resolved.

Which view do you think is the more creditable? Provide evidence to support your views.

## Sample HSC Exam Questions:

**1** Why did the Communists win in Vietnam in 1975?

**2** Why were there communist victories in Indochina in 1975? In your answer you may discuss EITHER Vietnam OR Cambodia OR both.

**3** To what extent were the Viet Cong responsible for the withdrawal of the United States from Vietnam and the eventual defeat of the South Vietnamese forces in the period 1968–1975?

**4** Assess the contribution of the media in determining the outcomes of war in Indochina from the overthrow of Diem to the withdrawal of US troops from Vietnam in 1975.

### FURTHER READING

Useful surveys of the period covered in this chapter include: George C. Herring's, *America's Longest War: The United States and Vietnam, 1950–1975*, 3rd ed. (McGraw Hill, New York, 1996) Chapter VII; Marilyn Young's *The Vietnam Wars, 1945–1990* (Harper Perennial, New York, 1991) Chapters 12–14; George Donelson Moss' *Vietnam: An American Ordeal*, 4th ed., (Prentice Hall, Upper Saddle River, NJ, 2002), Chapters 8 and 9; James S. Olson and Randy Roberts' *Where the Domino Fell: America and Vietnam, 1945–1990* (St. Martin's Press, New York, 1991), Chapters 9 and 10. Henry Kissinger's *White House Years* (Little, Brown, Boston, 1979) is predictably self-serving.

# PART 4

## CONFLICT IN CAMBODIA, 1954–1979

# 12

# Cambodia, 1954–1975: Descent into Turmoil

IN THIS CHAPTER YOU WILL:

- be introduced to Cambodia's history before and during the period of French colonisation
- learn about Cambodia's role in the Indochinese conflict
- learn about the overthrow of Norodom Sihanouk and the impact of American intervention in Cambodia
- explore the factors behind Khmer Rouge victory in the 1970–1975 civil war.

## Background

For most of the 1950s and 1960s Cambodia was spared much of the violence that devastated neighbouring Vietnam. By the late 1960s, however, even the nimble leadership of Norodom Sihanouk could not prevent Cambodia being drawn into the Vietnam War. All protagonists in the Vietnamese conflict abused Cambodian neutrality. From early 1970, Cambodia was beset by a brutal civil war, which led in April 1975 to the installation of the murderous Khmer Rouge (KR) regime.

## Cambodia and the French Empire

For much of its history, Cambodia's fortunes have been shaped by its more powerful neighbours: Siam (Thailand) to the west and Vietnam to the east. From the 8th century CE until the 15th century the Cambodian Kingdom of Angkor was a dominant power in the region. Heavily influenced by Indian culture and religion, this was the 'golden age' of Khmer history. Between the 9th and 12th centuries, the massive complex of Hindu temples, known as Angkor Wat, was constructed. In 1434, the Thai kingdom of Ayudhya attacked the Khmer Kingdom, beginning a conflict that continued until the late 16th century. During this period Spain and Portugal took an often-unwelcome interest in Khmer affairs: in 1599 a Spanish contingent in Phnom Penh was massacred. From 1600 until the mid-19th century, Cambodia was ruled by a succession of weak kings.

In 1863, as France sought to expand and consolidate its emerging Indochinese empire, Cambodia's King Norodom signed a treaty, making Cambodia a French protectorate. Despite their contempt for much of Khmer culture and history, the French were interested in Cambodia: they considered the Mekong River, which ran through Cambodia, as a possible 'road' to China; and they were alarmed by Vietnamese rebels and bandits, who, after harassing French officials and merchants, sought sanctuary in Cambodia.

In 1884, France forced King Norodom to sign another treaty, effectively turning Cambodia into a French colony. In 1887 Cambodia formally became part of the Union of Indochina. Many Khmers resented the French presence. During the late-19th and early-20th centuries, France contended with Khmer resistance. Much of that opposition was unorganised and sporadic, but in 1916 a peasant uprising signalled the emergence of more systematic resistance. There was some Cambodian representation in the Indochinese Communist Party, established in 1930, and by the late 1930s Cambodian nationalism had become a serious concern to France.

## HISTORICAL ISSUE

### Cambodia, the Khmer Republic and Kampuchea

Since 1955 Cambodia has been known by a number of different names:
- 1955–1970: (The Kingdom of) Cambodia
- 1970 – April 1975: The Khmer Republic
- April 1975 – January 1979: Democratic Kampuchea (DK)
- January 1979 – May 1989: People's Republic of Kampuchea (PRK)
- 1989 – present: Kingdom of Cambodia

# Norodom Sihanouk's Cambodia: An Oasis of Peace?

During World War II, Japan occupied Cambodia, but left the Vichy French in nominal control. In 1941, France installed 19-year-old Prince Norodom Sihanouk as King. They hoped his youthfulness would make him compliant to their wishes. They were wrong. The young Sihanouk was an avid nationalist, who understood the nuances of Cambodian political life and who knew that Cambodia's geographical location required it to walk a fine line on the international stage.

Despite his popularity, despite the appearance of inclusiveness in political life and despite the nation's relative prosperity, Sihanouk's rule was less than democratic. Inevitably, there was political opposition: so long as this remained unorganised, there were few challenges to his government. From the mid-1960s, however, Sihanouk confronted growing opposition, which reflected dissatisfaction with his foreign, as well as domestic, policies. Sihanouk faced challenges from two sides.

1   From the 'right', elements of the Cambodian military became increasingly disenchanted with Sihanouk.
2   From the 'left', a communist guerrilla group, the Khmer Rouge ('Red Khmer') sought to overthrow Sihanouk.

**PERSONALITY**

**Norodom Sihanouk**

Norodom Sihanouk was born on 31 October 1922, the son of King Norodom Suramarit. Sihanouk was an influential, sometimes dominant figure in Cambodian political life and was long admired and respected by a majority of Cambodians.

When Japan overthrew the Vichy French regime in March 1945, France informed Sihanouk that Cambodia was independent. Two days later, on 12 March, Sihanouk declared independence himself. When the French returned, they sought to reduce Sihanouk's influence, but that proved impossible, as he identified himself with the nationalist cause. The 1954 Geneva Conference proclaimed Cambodian independence as a neutral nation and called for free elections. Sihanouk responded by abdicating as King to pursue a political career. He established his own political party, which advocated 'Nation, Buddhism, and Monarchy'. Sihanouk enjoyed great popularity amongst the peasantry and in March 1955 was elected Prime Minister. A ladies' man, with a penchant for filmmaking, he was known as an eccentric leader.

In 1960, after the death of his father, King Norodom Suramarit, Sihanouk again became Head of State. For most of the 1950s, until the late 1960s, Sihanouk's popularity ensured there was relatively little organised resistance to his regime – a stark contrast to governments in South Vietnam.

**HISTORICAL ISSUE**

*The Origins of the Khmer Rouge*

The Khmer Rouge (variously known as the Communist Party of Kampuchea or CPK; or the Khmer People's Revolutionary Party or KPRP) was established in 1951. The KR emerged from the anti-French nationalist movement and was connected to the Viet Minh. The early KR leadership was moderate, rural-based and Buddhist-educated. During the late 1950s and early 1960s, however, younger, urban-based and Paris-educated radicals, many of whom harboured strong resentment toward the Vietnamese, took control of the KR. For much of the 1960s the KR remained an almost-insignificant threat to Sihanouk's rule. That changed dramatically during the late 1960s; after Sihanouk's fall, the KR (which entered an alliance with the deposed Sihanouk) fought against Lon Nol's government.

# Cambodia, the United States and the Vietnam War

The United States took a keen interest in Cambodia. Cambodia was both a potential 'domino' (susceptible to communism) and a potential refuge for Vietnamese communists. Consequently, although Cambodia was officially neutral and Sihanouk sought to maintain friendly relations with China, the USSR and North Vietnam, the United States wanted to ensure Cambodia did not gravitate toward communism. During the 1950s and 1960s, the United States supplied military equipment to Cambodia, and some Cambodian politicians and officers supported the US in the conflict in Vietnam. This alarmed sections of the Cambodian population and exposed Sihanouk to the charge that he had abandoned neutrality and aligned his nation to the United States.

Ever the pragmatist, in 1965 Sihanouk denounced 'US imperialism', broke diplomatic relations with the United States and refused to accept any further American aid. As the war in Vietnam intensified, Sihanouk allowed the PAVN and PLAF to establish bases on the Cambodian side of the border. This frustrated the United States. Keen to eliminate the PAVN/PLAF presence in Cambodia and slow the supply of men and material being channelled into Cambodia from the Ho Chi Minh Trail (which extended into Cambodia), Westmoreland requested permission to launch air strikes into Cambodia and, if necessary, send ground troops across the border in pursuit of enemy forces. Johnson consistently denied Westmoreland's requests, although in May 1967 permission was granted for small teams of US Special Forces to cross into Cambodia. The primary purpose of these missions was intelligence gathering: in 1,835 missions, however, they captured just 24 prisoners.

Sihanouk's government knew of these incursions, but was prepared to tolerate small-scale violations of its neutrality by the United States. Moreover, it was difficult to denounce US violations of Cambodian neutrality when the PAVN/PLAF were engaging in much more significant activities. Sihanouk even allowed the port of Sihanoukville to be used to ship supplies to the PLAF. He hoped that if the DRV/NLF did win in South Vietnam, they would keep their promise to respect Cambodia's borders. Sihanouk also hoped that if he turned a blind eye to the activities of the PAVN and PLAF, they would not encourage or support the Khmer Rouge.

# The Khmer Rouge

There was some ground for Sihanouk's fears of a possible alliance between the Khmer Rouge and Vietnamese communists. The KR commitment to communism meant they had much in common with the DRV and the NLF. Some KR leaders, moreover, had been involved with the North Vietnamese and NLF leadership in the Indochinese Communist Party. Also there were contacts, and some instances of cooperation, between the KR leadership and PAVN/PLAF commanders. There were also differences between KR and DRV/NLF:

1   Cambodia has been linguistically influenced by India, whilst Vietnam has been shaped by Chinese influences.
2   Cambodia and Vietnam were not always allies, Cambodia controlled much of Southern Vietnam after Angkor domination, and the relationship between them had often been tense.
3   Reflecting those tensions, many nationalistic KR leaders were suspicious of DRV and NLF.

During the late 1950s and early 1960s the KR insurgency was a nuisance, rather than a significant threat to Sihanouk's government. Certainly the KR was unable to muster the same degree of support as the NLF in

South Vietnam. Nevertheless, despite Sihanouk's continuing popularity, during the late 1960s, the KR gathered force. In part, the Khmer Rouge was driven by left-wing politicians who became alienated from Sihanouk's government: some slipped into the forests to fight in the guerrilla war against the government; others found refuge in Paris. But the KR rebellion was also fuelled by Sihanouk's increasingly erratic politics. Widespread accusations of corruption contributed to a growing sense that Sihanouk was losing touch with Cambodians' day-to-day concerns.

## Sihanouk's Dilemma: Preserving Cambodian Neutrality

Sihanouk's government was also compromised by his willingness to tolerate PAVN/PLAF activities inside Cambodia. As the war in Vietnam escalated during 1966 and 1967, PAVN/PLAF activities inside Cambodia increased and tensions between Vietnamese and Cambodians living close to the border grew. Sihanouk's army, despite having received significant quantities of US aid during the early 1960s, was small and ineffective.

Troubled by increasing PAVN/PLAF activity within Cambodia, Sihanouk again demonstrated his pragmatism, by reversing direction again and improving relations with the United States. However, tiring of political life and losing interest in day-to-day administration, he appointed General Lon Nol as Prime Minister. Lon Nol had long called for closer relations with the United States. His crackdowns on a peasants' revolt and on urban dissent prompted a number of left-wingers to join the communist rebels in the countryside. Among them was Khieu Sampham, who became a key figure in the Khmer Rouge.

Sihanouk understood well that Cambodian foreign policy required a careful balancing act. The extent to which he could preserve Cambodian neutrality depended on his ability to maintain friendly relations with the United States, North Vietnam and the Provisional Revolutionary Government in South Vietnam: Cambodia was of little significance to those players however, beyond the role it could play in relation to Vietnam.

## 1969: US Bombing and Sihanouk's Deteriorating Position

Sihanouk's decision to elevate Lon Nol to the position of Prime Minister did not satisfy the demands of those Cambodians who believed the nation's security required a closer relationship with the United States. This group was driven by an opposition to communism and by a fear that a powerful, united Vietnam would inevitably threaten Cambodia. By early 1969 there was an estimated 40,000 PAVN/PLAF troops inside Cambodia. After Lon Nol became Prime Minister, those Cambodians dissatisfied with Sihanouk's government became increasingly confident. Sihanouk was apparently unaware of the crisis confronting Cambodia.

In March 1969 the United States began bombing Cambodia in order to slow the movement of communist supplies through Cambodia into Vietnam and strike at the PAVN/PLAF sanctuaries. The US Commander General Abrams believed he had intelligence locating the communists' Central Office of South Vietnam (COSVN), eight kilometres inside the Cambodian border. US intelligence also identified supply dumps and staging areas across the border. Henry Kissinger subsequently claimed that in 1968 Sihanouk had approved US plans to bomb Cambodia when the American Ambassador to India, Chester Bowles, had visited Phnom Penh. Sihanouk denied that claim.

Part of a Cambodian task force attempting to clear Route 7 east of Skoun watches as American air support bombs communist positions nearby

The US bombing campaign was entitled 'Menu'. It was followed by 'Breakfast', 'Lunch', 'Snack' and 'Dinner'. Those benign phrases masked a brutal campaign, which saw 100,000 tonnes of bombs dropped over Cambodia during a 14-month period. Nixon and Kissinger hoped to keep the bombing secret, from both the US Congress and the American public. To further ensure secrecy, the B-52s that flew from the Pacific Island of Guam had their flight logs falsified to suggest they had attacked targets in Vietnam.

However, the American press heard rumours about the raids and on 9 May the *New York Times* broke the story. The ensuing publicity enraged Nixon. He took the unusual step of ordering illegal wiretaps on the telephones of journalists and anyone else who came under his suspicion.

The US bombing of eastern Cambodia:
1   Had a serious impact on the production of rice in the area, straining the nation's economy.
2   Caused further political dislocation in Cambodia. The Army wanted to evict the PAVN/PLAF from Cambodia, but the American bombing also encouraged the growth of the Khmer Rouge, as growing numbers of disaffected Cambodians joined the KR.
3   Drove the Vietnamese communists further into Cambodia, in an effort to find sanctuary from the American bombers. This further angered those Cambodians who were determined to evict the Vietnamese.

Despite the obvious damage caused by the US bombing, in June 1969, Sihanouk formally restored diplomatic relations with Washington. The United States restored military and civilian aid and hoped the Cambodian army could limit PAVN/PLAF use of Cambodian territory as a sanctuary and transport route.

Yet even as Sihanouk improved relations with the United States, he continued in his efforts to balance Cambodia between the United States and North Vietnam. He maintained relations with the DRV and, in September 1969, attended Ho Chi Minh's funeral in Hanoi.

# The Overthrow of Sihanouk and the Rise of Lon Nol

Sihanouk's determination to preserve Cambodian neutrality frustrated those Cambodians, led by Lon Nol and Prince Sirik Matak (a cousin of Sihanouk), who sought closer ties with the United States. This group sought public support, using PAVN/PLAF encroachments into Cambodia to provoke long-standing Khmer concerns about Vietnamese domination.

**PERSONALITY**

**Lon Nol**

Lon Nol was born in 1913 and educated in French colonial schools in Cambodia. After a career as an administrator, he became Chief of the Cambodian police. He was transferred to the military, where he became army Chief of Staff in 1955. In 1959, he thwarted an attempted coup d'état against Sihanouk. By the end of the 1950s he was Minister for Defence and Commander-in-Chief.

After taking power in 1970, Lon Nol's strategic limitations were exposed, and his corrupt and repressive regime only survived as long as it did because it had US support. Lon Nol suffered a stroke in February 1971, which further incapacitated his leadership. On 1 April 1975, as KR forces closed in on Phnom Penh, Lon Nol fled Cambodia – after accepting a 'gift' of $500,000. He settled initially in Hawaii, before relocating to California in 1979. He died in 1985.

In January 1970, after ordering Lon Nol to organise anti-Vietnamese demonstrations in Phnom Penh, Sihanouk left Cambodia for a trip to France, the USSR and China. He planned to urge Soviet and Chinese leaders to pressure North Vietnam to withdraw its forces from Cambodia. If North Vietnam did so, Sihanouk hoped, the United States would stop bombing. Cambodian neutrality could then be restored.

On 11 March, an anti-Vietnamese demonstration in Phnom Penh led to the destruction of the North Vietnamese Embassy, as well as that of the South Vietnamese Provisional Revolutionary Government. Events then moved rapidly. On 12 March Sirik Matak told North Vietnam it could no longer use the port of Sihanoukville to ship supplies to its forces. The same day, Lon Nol demanded that all Vietnamese communist troops leave Cambodia within three days. Anti-Vietnamese protests continued throughout Cambodia. Sihanouk's control of Cambodia had become very precarious.

On 18 March, Lon Nol and Sirik Matak led a coup d'état overthrowing Sihanouk, who by that time was in Moscow. Lon Nol headed the new government, with Sirik Matak assuming the role of Prime Minister. Lon Nol's hostility toward North Vietnam and the Viet Cong endeared him to the United States, which promptly recognised the new regime in Phnom Penh. Within Cambodia, there was a mixed reaction to Sihanouk's downfall. In a number of areas there were protests against Lon Nol's seizure of power.

Accusing the United States of complicity in his downfall, Sihanouk claimed the CIA had played a role in Lon Nol's coup. Henry Kissinger denied those accusations, but it appears that Nixon's administration was not surprised by the coup. When asked about the overthrow of Sihanouk, Kissinger was very careful with his choice of words. He denied the US was involved in the coup, 'at least at the top level'.

Sihanouk, who had moved on to Beijing, was unable to control events in his homeland. On 23 March he announced the establishment of a 'National United Front of Kampuchea' (FUNK) and urged his supporters to wage a guerrilla war against Lon Nol's government. Sihanouk envisaged FUNK would include his former enemy, the Khmer Rouge, which was of course hostile to Lon Nol.

Lon Nol continued to encourage anti-Vietnamese sentiment in Cambodia. Over 400,000 Vietnamese lived in Cambodia in 1970 but there were significant animosities between that group and many Cambodians. Lon Nol promoted a wave of violence, which led to the deaths of thousands of Vietnamese civilians.

Lon Nol also sought to evict the PAVN and PLAF from Cambodia. He dramatically increased the size of the Cambodian Army, as over 70,000 volunteers rushed to enlist in the first month. But Lon Nol's forces were no match for the battle-hardened North Vietnamese and Viet Cong. Many of Lon Nol's 'troops' were young teenagers, who lacked military training and equipment.

Realising his army's limitations, Lon Nol stated he would welcome the 'assistance' of other nations: 'I am thinking of the possible intervention of all friendly countries.' In South Vietnam, Thieu was pleased Lon Nol had taken control of Cambodia. In late March Thieu ordered ARVN forces into areas across the Cambodian border to attack and harass PAVN/PLAF units. On 27 and 28 March American helicopters supported ARVN forces as they moved into Cambodia. Communist forces escaped westward, leaving their arms with Khmer Rouge forces. The United States also increased the flow of military supplies to Cambodia, as Nixon and Kissinger planned a larger, more controversial US involvement in Cambodian affairs.

# Kissinger, Nixon and Cambodia

Unlike Johnson, Nixon was willing to consider the idea of 'cleaning out' the PAVN/PLAF sanctuaries inside Cambodia. Having already ordered the bombing of Cambodia, in early 1970 Nixon took advantage of the change of regime in Phnom Penh to send American and South Vietnamese troops across the border into Cambodia. On 30 April Nixon explained his decision to the American people.

Nixon's decision to invade Cambodia in 1970 was one of the most controversial of his Presidency. In their memoirs, Nixon and Kissinger claimed the decision to send US forces into Cambodia had been reached only after a careful and deliberate debate amongst policymakers. In fact, the 'decision' revealed much about Nixon's paranoia and determination to concentrate decision-making in the hands of himself and Kissinger.

*Nixon announces that US troops have crossed into Cambodia*

Nixon's public statements that the US incursion of Cambodia was based on sound strategic and diplomatic needs should be viewed alongside suggestions that the invasion also reflected political and even psychological factors:

• Nixon and Kissinger went to considerable lengths to exclude the US Departments of State and Defense from the decision-making process. This reflected Nixon and Kissinger's determination to concentrate power in their own hands.

## HISTORICAL ISSUE

### *Richard Nixon Justifies the US Invasion of Cambodia*

Ten days ago … I announced a decision to withdraw an additional 150,000 Americans from Vietnam over the next year. I said then that I was making that decision despite our concern over increased enemy activity in Laos, in Cambodia, and in South Vietnam …

North Vietnam has increased its military aggression in all these areas, and particularly in Cambodia. After full consultation with the National Security Council, Ambassador Bunker, General Abrams, and my other advisers, I have concluded that the actions of the enemy in the last 10 days clearly endanger the lives of Americans who are in Vietnam … To protect our men who are in Vietnam and to guarantee the continued success of our withdrawal and Vietnamization programs, I have concluded that the time has come for action.

American policy … has been to scrupulously respect the neutrality of the Cambodian people … North Vietnam, however, has not respected that neutrality. For the past five years … North Vietnam has occupied military sanctuaries all along the Cambodian frontier with South Vietnam … For five years neither the United States nor South Vietnam has moved against these enemy sanctuaries … Thousands of [PAVN] soldiers are invading [Cambodia] from the sanctuaries; they are encircling … Phnom Penh … they have moved into Cambodia and are encircling the Capital. Cambodia … has sent out a call to the United States, to a number of other nations, for assistance …

Tonight American and South Vietnamese units will attack the headquarters for the entire Communist military operation in South Vietnam [COSVN] …

This is not an invasion of Cambodia. The areas in which these attacks will be launched are completely occupied and controlled by North Vietnamese forces. Our purpose is not to occupy the areas …

The action I have taken tonight is indispensable for the continuing success of [the US] withdrawal program [from Vietnam] …

The action I take tonight is essential if we are to accomplish [the] goal of keeping … casualties of our brave men in Vietnam at an absolute minimum. We take this action not for the purpose of expanding the war into Cambodia, but for the purpose of ending the war in Vietnam and winning the just peace we all desire … [W]e will continue to [strive] to end this war through negotiation …

If, when the chips are down, the world's most powerful nation, the United States of America, acts like a pitiful, helpless giant, the forces of totalitarianism and anarchy will threaten free nations and free institutions throughout the world. It is not our power but our will and character that is being tested tonight. The question all Americans must ask and answer tonight is this: Does the richest and strongest nation in the history of the world have the character to meet a direct challenge by a group which rejects every effort to win a just peace, ignores our warning, tramples on solemn agreements, violates the neutrality of an unarmed people, and uses our prisoners as hostages?

If we fail to meet this challenge, all other nations will be on notice that despite its overwhelming power the United States, when a real crisis comes, will be found wanting … I would rather be a one-term President and do what I believe is right than to be a two-term President at the cost of seeing America become a second-rate power and to see this nation accept the first defeat in its proud 190-year history.

## DOCUMENTARY EXERCISE

How did Nixon justify the decision to invade Cambodia? How did he justify the decision to ignore Cambodian neutrality?

- Nixon had suffered political setbacks in the months leading up to the invasion of Cambodia. Twice, his nominees for the US Supreme Court were rejected by the US Senate. 'Those Senators,' stated an angry Nixon, 'think they can push me around, but I'll show them who's tough'.
- Twice during the weeks preceding the invasion of Cambodia Nixon watched the movie *Patton*. The film reflected Nixon's own self-image. Secretary of State William P. Rogers was distressed that the President seemed to be using the film's lead character as a role model.

## Consequences of the US Invasion

Despite Nixon's explanation for the Cambodian 'incursion', the US Congress repealed the Gulf of Tonkin Resolution and demanded that American troops be withdrawn from Cambodia by 30 June. The antiwar movement found new life.

The US invasion only temporarily affected the ability of the PAVN and PLAF to use Cambodia. COSVN was not found. However, the invasion had a serious, destabilising impact on Cambodia: 200,000 refuges fled their homes in eastern Cambodia. The PAVN and PLAF were also forced further westward into Cambodia, causing further social and political dislocation. Lon Nol's government proved incapable of resisting the PAVN and PLAF.

In Beijing, China encouraged Sihanouk to establish a government-in-exile, in which the Khmer Rouge played a significant role. Although China had done much to support North Vietnam, it was keen to see Cambodia develop as a possible counter to Vietnamese power in the region. They were using Sihanouk and the KR to thwart possible Vietnamese – and, potentially, Soviet – ambitions elsewhere in Indochina or Asia.

The US invasion of Cambodia also encouraged the further growth of the KR, which could now present itself even more plausibly as an anti-American organisation. Sihanouk's alliance with the KR made it more acceptable to many Cambodians. Nixon's bombing, and then invasion, played significant parts in unravelling Cambodian society.

## Civil War: Lon Nol Versus the Khmer Rouge

By mid-1970, Lon Nol's Royal Cambodian Army was fighting a full-scale war against the Khmer Rouge. Lon Nol benefited from massive supplies of US aid ($US1.85 billion from 1970 to 1975). However, as in South Vietnam, that infusion of aid contributed significantly to the growing problem of corruption. The US involvement also fed suspicions that Lon Nol was a 'lackey' of the Americans.

Lon Nol's government did little to help 'ordinary' Cambodians. Concentrating increasing power in his own hands, in April 1971 he abolished the National Assembly. Many wealthy Cambodians fled overseas. The expanding civil war caused massive social dislocation, with hundreds of thousands of peasants forced from their lands. It was estimated that by 1972, up to one-third of the Cambodian population were refugees. Like Saigon, Phnom Penh's infrastructure was inadequate to cope with the massive influx of people.

American bombing of Cambodia continued until August 1973, when it was finally ended by the US Congress. This ongoing bombing, designed to support Lon Nol's forces, led to 383,851 tons of bombs being dropped over Cambodia. As in South Vietnam, however, the massive application of American firepower created more problems than it solved. The US bombing campaign further destabilised Cambodian society and economic life, and killed thousands of people. One estimate is that US bombing killed 150,000 Cambodians. The bombing further alienated many Cambodians from Lon Nol's regime, which supported both the United States and the bombing.

The Khmer Rouge argued that the only way to stop the American 'Killing Birds' was to overthrow Lon Nol. Many of those alienated Cambodians joined the KR. As US intelligence reports conceded, American bombing had assisted the KR. By 1973 the KR army numbered over 40,000.

The Cambodian civil war was a brutal conflict, with young boys in the front lines and prisoners rarely taken.

As was the ARVN in South Vietnam, Lon Nol's army was often undermined by poor leadership; on occasions, the troops fought bravely, but the regime for which they were fighting did not represent the needs and aspirations of the Cambodian people. The Khmer Rouge proved a vile substitute for Lon Nol's government, but from 1970–1975 it was a disciplined and highly motivated fighting force.

## The Khmer Rouge, the North Vietnamese and Sihanouk

The relationship between North Vietnam and the KR was characterised by mistrust, and by mid-1973 the KR leadership concluded North Vietnam had sold out by negotiating and signing a peace treaty with the United States. The rift between the KR and the DRV highlighted American misperceptions about 'monolithic communism' – upon which American interventions in Indochina were largely predicated.

The KR relationship with Sihanouk was one of convenience. KR leaders capitalised on Sihanouk's popularity amongst the peasantry, but did not allow him to influence policy. Sihanouk did not approve of the KR's hard-line communist ideology. Peasants were forced to relocate, private property was confiscated, religion was banned and even traditional Cambodian folks songs were prohibited. From 1970 to 1975, in their so-called 'liberated zones', the KR used terror and violence to quell potential opposition.

Sihanouk's attempts to assume a position of leadership within FUNK failed. In 1973 he stated that he and the KR hated each other and that when the KR had finished with him they would 'spit me out like a cherry stone'. He was right: after the KR victory in 1975, Sihanouk was soon marginalised.

# 1975: The Defeat of Lon Nol

When the United States ceased bombing in August 1973, Lon Nol's government controlled just one-third of Cambodia. Movement around the country was almost impossible, with the KR controlling most of the major roads. Food shortages were common and Lon Nol's administration was incapable of providing the social services and infrastructure to cope with the massive disorder arising from the war. Although the United States continued to supply weapons and munitions to Lon Nol's forces, the KR pushed closer toward Phnom Penh.

By early 1975, Lon Nol's rule was confined to Phnom Penh and a handful of other major towns. Some Cambodians hoped the United States would intervene to prevent a KR victory. President Gerald Ford (Nixon's successor) and Kissinger argued that the United States should provide further aid, but the US Congress was firmly opposed to any intervention or increased aid.

Lon Nol fled Cambodia on April Fool's Day. US Ambassador John Gunther Dean left on 11 April. On 17 April, the Khmer Rouge entered Phnom Penh. After five terrible years, Cambodia's civil war was over. Many residents of Phnom Penh celebrated and looked forward to peace. But the thousands of black-clad KR troops arriving in the city had other ideas, and within a few days – in some cases, hours – residents of Phnom Penh were being force-marched from their homes and ordered into the Cambodian countryside. This was 'Year Zero' and Cambodia was about to be subjected to the incomprehensible horrors of KR rule.

---

### POINTS TO REMEMBER

- Geography meant Cambodia always needed to walk a fine line in international relations. There was a history of animosity between the Cambodians and the Vietnamese.
- To maintain Cambodian neutrality Sihanouk had to balance the conflicting interests of the North Vietnamese, the South Vietnamese communists and the United States.
- North Vietnamese and Viet Cong bases inside Cambodia made them targets for US escalation of the war.
- The war in Vietnam caused political instability in Cambodia, which resulted in the Lon Nol coup in 1970 and then a civil war that was eventually won by the communist Khmer Rouge.

## ACTIVITIES

**1** To what extent was Cambodia neutral under Sihanouk?

**2** Was Sihanouk a successful nationalist leader in Cambodia?

**3** Assess the impact of US intervention in Cambodia from 1969.

**4** Can history be interpreted as a series of causes and effects? Starting with the 1967 decision by Sihanouk to improve relations with the United States, draw a graph showing 'causes' and 'effects' of major events in Cambodian history until 1975.

| Cause | Effect |
|---|---|
| 1967 Sihanouk to improve relations with the US | General Lon Nol appointed PM – suppresses peasant revolts |

**5** Draw a timeline of Cambodian history covered by this chapter.

**6** Sihanouk was unrealistic to try and remain neutral in the Indochina conflict. Do you agree?

**7** Why were the communists successful in the Cambodian Civil War?

### Sample HSC Exam Questions:

**1** How was EITHER Vietnam OR Cambodia affected by war in the 1970s?

**2** Assess the impact of the spread of conflict from Vietnam had on Cambodia in the period up to 1979.

### FURTHER READING

William Shawcross's *Sideshow: Kissinger, Nixon and the Destruction of Cambodia*, Rev. Ed. (Touchstone/Simon & Schuster, New York, 1987) offers a provocative account. Ben Kiernan, *How Pol Pot Came to Power: A History of Communism in Kampuchea, 1930–1975* (Verso, London, 1985) explores the contentious argument that American bombing contributed to KR success. David P. Chandler's, *A History of Cambodia*, 2nd ed. (Allen & Unwin, North Sydney, NSW, 1992) and *Facing the Cambodian Past: Selected Essays, 1971–1994* (Allen & Unwin, North Sydney, 1996) provide useful analyses. See also Milton Osborne, *Sihanouk: Prince of Light, Prince of Darkness* (Allen & Unwin, St Leonards, NSW, 1994); Philip Short, *Pol Pot: The History of a Nightmare* (John Murray, London, 2004); and David P. Chandler, *Brother Number One: A Political Biography of Pol Pot* (Allen & Unwin, St Leonards, NSW, 1993).

# The Killing Fields and Beyond: Indochina, 1975–1979

IN THIS CHAPTER YOU WILL:
- be introduced to the ideology and policies of the Khmer Rouge in Democratic Kampuchea and their disastrous consequences
- explore the tensions and rivalries between Kampuchea and Vietnam that culminated in the Third Indochina War
- examine how rivalries between Kampuchea and Vietnam fuelled existing tensions between Vietnam and China, and how these culminated in a fourth Indochina War
- understand Soviet and American positions on Indochina from 1975–1979.

## Background

The history of Cambodia from 1975 to 1979 is one of the most distressing chapters in the 20th century. At its centre was the newly founded Democratic Kampuchea (DK) – the new name for the Khmer Rouge-dominated Cambodia. For four years Cambodia endured perhaps the greatest per capita loss of life in a single nation. The repercussions of this event were felt elsewhere in Indochina and were a contributing factor to a fourth Indochina War, when Vietnamese and Chinese rivalries led to yet another conflict

## Year Zero

Following their capture of Phnom Penh, the Khmer Rouge (KR) set about realising their revolutionary vision for their new nation of Democratic Kampuchea. They did so without revealing the Party or its leadership to the world. Pol Pot's siblings were allegedly not even aware that their brother and the leader of the KR were one and the same. The Party transformed into the shadowy 'Angka' – the 'organisation' that governed the new Cambodia through the party's senior officials, known as the 'Centre'.

**PERSONALITY**

**Pol Pot**

Brother Number One of the Khmer Rouge regime was born Saloth Sar, near Kompong Thom, on 19 May 1928. Saloth Sar was the son of a prosperous small landowner who had connections to the royal court. This background greatly

embarrassed him. Despite being a poor student, he won a scholarship to study radio electronics in Paris. In France he became increasingly interested in communism and after repeatedly failing his exams, returned to Cambodia in 1953, joined the Viet Minh and began working as a teacher.

In 1960 he was elected to the Central Committee of the Communist Party of Kampuchea. Two years later he was Party Secretary, living in hiding in north-eastern Cambodia. After the overthrow of Sihanouk in 1970 Pol Pot became the leader of united guerrilla front seeking to overthrow the Khmer Republic. With victory in 1975 he became Prime Minister of Democratic Kampuchea, although his position was kept secret until 1976. Following the Vietnamese invasion, he returned to the jungle to wage guerrilla war. After the Vietnamese withdrawal and the United Nations-brokered peace deal, the Khmer Rouge's position was increasingly compromised, undermining Pol Pot's position. In the 1990s he was placed under house arrest by his own party for 'treason' and died in April 1998. In an interview before his death he claimed: 'My conscience is clear.'

*Victorious Khmer Rouge troops enter Phnom Penh*

The Centre's vision for Cambodia was influenced by communism, nationalism and revulsion for colonialism. KR leaders had four main aims for Kampuchea:

1 Total independence and self-reliance.
2 Preservation of the dictatorship of the proletariat.
3 Total and immediate economic transformation.
4 A complete recasting of social values.

The KR shared the Chinese communist conviction that the peasantry was the heart of society. Their aim was to create a 'complete communist society ... without wasting time on intermediate steps'. The KR claimed its communist vision was the 'most beautiful and most pure', surpassing Lenin and going further than Mao. So revolutionary was the KR approach and so informed was it by indigenous goals and methods that it could learn nothing from Chinese or Vietnamese communism. As elsewhere in the communist world, nationalism was a powerful force driving change in Cambodia.

The watchword for the new Kampuchea was 'self-reliance'. Forgetting the earlier assistance given by the Vietnamese and the Chinese, the KR claimed their victory was the clearest evidence of the strength of Cambodian independence. Furthermore, KR propaganda insisted the United States was also defeated in Cambodia in 1975.

Self-reliance was further consolidated in Cambodia by effectively cutting

## HISTORICAL DOCUMENT

### Ieng Sary (KR Deputy Prime Minister) Reflects on the Khmer Revolutionary Experience

The Cambodian revolutionary experience is unprecedented. What we are trying to bring about has never occurred before. That is why we are not following any model, either Chinese or Vietnamese. We are reorganising the country, taking agriculture as the base; and with what we are able to recover we are building an industry whose aim is, in any case, to serve agriculture. The Cambodian people have had their own experience in the paddies for centuries, and we must start with the paddies.

the nation off from the Western world. A program was introduced to expunge any trace of European colonialism's legacy. International trading was stopped. All foreigners were forced to leave; all telephone, telegram and mail services were cut. The borders were mined. The only flights leaving Cambodia were rare flights to Hanoi or Beijing. So effective was the isolation of the country that for many years what exactly was going on in Democratic Kampuchea was a mystery to the rest of the world.

The KR believed that Cambodia's cities symbolised the external influences and foreign domination that had damaged the Cambodian people. Kampuchea had to be rid of cities, which housed the revolution's opponents. Only the countryside held the true spirit of the Khmer people. The KR evacuated the cities, often on the grounds that American air raids were imminent and on the lie that such an inconvenience would only last a few days. To assist the evacuation, Phnom Penh's electricity and water supplies were cut. To further ensure that the evils of the city would no longer contaminate the countryside, roads, bridges and motor vehicles were destroyed.

With the city crowded with rural Cambodians who had fled the fighting, over three million residents of Phnom Penh were forcibly evacuated. Hospitals were emptied of the sick and injured without compassion. Perhaps over 400,000 people died during the evacuation. When Pol Pot entered Phnom Penh for the first time in 12 years, on 23 April 1975, the city was virtually deserted except for the members of the Centre, who now made the capital their home and ensured the electricity remained on in their newly acquired houses.

Once in the countryside, urban dwellers were disbursed to ensure they had little chance of orchestrating a counter-revolution. Many of those deemed representative of the ruinous effects of foreign influence were killed, so they did not pollute the countryside. As well as members of the military and government of the

*The National Bank of Cambodia was another victim of the Khmer Rouge. The Bank was destroyed and all currency deemed worthless*

old regime, who were automatically enemies of Angka, bureaucrats, skilled labourers, landowners and those who had received a Western-style education (teachers, doctors, engineers, for example) were singled out for eradication.

While the KR plan for Cambodia is often identified as an effort to take the nation back to a pre-modern, pre-Western past, this was actually not the motivation of the Centre. Rather than looking to the past, Angka looked to the future – a new communist modernity. To reinforce this notion the Western calendar was dispensed with. Time was starting again as Cambodia entered 'Year Zero'.

## Khmer Rouge Economic Transformation

Democratic Kampuchea's greatest assets were the peasantry and their rice crop. If agricultural production was increased, the new nation could feed its people and fund its industrialisation. In 15 to 20 years Cambodia would be transformed from a 'backward agricultural country' into a 'country endowed with an industrial base'. The first step was to quickly increase the nation's rice crop for export.

Such increases could only come from the sweat of the people. The plan called for the Cambodian people to produce 'Three tons per hectare'. This roughly translated into 26.7 million tons of rice annually, three times greater than the national output prior to the war. Half of this crop would be used for food and seed, while the rest would be sold on the international export market.

Rural peasants who had not previously been corrupted would be the new residents of the cities, working in the factories that would mark the beginnings of the new industrialisation.

To ensure maximum productivity, significant social and administrative changes were required. Cambodia was divided into a number of zones that would then report to the Centre. With the abolition of private property, people worked the land as members of cooperatives, often formed through the consolidation of several local villages.

It was hoped the cooperatives would deliver greater productivity than the old system, which had long exploited the peasantry. Again, this involved the transformation of social relations. For example, women were absolved of most of their domestic chores. All meals would be prepared by the cooperative and all children would be cared for by the cooperative. This freed women to work in the fields. Indeed, the family home no longer existed. Husbands and wives and their children were separated into separate dormitory accommodation or worse, sent to different cooperatives. Angka was more important than any family.

The plans for Kampuchea's economic and social transformation were never realized because the nation reputedly had just a week's supply of rice when the KR took control. By the end of the first year Cambodia was enduring a famine. Starvation, disease and overwork killed many Cambodians. Western medicine was rejected in favour of traditional techniques, yet many of the new nation's 'doctors' had no qualifications. Disease became a crippling problem. Over 100,000 people died in a cholera epidemic soon after the evacuation of the cities. International aid was rejected in the name of self-reliance.

**HISTORICAL ISSUE**

### The Children of the Killing Fields

Considerable effort was devoted to inculcating children – the inheritors of the new Kampuchea – with 'proper' values. They were separated from their families and instructed to reject 'familyism'. One instruction was to not call their parents 'mother' and 'father', but the generic KR approved terms for all adults – 'uncle' or 'aunt'. Of course, for thousands of Cambodian children there were no parents alive to call anything. Devotion to family was to be replaced by devotion to Angka. As one children's song suggested:

> We children love Angka limitlessly
> Because of you we have better lives and live quite happily,
> Before the revolution, children were poor and lived like animals,
> We were cold and suffered
> But the enemy didn't care about us.
> Only skin covered our bones, so thin we were worried
> All night we slept on the ground,
> We begged and looked for food in trashcans during the day.
> Now Angka brings us good health, strength.
> And now we live in the commune.
> We have clothes, we are not cold and miserable anymore
> The light of revolution, equality, and freedom shines gloriously
> Oh Angka we deeply love you
> We resolve to follow your red way

Much of the bad news coming from the zones did not reach the Centre. Phnom Penh was often sheltered from such bad news by local commanders fearful of being punished for their failings. The Centre was lied to about the crop. Cultivated rice was often sent for export and not left in the zone to feed the population. While life differed from region to region, zone to zone, the four years of KR rule brought starvation, misery and death for the Cambodian people.

# The Killing Fields

The most notorious aspect of the Khmer Rouge's four years of rule in Cambodia was its wholesale killing of its enemies – real and perceived. The scale of the horror visited on the people became an orgy of violence that grew out of control. Obsessed with seeking out and destroying its enemies, the KR's first targets were the soldiers and officials of the former regime. These men and their families were systematically rounded up and executed.

With these enemies neutralised, the KR then turned on its former allies in FUNK. Those who had fought alongside the KR now found themselves targeted and killed as the Party took power for itself. Sihanouk was made President of Democratic Kampuchea in 1975, but resigned in April 1976, as he had been unable to exercise any power in the role. He then spent nearly three years under house arrest in Phnom Penh.

In February 1976 soldiers who had been ordered to assist with rice cultivation began expressing discontent. The ensuring unrest sparked a witchhunt, which trapped a number of senior KR military leaders. Under torture these men claimed the Party had been infiltrated by a 'string of traitors'. So began a purge of the Khmer Rouge. Terror turned inward. By September 1976 the purge was in full swing, capturing thousands of loyal Party members in its trap. 'Enemies' were everywhere and the signed confessions of the 'traitors' showed the 'sickness in the Party'. No one, from the lowest functionary to a government minister, was safe. Ministers with decades of faithful service to the Party were suddenly 'exposed' as CIA operatives, who allegedly established spy networks throughout the Party.

The purge was renewed with increased vigour following the disappointing rice crop of early 1977. It is estimated that between 1.671 and 1.871 million Cambodians died between 1975 and 1979. This constituted 21 to 24% of Cambodia's population in 1975.

Historians have sought to understand the reasons for the events that gripped Cambodia in those terrible years. Revolutions are usually characterised by the purposive use of violence. Often more people die *after*, rather than *during* a revolution. Such historical truths, however, do little to explain Cambodia's Killing Fields. The argument that the events were the product of a collective madness within the KR is also an inadequate historical explanation for Cambodia's horrors. Nevertheless, the answers are to be found in the KR:

- their world view was driven by threat and secrecy
- their uncompromising ideology sanctified their actions
- their administration permitted a society to function without restraint and made the irrational appear rational because it was the product of a 'process'
- from the 1960s their history (including the means by which they had gained power and in their dreams) was one of relentless brutality.

## HISTORICAL ISSUE

### *Tuol Sleng*

The KR had many locations where Cambodians were detained, tortured and killed. The most infamous of these was S-21 (or Tuol Sleng): it was known as 'the place where the people went in and never came out'. Between 1975 and 1978 as many as 14,000 to 20,000 people entered S-21 – only a handful survived. Most were guilty of no crime. They were victims of the paranoia of the purges and a KR slogan: 'It is better to arrest 10 people by mistake than to let one guilty person go free.' Toul Sleng's administrators kept detailed records and photographs of all the inmates – before and after their execution. With no judiciary in Democratic Kampuchea, there were never any trials. Being captured was taken as evidence of guilt, and this guilt was extended to family members who were usually killed soon after their arrival.

Each interrogated captive was expected to name co-conspirators. Many prisoners betrayed innocent friends just to stop their torture and be freed by death. Their friends would themselves be purged, confirming the regime's paranoia and starting the process again. Being on the other side of the cell did not guarantee safety. Sixty per cent of the prison staff was also executed. Most of the records of Tuol Sleng were found intact after the Vietnamese invasion: they provide a chilling insight into the Khmer Rouge.

*Tuol Sleng*

While these terrible events remain the subject of historical debate and conjecture, one fact remains beyond dispute; the 'Genocide' in Cambodia only stopped after the successful invasion of the country in December 1978 by the unified Socialist Republic of Vietnam (SRV).

## HISTORICAL ISSUE

### *Romanticising the Khmer Rouge: The Case of Malcolm Caldwell*

Within the West some left-wing academics celebrated the rise of the Khmer Rouge and reported favourably on its progress. These academics often relied not on substantial evidence, but on the publicly expressed ideology of the Party. None could conceive that the practice differed so much from what appeared as the purity of the ideology. Consequently, they questioned many of the early allegations made by refugees and dismissed much of the early media coverage on the grounds of Cold War Western anti-communism. Democratic Kampuchea's 'leading academic supporter' was Malcolm Caldwell, a Scottish economic historian based at the University of London's School of Oriental and African Studies. Caldwell was the founder the *Journal of Contemporary Asia*. The journal tended to support revolutions and revolutionary groups in Asia.

In December 1978, as Vietnam was preparing to invade Cambodia, Caldwell and two journalists were invited to Kampuchea. On arrival they took part in a number of 'guided tours' and Caldwell was even granted a personal interview with Pol Pot. In talks with the two journalists, Caldwell suggested that his position on the Cambodian revolution had been justified.

On the evening of 23 December 1978 gunmen entered Caldwell's accommodation in Phnom Penh and shot him dead. While the regime blamed Vietnamese traitors, it is assumed the KR murdered one of their most passionate advocates in the hope that it could be blamed on Vietnam, whose international position would be further weakened. Caldwell's strongest defence of the regime that killed him was published posthumously in 1979 by an Australian university and was titled 'Cambodia: Rationale for a Rural Policy'.

## The Third Indochina War

In understanding communist victory in Vietnam and Cambodia, the strategic alliance between the Lao Dong and the Khmer Rouge is yet another key to their successes in 1975. One KR official noted upon the capture of Saigon: 'Vietnam owes its victory in large part to the heroic struggle of our people.' This alliance, which dated back to the old days of the Indochinese

Communist Party, quickly unravelled, however, even before final victory had been secured. Nationalism, which had been at the centre of both communist parties, produced frictions between the two communist states that culminated in war.

Two issues were at the centre of Cambodian/Vietnamese tensions. The first was Cambodia's traditional fear of an expansionary Vietnam. This dated back to at least the 18th century, when Vietnamese had migrated into the Mekong Delta, which was then part of the Cambodian Kingdom. Additionally, Cambodians believed the border formulated by the French in 1939 favoured the Vietnamese. The KR wanted to see the return of much of southern Vietnam.

The second issue was the continuing presence of PLAF and PAVN troops in the Cambodian sanctuaries, despite the fact that the war was over. This was regarded as clear evidence that 'ungrateful Vietnamese crocodiles' were determined to extend their influence in Cambodia, as they had in Laos.

On 1 May 1975 Cambodian troops entered South Vietnam 'to liberate Vietnamese territory because it is all our territory'. The United States became caught up with this tussle on 12 May 1975 when a private American ship, the *Mayaguez*, was captured by KR forces as it passed seemingly too close to a Cambodian held island. When the KR failed to comply with a US ultimatum for the ship's return, the United States stormed the island, saved the crew and the ship and destroyed a number of surrounding KR bases. Vietnam saw the American attack as an opportunity to regain control of the island of Poulo Wau.

These skirmishes became the central discussion point when Pol Pot visited Hanoi in June 1975. The Cambodians claimed Hanoi was reneging on an earlier boundary resolution that Sihanouk had secured with the Vietnamese in 1966. The Cambodian delegation also asked when Vietnamese troops would leave Cambodia. On both counts the Cambodians were unsatisfied by the Vietnamese response. Nevertheless, the discussions did lead to a de-escalation of the skirmishes and in August, Le Duan visited Phnom Penh to sign an economic agreement.

Vietnam's desires for a more formal friendship treaty or memorandum of understanding between the two nations were rejected by the KR, which remained sceptical of Vietnamese intentions. Vietnam was allegedly trying to create an 'Indochina Federation', with Hanoi as its power base. This had been the stated aim of the Vietnamese communists since 1935 and was evidenced by increasing Vietnamese influence in Laos.

KR perceptions of Vietnamese 'arrogance' fuelled the desire to remove any trace of Vietnamese influence from national life. In May 1975 Angka decided to expel all ethnic Vietnamese. Reports also reached the west that more than 2,000 Cambodians were killed after returning from Vietnam. Even officials of the Party who had been sent to Vietnam often found themselves at Tuol Sleng on their return to Cambodia.

It is alleged that the real trigger for the purges was that some moderates dared to continue to suggest the Party had been formed in 1951 as the Khmer People's Revolutionary Party (KPRP). The extremist position was that the Party had not formed until 1960 when Pol Pot became Deputy Secretary and the overt connections to Vietnam were severed.

From late 1975 there were renewed border clashes between the two countries. Phnom Penh refused to negotiate. The efforts of some KR moderates to resist the extremists were further used to distance Kampuchea from Vietnam, with claims that the 'internal power coups' had been 'Hanoi inspired'. Such allegations became the justification for the largest KR intrusion into Vietnam. Over 60 border villages were attacked and more than 200 Vietnamese were killed. The attacks caused an outrage in southern Vietnam and damaged the credibility of the new government because of its inability to prevent them. Caught off guard, Hanoi called for a ceasefire. Phnom Penh refused and demanded a correction of the frontier. In response, Vietnamese forces raided Cambodia.

In July 1977 Vietnam and Laos signed a treaty of friendship. Phnom Penh regarded this as further evidence of Vietnam's desire to encircle and destroy Cambodia. Although this was untrue, Hanoi was increasingly convinced that something had to be done about the Phnom Penh regime. In October 1977 Hanoi sent troops into Cambodia on a secret mission under the charge of General Giap. Their aim was to either force the KR to the negotiating table to improve relations or fuel a general uprising that would overthrow the KR. By December over 20,000 Vietnamese troops had penetrated over 20 kilometres into Cambodia. When the Cambodians counteracted with raids into southern Vietnam, the Vietnamese force was increased to 58,000.

Until December this virtual war between Democratic Kampuchea and the Socialist Republic of Vietnam remained a secret. Neither side was alerting the world's media to the situation. As the Cambodian military position in the Eastern Zone deteriorated, however, Phnom Penh announced the Vietnamese had invaded Cambodia and that by 'acts of aggression and criminal schemes' were trying to 'overthrow the Government of Democratic Kampuchea'. The Centre then cut diplomatic relations with Hanoi.

Phnom Penh's statement was a public relations coup. Hanoi appeared the aggressor and some international sympathy was expressed for the Cambodians. Hanoi announced a withdrawal of its forces on 6 January 1978. Phnom Penh claimed it was a Vietnamese retreat and celebrated a massive victory. The KR also claimed that thousands of Cambodians who had fled to Vietnam during the fighting were not seeking refuge from the KR; rather, they had been 'abducted' by the Vietnamese.

In celebrating its military victory, the Centre told Cambodians that 'the worst enemy remains the enemy within'. Knowing that in reality the Eastern Zone army's performance had been poor, Pol Pot claimed that military and officials there were in fact traitors – 'henchmen of Vietnam'. Senior officials 'disappeared'. Army officers were executed. Some eastern zone soldiers slipped into the jungle to conduct a guerrilla war, while others crossed the frontier and found refuge with the Vietnamese. By May Angkor had decided that the whole zone needed to be 'purified' and that all its inhabitants – 'Khmer bodies with Vietnamese minds' – had to be either killed or relocated. Thousands of people were relocated and thousands fled to Vietnam. Another 100,000 eastern zone residents were murdered.

Having refused repeated calls from Hanoi for negotiations and the international monitoring of the frontier, Phnom Penh changed its tune in May 1978 when it suggested it would negotiate if Vietnam stopped its military and subversive activities in Cambodia and ended its plans for an Indochinese federation. Hanoi did not respond to the call – to do so would have been an admission they were doing things they had repeatedly denied. Hanoi had already decided that the only way to protect Vietnam's security was to remove the Khmer Rouge.

Hanoi began to build a new Cambodian army from the fleeing eastern zone soldiers. Plans were also made for an alternate Cambodian Communist Party. After a Vietnamese incursion into Cambodia the Kampuchean National United Front for National Salvation was unveiled on 2 December 1978.

Clearly Vietnam had tired of negotiating and the KR now had to contend with the very real possibility of a Vietnamese invasion. Phnom Penh again sought international sympathy. China was asked to increase its aid to Kampuchea and Pol Pot requested Chinese troops to bolster his forces. Beijing refused. The second four-year plan was built around the theme of defending Cambodia against Vietnamese aggression.

On 25 December 1978 Vietnam launched its long-expected invasion of Democratic Kampuchea. Communist had turned against communist. As the Vietnamese headed west they were usually welcomed as heroes by the Cambodian people. In a symbolic gesture the Vietnamese gave Cambodians individual cooking pots. The days of forced communalism were over. In anticipation of their arrival, some Cambodian communities turned against the cadres and soldiers who had enslaved them for four years. So began another wave of violence fuelled by revenge.

As the Vietnamese converged on Phnom Penh – using the tactics and weapons of modern warfare, rather than the methods of 'People's War' – the KR appealed to the world for assistance against what it claimed was an invasion by the Soviet-controlled Warsaw Pact of European communist nations. Prince Sihanouk was called on to act as the spokesmen for the nation. He flew to Beijing whereupon he criticised the Vietnamese – and the Khmer Rouge.

*Phnom Penh shortly after its capture by the Vietnamese*

Once they had taken Phnom Penh, the Vietnamese installed a new communist government – led by the former eastern zone senior officer Heng Semrin – that was sympathetic to Hanoi. He would be replaced as leader of Cambodia by Hun Sen, another eastern zone officer who had fled to Vietnam. Elements of the KR, and other opponents of the Vietnamese, fought a protracted guerrilla war against the regime. From his jungle hideout Pol Pot refused to accept the blame for the 'genocide' that had nearly destroyed the nation. He claimed that most of those who had died were victims of the invading Vietnamese.

Some left-wing American academics – notably Noam Chomsky – who had supported the Khmer Rouge, questioned the 'truthfulness' of 'alleged' KR crimes in the months preceding the regime's demise. But as the weight of evidence grew, their support evaporated.

One consequence of Vietnam's embrace of the USSR was that during the Third Indochina War the United States sided with Kampuchea and publicly attacked Vietnam. Such positions became embarrassing when Hanoi proved the brutality of the KR and represented its invasion as a mercy dash that saved hundreds of thousands of Cambodian lives.

*Phnom Penh, December, 1992. Part of the Cheung Ek Killing Fields*

## Sino–Vietnamese Rift

Instability in Indochina was compounded by Vietnam's deteriorating relationship with China. Tensions between these two former allies also reflected the continuing power of nationalism over ideology and the repercussions of the ongoing Sino–Soviet rift.

Despite their claims of self-reliance, KR leaders had expended considerable efforts in securing assistance from other communist nations, particularly China. Whether it was because of respect for China's position or because of Vietnam's perceived allegiance to the Soviet Union, the KR leadership had little regard for the USSR. Enemies were not only CIA or Vietnamese agents. They might also be spies for the KGB.

China supported Democratic Kampuchea because it saw it as a useful counterweight to Vietnam in Indochina. Over 200 Chinese military advisers arrived in Cambodia in October 1975 to assist the KR Army. China was either unaware or turned a blind eye to the fact that the evacuation of Phnom Penh had led to the death of much of the city's 14% Chinese minority.

In Hanoi, the pro-Soviet faction dominated the Politburo, but the public line remained one of trying to maintain a neutral position on the Sino–Soviet rift. This neutral position continued despite the fact China had adopted an aggressive position with regard to border issues. In January 1974 China seized Hoang Sa (Paracel) Island from South Vietnam. Although the island was controlled by South Vietnam, Hanoi claimed territorial rights. China raised other territorial disputes, including the Spratley Islands and a small parcel of land on the Sino–Vietnamese frontier. In 1974 these disputes led to over a hundred border 'clashes' between Chinese and Vietnamese troops. The number of these incidents doubled in 1975.

Hanoi's reluctance to be beholden to either China or the USSR was reflected in the period after reunification when plans were laid to rebuild Vietnam. Hanoi looked to neither China nor the USSR to fund its reconstruction. Despite Soviet requests, Hanoi refused to become a fully-fledged member of the Soviet bloc by joining the Council for Mutual Economic Cooperation (COMECON). It refused Chinese and Soviet requests to place consuls in the liberated South. Unhappy with Hanoi, Soviet aid to Vietnam actually declined in 1976.

In contrast, Western journalists and diplomats were granted access to South Vietnam. Instead of looking to its old wartime allies, Hanoi looked to its old adversaries, France and the United States. Vietnam also joined the International Monetary Fund.

The main reason for courting the United States was the secret deal struck with the Nixon Administration in Paris. The United States had promised the North Vietnamese $4.7 billion in aid. In Hanoi this money increasingly came to be considered a form of American war reparation. In Washington it was viewed as a pragmatic offer that had been made, but was no longer valid, because the North had not abided by the terms of the agreement. Hanoi's demands for the promised money dashed early American hopes for 'normalising' relations with Vietnam. Reparations suggested guilt and defeat and American was unwilling to concede they owed anything to their former enemies.

US President Jimmy Carter, however, sought resolution to the issue of those Americans still missing in action (MIA) in Indochina. Initially, Hanoi linked any discussion of the issue to reparations; eventually, however, it agreed to treat the two issues separately. Phnom Penh refused to discuss the MIA issue with the United States.

In late 1977, US and Vietnamese officials returned to Paris. While some progress was made on the MIA issue, little progress was forthcoming on the question of reparations or American financial aid to Vietnam. Casting an invisible hand over proceedings was the American relationship with China. Carter hoped to build on Nixon and Ford's efforts to normalise relations with China. Some US State Department officials insisted that the emerging rivalries between China and Vietnam meant the United States could not simultaneously normalise relations with both nations. If a choice had to be made, it had to be China. Carter's national security adviser, Zbigniew Brzezinski, agreed: 'Moving ahead on relations with Vietnam would only be an irritant to expanding our relations with China.' The United States, therefore, walked away from normalising relations with Vietnam.

With echoes of 1945, Hanoi had few options. To compound its problems, Vietnam's relationship with China was deteriorating. As the border clashes continued, China was dismayed by Hanoi's plan to unify the country by forming the Socialist Republic of Vietnam in 1976. China had insisted, perhaps in the hope of influencing southern communists, that reunification not take place for at least two years. China denied Vietnam's October 1976 request for an increase in aid, further antagonising Hanoi – which was also angered by China's increasing aid to Kampuchea.

Eventually, Chinese frustration with Vietnam was vented publicly. When Phnom Penh announced in April 1977 its success in purging the KR of pro-Vietnamese elements, Beijing publicly applauded the move. China's rhetoric became increasingly anti-Vietnamese and – despite its reservations on the course of the KR revolution – pro-Kampuchean.

Pol Pot told his colleagues in 1977 that 'China can help us scare our enemies'. Vietnam was apprehensive and the only nation that seemed prepared to help was the USSR. Moscow identified a number of advantages in building its relationship with Vietnam. A strategic alliance would:

- allow the USSR to project its military globally with the assistance of the PAVN

- allow Soviet air and naval forces to forward deploy into South-East Asia
- increase Soviet intelligence-gathering in Asia.

# Sino–Vietnamese Clashes

Following Phnom Penh's revelations about the first Vietnamese invasion in December 1977, Hanoi made one final attempt to maintain its relationship with China. In early January Le Duan travelled to Beijing, hoping that Chinese influence might bring the KR to the negotiating table. China, however, urged Vietnam to withdraw from Cambodia before it would consider playing any such role. China's public pronouncements continued to inflame the situation. Le Duan returned to Hanoi fearful that China might join with Cambodia in an attack on Vietnam. Further evidence came from the Sino–Vietnamese border where clashes continued during 1976. Both sides were reinforcing the border with more troops, which led to further clashes. During 1977 there were over 900 such incidents.

In March 1978, the Vietnamese Politburo discussed the question of its deteriorating relationship with China. The same month an 'anti-capitalist raid' was launched against the Ho Chi Minh City suburb of Cholon. Cholon had long been Saigon's Chinatown and the Hoa Kieu (ethnic Chinese) had long played an important role in Vietnam's economic system. Dismantling the capitalist edifice in the south was an important dimension of unification, but its timing and its concentration on Chinese, first in Cholon and then elsewhere, led many commentators to conclude the raids were part of Hanoi's preparations for the inevitable clash with China.

The raids were described as necessary to remove a potential fifth column. Despite the acculturation of many ethnic Chinese into the Vietnamese way of life, the Chinese had remained second-class citizens in the eyes of the law and in the opinion of many Vietnamese. China, moreover, made a number of pronouncements in early 1978 about 'Overseas Chinese' being members of the 'Chinese nation'.

Hanoi intensified its anti-Chinese activities. That this was more than just an anti-capitalist exercise was highlighted by the fact that northern Chinese were also persecuted. Tens of thousands of Chinese fled into China before Beijing closed its frontier with Vietnam. Over 200,000 Chinese sought to find another way out of the country. The Chinese Government announced it would send two ships to start to collect Vietnamese Chinese. But the first ship sat off the Vietnamese coast for six weeks, before returning to China empty.

Wishing to see the Chinese leave, Hanoi reputedly stepped in with what Western diplomats in Hanoi called 'Rust Bucket Tours Inc'. For large amounts of money the Vietnamese Government helped organise the exodus of tens of thousands of Chinese. Other Chinese–Vietnamese organised to leave in their own boats. Over 250,000 'boat people' (not all ethnic Chinese) left Vietnam. Tens of thousands died when their overburdened vessels sank or stopped, or became victims of pirates. While many would find new lives in Canada, France, the United States and Australia, others endured many years' captivity in squalid refugee camps in Hong Kong, Thailand and Malaysia.

China continued to protest over the treatment of the ethnic Chinese and called for an end to the persecution. When it did not, in May 1978 Beijing cut all aid to Vietnam. In response, Hanoi noted Beijing's silence regarding the treatment of ethnic Chinese in Cambodia. It suggested that perhaps China should take responsibility for the 1,500 'victimised Chinese' who had fled Cambodia and were now refugees in Vietnam. Moscow also weighed into the fracas in defence of Hanoi. Chinese concerns were no more than 'crocodile tears'.

With the cessation of Chinese aid, Hanoi accelerated its negotiations with the Soviets. In June the USSR began sending enormous quantities of military aid to Vietnam. Soviet military aid to Vietnam in 1977 had been US$80 million. During 1978 it topped US$700 million. In response to the arrival of this aid Vietnam joined COMECON on 28 July 1978. The same month, China began a massive airlift of military supplies into Phnom Penh.

In November, Vietnam and the USSR signed a Treaty of Friendship. In the case of an attack, or threat of attack, on 'either Party' Vietnam and the USSR agreed to 'consult each other with a view to eliminating that threat and taking appropriate and effective measures to ensure the peace and security of the two countries'.

The Friendship Treaty was the first step in a Vietnamese strategy aimed at avoiding a two-front war with China and Cambodia. It was hoped the Treaty would reduce the chances of Chinese intervention if Vietnam invaded Cambodia. In reality, however, it firmed the resolve of a previously split Chinese Politburo. When placed beside Russian endeavours in Afghanistan, China feared it was being encircled by the USSR and its satellites. Furthermore, while China's invasion of Vietnam in February 1979 is usually viewed as a response to the Vietnamese invasion of Cambodia a few weeks earlier, the Chinese army had been mobilising on the border for many weeks before the PAVN entered Cambodia.

## The Fourth Indochina War: China Versus Vietnam

Following the cessation of aid to Vietnam, Beijing contemplated the possibility of 'teaching Hanoi a lesson'. This was a military strategy to invade a neighbour for a time and compel the neighbour to correct their behaviour. With set limited goals, it was believed the strategy would prevent a deterioration into full-scale war. Reputedly, Beijing informed the United States of its punitive mission. Washington was delighted.

Vietnam's invasion of Cambodia ensured that the mobilising Chinese forces would attack. Vietnam's actions were again perceived as an insult to China. A regime China had vowed to protect had been defeated. The capture of 10,000 Chinese 'advisors' rubbed salt into the wound.

On 17 February 1979 China acted. Over 250,000 Chinese troops entered northern Vietnam, virtually all the way along the frontier. The Chinese tactic reflected that used by General Westmoreland a decade before. The Chinese People's Liberation Army would act as a 'meat-grinder', destroying Vietnamese units and damaging the PAVN's ability to wage war for years to come.

Vietnam was aware that Chinese aims were limited. The PAVN held its regular divisions in reserve to defend Hanoi and instead used 100,000 militia troops to resist the enemy. The majority of these Vietnamese militia soldiers were seasoned veterans. By contrast the PLA battlefield inexperience showed. Yet, the sheer size of the PLA enabled it to advance over 40 kilometres into Vietnam.

Having captured the major centres of Lang Son and the coastal town of Quang Yen on 3 March, China felt the lesson was over. On 6 March it began to withdraw over the border and within two weeks had left Vietnam. China declared its 'punitive military operation' a success. But many Vietnamese and international observers disagreed. Politically, Vietnam was hardly taught a lesson. It did not prevent the Vietnamese occupation of Cambodia and, rather than severing the Vietnamese relationship with the USSR, it saw the Soviets gain that which they most coveted: in 1980 they secured naval access to Cam Ranh Bay. Vietnam claimed China had retreated because it had endured an unmitigated defeat. The PLA admitted to over 20,000 casualties as a result of their 29 days in Vietnam: more than the losses the United States endured in a single month during its war in Vietnam. As usual, Vietnam refused to disclose its casualties. The short war revealed the inadequacies of the PLA. Chinese leader Deng Xiao Peng used the experience to justify a modernisation of the PLA during the 1980s. The operational doctrine of the Chinese military was no longer characterised by Mao's People's War doctrine.

Following the invasion, Hanoi published a long indictment of Chinese wrongdoings over three decades. It was claimed that China sacrificed Vietnam at Geneva in 1954 to protect itself. Beijing was charged with having sabotaged peace negotiations between the United States and Vietnam during the 1960s. Hanoi accused China of 'revisionist crimes' during the Cultural Revolution and claimed Beijing was organising anti-Vietnamese activities amongst ethnic Chinese with Vietnam. Furthermore, the Chinese Navy was allegedly intefering with the delivery of Soviet aid. Vietnamese–Chinese estrangement continued and deepened during the 1980s.

# Conclusion

Cambodia's history remains a breathtaking example of inhumanity in the 20th century. It is a past that still haunts modern-day Cambodia.

The Third and Fourth Indochinese Wars challenged many French and American politicians' and military planners' ideas concerning the character of communism and the nature of Indochina. Where the first two Indochinese wars showed the power of ideology to unite neighbours in a shared cause, the second two showed that in this part of Asia, at least, nationalism (even when constructed out of colonialism) was ultimately more important than communism. This reopens that enduring historical debate about the roles of communism and nationalism in Indochinese decolonisation.

**POINTS TO REMEMBER**

- The Khmer Rouge planned to de-Westernise and de-modernise Cambodia by rebuilding the country on an agricultural model. This was symbolised by 'Year Zero.'
- These economic reforms failed miserably.
- A notorious aspect of the Khmer Rouge's four-year rule was the wholesale killing of its enemies. An estimated 1.6 to 1.8 million Cambodians, or just over 20% of the population, died.
- Tensions between the Khmer Rouge and Vietnam increased over the national boundary and the presence of PAVN troops inside Cambodia. Eventually, war erupted on 25 December 1978 when Vietnam invaded Cambodia. Vietnamese troops were welcomed as liberators by the Cambodian population.
- During this period, relations between Vietnam and China deteriorated. Shortly after Vietnam's invasion of Cambodia, China launched a 'punitive' invasion of Vietnam.

## ACTIVITIES

**1** What economic plans did the Khmer Rouge have for Cambodia? Were these successful?

**2** Account for the Khmer Rouge's reign of terror in Cambodia. Was this genocide?

**3** 'Pol Pot does not believe in God, but he thinks that heaven, destiny, wants him to guide Cambodia in the way he thinks is best for Cambodia, that is to say, the worst. Pol Pot is mad, you know, like Hitler' (Norodom Sihanouk). How accurate is this assessment of Pol Pot?

**4** Why did Vietnam invade Cambodia in 1978?

**5** Account for the increase in tensions between Vietnam and China.

**6** How did events in Indochina become tied up with superpower relations?

**7** Did Vietnam's wars with Cambodia and China prove that the conflict in Indochina had always been a nationalistic response to imperialism and not a communist one?

### FURTHER READING

Karl Jackson's *Cambodia: 1975–1978: Rendezvous with Death* (Princeton University Press, Princeton, 1989) and Molyda Szymusiak's *The Stones Cry Out: A Cambodian Childhood, 1975–1978* (Indiana University Press, Bloomington, 1999) offer intriguing insights. Audio-visually the 1984 film *The Killing Fields* is a powerful testament.

# Epilogue

What some people called the '30 Year War' in fact lasted much longer, as Vietnam and Cambodia went to war, and then Vietnam and China also fought their short but bitter war in 1979. Millions of people were killed in Indochina; many as a consequence of the struggles for independence, and in Vietnam, reunification; and, in Cambodia, as a consequence of Khmer Rouge brutality. Indochina has also been forced to cope with the vast human and physical devastation resulting from the wars. Millions of Indochinese were physically or emotionally damaged. Agricultural and industrial outputs in Vietnam, Cambodia and Laos were devastated. Millions of litres of Agent Orange caused massive environmental damage.

Following the 'end' of the war, hundreds of thousands of people fled Indochina. Many died in desperate attempts to find safety. Many others spent years in refugee camps throughout South-East Asia. A smaller, but significant number found sanctuary in France, the United States, Australia or in other Western nations. There, despite some hostility, these so-called 'boat people' have become valued members of their new communities.

In the West, the Indochinese conflicts have left deep scars. For France, the loss of Indochina was further evidence that it was no longer a great power. Nearly 59,000 Americans died in the war. Their names are inscribed in the Vietnam Veterans' Memorial in Washington, DC, one of the most-visited historical monuments in America.

The divisions caused by the war have left a long legacy. Within the United States, the Vietnam War is at the centre of a larger political and cultural contest over the 1960s. On a range of issues, conservatives and liberals continue to squabble over the legacies of the 1960s. Conservatives claim the antiwar movement, and the

*Anguished Memories: Visiting the Vietnam Veterans' Memorial, Washington, DC*

'liberal press', undermined American efforts to win the Vietnam War. Others contend that 'Vietnam was the wrong war in the wrong place at the wrong time for the wrong reason'.

The conflict in Indochina also affected US foreign policy. The war exposed the limits of American power. During the period from 1975 until Ronald Reagan took office in early 1981, US foreign policy was purportedly constrained by the so-called 'Vietnam Syndrome'. According to this theory, policymakers refused to involve the United States in conflicts unless they were assured of victory.

If the Vietnam Syndrome existed at all, however, it did so only briefly: the Reagan years witnessed a return to a more muscular US foreign policy. Yet Reagan understood well that Vietnam had divided America. In 1988, speaking at a Veterans' Day ceremony, Reagan articulated a message of healing, which captured many Americans' desire for unity. After praising the sacrifices made by Vietnam veterans, he conceded there had been 'deep divisions about the wisdom and rightness of the Vietnam war'. 'Both sides,' he continued, 'spoke with honesty and fervour. And what more can we ask for in our democracy?' By reminding Americans that their sense of patriotism – indeed, their understanding of nationalism – rests on commonly held assumptions about the nature of their political system and culture, Reagan sought to unite the United States after the divisions caused by its failed attempt to thwart Vietnamese nationalism.

The US experience in Vietnam has shaped the way it has fought wars since the 1960s. In subsequent conflicts commanders have been careful to 'manage' the media, in an effort to ensure there were no unrealistic expectations concerning the task at hand. The US military has done its best to ensure the public is not exposed to disturbing images of the consequences of American military actions. On both counts, as the wars against Iraq highlight, they have not entirely succeeded.

The United States did not recognise Vietnam until 1995, when President Bill Clinton (who, during the 1992 election campaign, had been forced to fend off accusations that he dodged the draft during the 1960s) decided it was time for the United States to re-establish relations with its former adversary. Clinton's decision provoked controversy, as he was accused of betraying the memories and sacrifices of those Americans who had fought in the war.

As is often the case, international politics lagged behind international commerce: by the mid-1990s multinational corporations were already busily establishing themselves in Vietnam. Today, Saigon (officially 'Ho Chi Minh City') resembles any number of Asian cities, as capitalism develops apace. The difference is that these changes are taking place in a nation still nominally under communist control.

*The Australian Welcome Home Parade, 1987. In Australia, as in the US, many Vietnam veterans were ostracised and sometimes blamed for losing a war that was not of their own making. In 1987, Australia formally 'welcomed' home its Vietnam veterans.*

In Vietnam, as in China, it remains to be seen how long capitalism and communism can co-exist. As the older generation of political leaders give way to a younger generation, whose political consciousness is less influenced by the wars of 1945–1975, it is conceivable that the pace of change in Vietnam will accelerate.

What would Ho Chi Minh make of the changes taking place in Vietnam? Despite American assumptions – and assertions – to the contrary, Ho was as much a pragmatist as he was an ideologue. He might express reservations about the capitalist 'revolution' that is transforming Vietnam, but he would probably smile at the sight of thousands of Western tourists visiting – and spending money – at the tunnels of Cu Chi, at Khe Sanh or at other sites that are etched in our collective consciousness. And he would probably hope that in their travels, these tourists will appreciate that 'Vietnam' is a country, not just a war.

# Glossary

**Agent Orange**   Chemical herbicide used by the USA to destroy the PLAF's jungle cover.

**Agrovilles**   South Vietnamese re-settlement program, launched in 1959, designed to force peasants into areas where they could be 'protected' from communist insurgents. The scheme was abandoned in 1961. Strategic Hamlets were later versions of a similar program.

**American War**   Vietnamese name for the Second Indochina War.

**Annam**   Central Vietnam. A French protectorate during the colonial days.

**appeasement**   Label given to the policies adopted by European democracies to deal with the rise of German Nazism in the 1930s. Early German expansion was accepted in the hope that appeasing Hitler would stop further expansion. The USA believed Russia could not be 'appeased' during the Cold War.

**Army of the Republic of Vietnam (ARVN)**   South Vietnamese Army. Members called 'Marvin' by American troops.

**battalion**   A military unit of around 800 persons.

**black market**   An alternative to the legal trading system, where goods are sold without permission of the government and without the collection of government taxes.

**Buddhism**   A religion based on the teachings of the Buddha. Seeks the acquisition of 'enlightenment' and opposes violence and cruelty. A major spiritual force in Vietnam.

**cadres**   A small military or political unit (cell) that can form the nucleus for an expanding military and/or political oraganisation.

**capitalism**   A socio-economic system characterised by private or corporate ownership of the means of production. Goods and services are produced and exchanged in a free market with little government control.

**Central Committee**   A senior echelon of administrative control that reports to the Politburo in Indochinese communist parties.

**CIA**   Central Intelligence Agency.

**Cochin China**   Southern Vietnam. Annexed outright by France in 1867.

**Cold War**   The post-World War II struggle between the USA and the Soviet Union.

**colonialism**   The political, economic and social domination of one country by another. Practised by European states in places such as Africa and Asia. The act of domination is also often referred to as 'Imperialism'.

**COMECON**   Council for Mutual Economic Assistance. Soviet aid program for communist countries.

**Comintern**   The Communist International. An organisation designed to unite communists around the world and advance the communist struggle.

**communism**   Theory of political and economic development developed by Karl Marx, and first implemented by V. I. Lenin. Rejects the capitalist system as a form of oppression. Seeks to use collective or state ownership to eliminate inequality. Workers are paid according to their needs and abilities.

**constitutional monarchy**   A political system where a monarch is Head of State, but their powers are limited by a constitution and a parliament controls government. Australia is a constitutional monarchy.

**conventional warfare**   The waging of armed conflict on land, sea and in the air between the militaries of sovereign states or between an established government and a dissident group. Conventional warfare is framed by international agreements and does not involve chemical, biological or nuclear weapons of mass destruction.

**Democratic Republic of Vietnam (DRV)**   'North Vietnam'.

**détente**   From the French word for 'relaxing' or easing tension. Usually refers to the easing of tensions between the USA and the USSR in 1970s.

**Dien Bien Phu**   Site of a major French military defeat in 1954.

**division**   A large military unit of around 10,000 to 20,000 persons. The basic unit for large-scale conventional warfare.

**DMZ**   Demilitarised Zone: According to the 1954 Geneva Accords, this stretch of land divided North and South Vietnam at the 18th parallel. Neither side was to place military force in this zone. It was intended as a temporary administrative line, rather than national boundary.

**Domino Theory**   An American principle that held that if a nation fell to communism its neighbours would also be immediately susceptible to communist domination.

**dust off**   Term used for the medical evacuation by helicopter of wounded American (and Australian) personnel.

**ecocide**   The deliberate or accidental destruction of the environment.

**fire support**   Military term for the assistance provided to an infantry unit by heavy weapons such as mortars and artillery, and aircraft. A crucial component of American military doctrine in Vietnam.

**fragging** The deliberate killing of an American officer by his men. Derived from 'fragmentation grenade'.

**Francophile** A person enamoured of French culture.

**free world** The label used by the USA and its Allies to identify their own side in the Cold War.

**genocide** Systematic and planned extermination of an entire national, racial, political or ethnic group.

**guerrilla warfare** From the Spanish 'guerre' meaning 'war', the term is used to describe unconventional/asymmetric warfare conducted by small mobile groups. Tactics are often based on ambush and sabotage. The objective is to destabilise the enemy through long/low intensity activity. Often utilised in anti-colonial struggles.

**Gulf of Tonkin Resolution** Passed by the US Congress (August 1964), soon after the Gulf of Tonkin Incidents, the Resolution gave President Lyndon Johnson a 'blank cheque' to send American troops to Vietnam.

**Guomindang** Chinese Nationalist Party.

**GVN** Government of Vietnam (South Vietnamese Government).

**Ho Chi Minh Trail** A supply and communications trail through Laos and Cambodia that helped the North supply the NLF with personnel and materials.

**Indochina** Region between Thailand and China in South-East Asia, colonised by France in the 19th century. Comprises Vietnam, Laos and Cambodia.

**Indochina wars** Also known as the Indochinese conflicts. A series of 20th century wars fought in Indochina.

**insurgency** Subversive political and military activity conducted by an organised movement that aims to overthrow an established government.

**Khmer Rouge** Literally the 'Red Khmers'; Cambodian communists.

**Lao Dong** The Vietnamese Workers' Party. (Vietnamese Communist Party that governed in Vietnam.)

**logistics** In military terms, the process of designing and strategically managing the acquisition, movement, storage and delivery of supplies for an armed force.

**Lycée** French-run schools in Vietnam.

**LZ** (Helicopter) Landing Zone.

**MAAG** Military Assistance and Advisory Group. Organisation through which the USA administered military aid to South Vietnam

**MACV** Military Assistance Command Vietnam. Established in 1962, MACV was the successor to MAAG. This was the apparatus through which the USA provided military support to South Vietnam.

**napalm** Gelled gasoline-based incendiary bomb used first by the USA in World War II. Used as a defoliant and antipersonnel weapon during the Vietnam War.

**nationalism** A consciousness by which a group of people distinguish themselves from others through bonds such as language, ethnicity, culture, history and geography.

**NATO** North Atlantic Treaty Organisation. Defence pact signed by Western European nations, and the USA, in 1949.

**Nixon Doctrine** Also known as the Guam Doctrine. Announced July 1969, Nixon declared the USA would support its allies, but would expect them to provide the bulk of the manpower for their own defence.

**NLF** National Liberation Front: A southern Vietnamese organisation dominated by communists who sought to overthrow the South Vietnamese Government.

**Office of Strategic Services** The forerunner to the US Central Intelligence Agency. Conducted intelligence and covert operations during World War II.

**one slow, four quick** A military tactic developed by General Giap that relied on slow and deliberate preparation for battle before engaging and disengaging the enemy at speed.

**pacification** A military tactic aimed at pacifying into submission a rebellious area or people. In Vietnam it was constructed as the need of the USA and its allies to win the 'Hearts and Minds' of the Vietnamese people. Sometimes known in South Vietnam as 'Revolutionary Development'.

**Pathet Lao** Laotian communists.

**peaceful co-existence** A communist Cold War doctrine. Challenging earlier ideological positions it suggested communist states could peacefully co-exist with non-communist nations.

**peasantry** The agricultural class that comprised the bulk of the Vietnamese population. Usually economically disadvantaged.

**People's Army Vietnam (PAVN)** The North Vietnamese Army. Also known as the NVA.

**People's Liberation Army (PLA)** The Chinese Army.

**People's Republic of China** Communist China.

**People's War** An approach to revolutionary war designed by Mao Zedong. Involves guerrilla war and relies on the support of the people and the spiritual power of civilians and soldiers who fight for the cause.

**PLAF** People's Liberation Armed Forces. Also known as the 'Viet Cong'. South Vietnamese forces who fought against the Americans. The PLAF had three different types of units: Main Force, Regional and Local.

**Politburo** Short for Political Bureau. The day-to-day governing body of the Lao Dong. Elected from the membership of the Central Committee. The highest and most powerful group of policymakers in North Vietnam.

**popular front**   Alliances by left-wing political groups and communists to destroy a common enemy.

**Provisional Revolutionary Government (PRG)**   Established in June 1969, as the successor to the NLF

**real-politik**   Politics or diplomacy informed by practical rather than ideological or moral considerations.

**Republic of Vietnam (RVN)**   The South Vietnamese state, or 'South Vietnam'.

**rules of engagement**   The rules American forces were bound to abide by in their fight against the NLF and the North Vietnamese. For example, the rules of engagement forbade US combat troops crossing the DMZ into North Vietnam. The earlier Geneva Protocols, the Gulf of Tonkin Resolution and US military doctrine help set the rules of engagement.

**self-determination**   The right of all peoples to determine the political future of their country or group without coercion or influence from external powers. Also known as 'self-rule'.

**Soviets**   Can be citizens of the USSR or communities where communist principles operate.

**Strategic Hamlet Program**   A scheme commenced in 1962 to relocate southern villagers into stockaded hamlets where they could be protected from the Viet Cong. Strategic Hamlets were generally unpopular amongst the peasantry.

**strategy**   Branch of military science that dealt with the planning, conduct and command of war.

**Students for a Democratic Society (SDS)**   Established in 1960, this group was an important part of the antiwar movement in the USA.

**Sureté**   colonial French secret police

**tactics**   Branch of military science dealing with the techniques and maneuvers to achieve objectives set down by strategy.

**Tet**   The Vietnamese Lunar New Year.

**Tonkin**   Northern Vietnam. The area became a French protectorate during the colonial period.

**Union of Soviet Socialist Republics (USSR)**   Also known as the Soviet Union. Often used interchangeably with 'Russia'.

**Viet Cong**   A phrase coined by the Diem regime to label communist insurgents in South Vietnam. Their proper title was People's Armed Liberation Forces (PLAF). Americans called the Viet Cong a variety of names including; 'VC', 'Victor Charles', 'Charlie' and 'Sir Charles'.

**Viet Minh**   Vietnamese independence fighters who fought for independence between 1941 and 1954. Dominated by the Indochinese Communist Party and Ho Chi Minh.

**Vietnam War**   American name for the Second Indochina War.

**Vietnam Veterans against the War (VVAW)**   Antiwar group comprised of American veterans of the Indochinese conflict.

**Vietnamese National Army (VNA)**   A French-created force of loyal Vietnamese. Plagued by desertion, the VNA proved no match for the Viet Minh.

**Vietnamisation**   American policy of handing over responsibility for fighting the war to South Vietnam's armed forces. The USA would continue to supply weapons and supplies.

**Warsaw Pact**   A defence alliance comprising the USSR and its Eastern European allies.

# Index

For EU product safety concerns, contact us at Calle de José Abascal, 56–1°,
28003 Madrid, Spain or eugpsr@cambridge.org.

www.ingramcontent.com/pod-product-compliance
Ingram Content Group UK Ltd.
Pitfield, Milton Keynes, MK11 3LW, UK
UKHW050232160625
459711UK00020B/284